St. Paul's Epistles To The Corinthians

EXPOSITIONS OF HOLY SCRIPTURE

ST. PAUL'S EPISTLES TO THE

CORINTHIANS

(TO II CORINTHIANS, CHAPTER V)

BY

ALEXANDER MACLAREN

D.D., Litt.D.

NEW YORK

A. C. ARMSTRONG AND SON

3 & 5 WEST EIGHTEENTH STREET

LONDON: HODDER AND STOUGHTON

MCMX

CONTENTS

v

CONTENTS

I. CORINTHIANS

CALLING ON THE NAME

'All that in every place call upon the name of Jesus Christ our Lord, both theirs and ours.'—1 Cor. i. 2.

THERE are some difficulties, with which I need not trouble you, about both the translation and the connection of these words. One thing is quite clear, that in them the Apostle associates the church at Corinth with the whole mass of Christian believers in the world. The question may arise whether he does so in the sense that he addresses his letter both to the church at Corinth and to the whole of the churches, and so makes it a catholic epistle. That is extremely unlikely, considering how all but entirely this letter is taken up with dealing with the especial conditions of the Corinthian church. Rather I should suppose that he is simply intending to remind 'the Church of God at Corinth ... sanctified in Christ Jesus, called to be saints,' that they are in real, living union with the whole body of believers. Just as the water in a little land-locked bay, connected with the sea by some narrow strait like that at Corinth, is yet part of the whole ocean that rolls round the world, so that little community of Christians had its living bond of union with all the brethren in every place that called upon the name of Jesus Christ.

Whichever view on that detail of interpretation be taken, this phrase, as a designation of Christians, is

A

worth considering. It is one of many expressions found in the New Testament as names for them, some of which have now dropped out of general use, while some are still retained. It is singular that the name of 'Christian,' which has all but superseded all others, was originally invented as a jeer by sarcastic wits at Antioch, and never appears in the New Testament, as a name by which believers called themselves. Important lessons are taught by these names, such as disciples, believers, brethren, saints, those of the way, and so on, each of which embodies some characteristic of a follower of Jesus. So this appellation in the text, 'those who call upon the name of our Lord Jesus Christ,' may yield not unimportant lessons if it be carefully weighed, and to some of these I would ask your attention now.

I. First, it gives us a glimpse into the worship of the primitive Church.

To 'call on the name of the Lord' is an expression that comes straight out of the Old Testament. It means there distinctly adoration and invocation, and it means precisely these things when it is referred to Jesus Christ.

We find in the Acts of the Apostles that the very first sermon that was preached at Pentecost by Peter all turns upon this phrase. He quotes the Old Testament saying, ' Whosoever shall call on the name of the Lord shall be saved,' and then goes on to prove that ' the Lord,' the 'calling on whose Name' is salvation, is Jesus Christ ; and winds up with 'Therefore let all the house of Israel know assuredly that God hath made that same Jesus, whom ye have crucified, both Lord and Christ.'

Again we find that Ananias of Damascus, when

Jesus Christ appeared to him and told him to go to Paul and lay his hands upon him, shrank from the perilous task because Paul had been sent to 'bind them that call upon the name of the Lord,' and to persecute them. We find the same phrase recurring in other connections, so that, on the whole, we may take the expression as a recognised designation of Christians.

This was their characteristic, that they prayed to Jesus Christ. The very first word, so far as we know, that Paul ever heard from a Christian was, 'Lord Jesus! receive my spirit.' He heard that cry of calm faith which, when he heard it, would sound to him as horrible blasphemy from Stephen's dying lips. How little he dreamed that he himself was soon to cry to the same Jesus, 'Lord, what wilt thou have me to do?' and was in after-days to beseech Him thrice for deliverance, and to be answered by sufficient grace. How little he dreamed that, when his own martyrdom was near, he too would look to Jesus as Lord and righteous Judge, from whose hands all who loved His appearing should receive their crown! Nor only Paul directs desires and adoration to Jesus as Lord; the last words of Scripture are a cry to Him as Lord to come quickly, and an invocation of His 'grace' on all believing souls.

Prayer to Christ from the very beginning of the Christian Church was, then, the characteristic of believers, and He to whom they prayed, thus, from the beginning, was recognised by them as being a Divine Person, God manifest in the flesh.

The object of their worship, then, was known by the people among whom they lived. Singing hymns to Christus as a god is nearly all that the Roman proconsul in his well-known letter could find to tell his

master of their worship. They were the worshippers
—not merely the disciples—of one Christ. That was
their peculiar distinction. Among the worshippers of
the false gods they stood erect; before Him, and Him
only, they bowed. In Corinth there was the polluted
worship of Aphrodite and of Zeus. These men called
not on the name of these lustful and stained deities,
but on the name of the Lord Jesus Christ. And everybody knew whom they worshipped, and understood
whose men they were. Is that true about us? Do we
Christian men so habitually cultivate the remembrance
of Jesus Christ, and are we so continually in the habit
of invoking His aid, and of contemplating His blessed
perfections and sufficiency, that every one who knew us
would recognise us as meant by those who call on the
name of the Lord Jesus Christ?

If this be the proper designation of Christian people,
alas! alas! for so many of the professing Christians of
this day, whom neither bystanders nor themselves
would think of as included in such a name!

Further, the connection here shows that the divine
worship of Christ was universal among the churches.
There was no 'place' where it was not practised, no
community calling itself a church to whom He was not
the Lord to be invoked and adored. This witness to
the early and universal recognition in the Christian
communities of the divinity of our Lord is borne by an
undisputedly genuine epistle of Paul's. It is one of
the four which the most thorough-going destructive
criticism accepts as genuine. It was written before
the Gospels, and is a voice from the earlier period of
Paul's apostleship. Hence the importance of its attes-
tation to this fact that all Christians everywhere,
both Jewish, who had been trained in strict mono-

theism, and Gentile, who had burned incense at many a foul shrine, were perfectly joined together in this, that in all their need they called on the name of Jesus Christ as Lord and brought to Him, as divine, adoration not to be rendered to any creatures. From the day of Pentecost onwards, a Christian was not merely a disciple, a follower, or an admirer, but a worshipper of Christ, the Lord.

II. We may see here an unfolding of the all-sufficiency of Jesus Christ.

Note that solemn accumulation, in the language of my text, of all the designations by which He is called, sometimes separately and sometimes unitedly, the name of 'our Lord Jesus Christ.' We never find that full title given to Him in Scripture except when the writer's mind is labouring to express the manifoldness and completeness of our Lord's relations to men, and the largeness and sufficiency of the blessings which He brings. In this context I find in the first nine or ten verses of this chapter, so full is the Apostle of the thoughts of the greatness and wonderfulness of his dear Lord on whose name he calls, that six or seven times he employs this solemn, full designation.

Now, if we look at the various elements of this great name we shall get various aspects of the way in which calling on Christ is the strength of our souls.

'Call on the name of—the Lord.' That is the Old Testament Jehovah. There is no mistaking nor denying, if we candidly consider the evidence of the New Testament writings, that, when we read of Jesus Christ as 'Lord,' in the vast majority of cases, the title is not a mere designation of human authority, but is an attribution to Him of divine nature and dignity. We have, then, to ascribe to Him, and to call on Him as

possessing, all which that great and incommunicable
Name certified and sealed to the Jewish Church as
their possession in their God. The Jehovah of the Old
Testament is our Lord of the New. He whose being
is eternal, underived, self-sufficing, self-determining,
knowing no variation, no diminution, no age, He who
is because He is and that He is, dwells in His fulness
in our Saviour. To worship Him is not to divert
worship from the one God, nor is it to have other gods
besides Him. Christianity is as much monotheistic as
Judaism was, and the law of its worship is the old law
—Him only shalt thou serve. It is the divine will
that all men should honour the Son, even as they
honour the Father.

But what is it to call on the name of Jesus? That
name implies all the sweetness of His manhood. He
is our Brother. The name 'Jesus' is one that many a
Jewish boy bore in our Lord's own time and before it;
though, afterwards, of course, abhorrence on the part
of the Jew and reverence on the part of the Christian
caused it almost entirely to disappear. But at the
time when He bore it it was as undistinguished a name
as Simeon, or Judas, or any other of His followers'
names. To call upon the name of Jesus means to
realise and bring near to ourselves, for our consolation
and encouragement, for our strength and peace, the
blessed thought of His manhood, so really and closely
knit to ours; to grasp the blessedness of the thought
that He knows our frame because He Himself has worn
it, and understands and pities our weakness, being
Himself a man. To Him whom we adore as Lord we
draw near in tenderer, but not less humble and
prostrate, adoration as our brother when we call on
the name of the Lord Jesus, and thus embrace as

harmonious, and not contradictory, both the divinity
of the Lord and the humanity of Jesus.

To call on the name of Christ is to embrace in our
faith and to beseech the exercise on our behalf of all
which Jesus is as the Messiah, anointed by God with the
fulness of the Spirit. As such He is the climax, and
therefore the close of all revelation, who is the long-
expected fruition of the desire of weary hearts, the
fulfilment, and therefore the abolition, of sacrifice and
temple and priesthood and prophecy and all that
witnessed for Him ere He came. We further call on
the name of Christ the Anointed, on whom the whole
fulness of the Divine Spirit dwelt in order that, calling
upon Him, that fulness may in its measure be granted
to us.

So the name of the Lord Jesus Christ brings to view
the divine, the human, the Messiah, the anointed Lord
of the Spirit, and Giver of the divine life. To call on
His name is to be blessed, to be made pure and strong,
joyous and immortal. 'The name of the Lord is a
strong tower, the righteous runneth into it and is
safe.' Call on His name in the day of trouble and ye
shall be heard and helped.

III. Lastly, this text suggests what a Christian life
should be.

We have already remarked that to call on the name
of Jesus was the distinctive peculiarity of the early
believers, which marked them off as a people by themselves. Would it be a true designation of the bulk of
so-called Christians now? You do not object to profess yourself a Christian, or, perhaps, even to say that
you are a disciple of Christ, or even to go the length
of calling yourself a follower and imitator. But are
you a worshipper of Him? In your life have you

the habit of meditating on Him as Lord, as Jesus, as Christ, and of refreshing and gladdening dusty days and fainting strength by the living water, drawn from the one unfailing stream from these triple fountains? Is the invocation of His aid habitual with you?

There needs no long elaborate supplication to secure His aid. How much has been done in the Church's history by short bursts of prayer, as 'Lord, help me!' spoken or unspoken in the moment of extremity! 'They cried unto God in the battle.' They would not have time for very lengthy petitions then, would they? They would not give much heed to elegant arrangement of them or suiting them to the canons of human eloquence. 'They cried unto God in the battle'; whilst the enemy's swords were flashing and the arrows whistling about their ears. These were circumstances to make a prayer a 'cry'; no composed and stately utterance of an elegantly modulated voice, nor a languid utterance without earnestness, but a short, sharp, loud call, such as danger presses from panting lungs and parched throats. Therefore the cry was answered, 'and He was entreated of them.' 'Lord, save us, we perish!' was a very brief prayer, but it brought its answer. And so we, in like manner, may go through our warfare and work, and day by day as we encounter sudden bursts of temptation may meet them with sudden jets of petition, and thus put out their fires. And the same help avails for long-continuing as for sudden needs. Some of us may have to carry lifelong burdens and to fight in a battle ever renewed. It may seem as if our cry was not heard, since the enemy's assault is not weakened, nor our power to beat it back perceptibly increased. But the appeal is not in vain, and when the fight is over, if not before, we shall know what reinforcements of strength to our weakness were due to our poor cry entering into the ears of our Lord and Brother. No other 'name' is permissible as our plea or as recipient of our prayer. In and on the name of the Lord we must call, and if we do, anything is possible rather than that the promise which was claimed for the Church and referred to Jesus, in the very first Christian preaching on Pentecost, should not be fulfilled— 'Whosoever shall call on the name of the Lord shall be saved.'

'In every place.' We may venture to subject the words of my text to a little gentle pressure here. The Apostle only meant to express the universal characteristics of Christians everywhere. But we may venture to give a different turn to the words, and learn from them the duty of devout communion with Christ as a duty for each of us wherever we are. If a place is not fit to pray in it is not fit to be in. We may carry praying hearts, remembrances of the Lord, sweet, though they may be swift and short, contemplations of His grace, His love, His power, His sufficiency, His nearness, His punctual help, like a hidden light in our hearts, into all the dusty ways of life, and in every place call on His name. There is no place so dismal but that thoughts of Him will make sunshine in it; no work so hard, so commonplace, so prosaic, so uninteresting, but that it will become the opposite of all these if whatever we do is done in remembrance of our Lord. Nothing will be too hard for us to do, and nothing too bitter for us to swallow, and nothing too sad for us to bear, if only over all that befalls us and all that we undertake and endeavour we make the sign of the Cross and call upon

the name of the Lord. If 'in every place' we have
Him as the object of our faith and desire, and as the
Hearer of our petition, in 'every place' we shall have
Him for our help, and all will be full of His bright
presence; and though we have to journey through the
wilderness we shall ever drink of that spiritual rock
that will follow us, and that Rock is Christ. In every
place call upon His name, and every place will be a
house of God, and a gate of heaven to our waiting
souls.

PERISHING OR BEING SAVED

'For the preaching of the Cross is to them that perish foolishness; but unto us
which are saved it is the power of God.'—1 Cor. i. 18.

THE starting-point of my remarks is the observation
that a slight variation of rendering, which will be
found in the Revised Version, brings out the true
meaning of these words. Instead of reading 'them
that perish' and 'us which are saved,' we ought to read
'them that *are perishing*,' and 'us which *are being* saved.'
That is to say, the Apostle represents the two contrasted
conditions, not so much as fixed states, either present
or future, but rather as processes which are going on,
and are manifestly, in the present, incomplete. That
opens some very solemn and intensely practical considerations.

Then I may further note that this antithesis includes
the whole of the persons to whom the Gospel is preached.
In one or other of these two classes they all stand.
Further, we have to observe that the consideration
which determines the class to which men belong, is the

attitude which they respectively take to the preaching
of the Cross. If it be, and because it is, 'foolishness'
to some, they belong to the catalogue of the perishing.
If it be, and because it is, 'the power of God' to others,
they belong to the class of those who are in process of
being saved.

So, then, we have the ground cleared for two or three
very simple, but, as it seems to me, very important
thoughts.

I. I desire, first, to look at the two contrasted conditions, 'perishing' and 'being saved.'

Now we shall best, I think, understand the force of
the darker of these two terms if we first ask what is
the force of the brighter and more radiant. If we
understand what the Apostle means by 'saving' and
'salvation' we shall understand also what he means by
'perishing.'

If, then, we turn for a moment to Scripture analogy
and teaching, we find that that threadbare word 'salvation,' which we all take it for granted that we understand, and which, like a well-worn coin, has been so
passed from hand to hand that it scarcely remains
legible—that well-worn word 'salvation' starts from a
double metaphorical meaning. It means either—and
is used for both—being healed or being made safe. In
the one sense it is often employed in the Gospel narra-
tives of our Lord's miracles, and it involves the metaphor
of a sick man and his cure; in the other it involves the
metaphor of a man in peril and his deliverance and
security. The negative side, then, of the Gospel idea of
salvation is the making whole from a disease, and the
making safe from a danger. Negatively, it is the removal from each of us of the one sickness, which is sin;
and the one danger, which is the reaping of the fruits

and consequences of sin, in their variety as guilt, re-morse, habit, and slavery under it, perverted relation to God, a fearful apprehension of penal consequences here, and, if there be a hereafter, there, too. The sick-ness of soul and the perils that threaten life, flow from the central fact of sin, and salvation consists, nega-tively, in the sweeping away of all of these, whether the sin itself, or the fatal facility with which we yield to it, or the desolation and perversion which it brings into all the faculties and susceptibilities, or the per-version of relation to God, and the consequent evils, here and hereafter, which throng around the evil-doer. The sick man is healed, and the man in peril is set in safety.

But, besides that, there is a great deal more. The cure is incomplete till the full tide of health follows convalescence. When God saves, He does not only bar up the iron gate through which the hosts of evil rush out upon the defenceless soul, but He flings wide the golden gate through which the glad troops of blessings and of graces flock around the delivered spirit, and enrich it with all joys and with all beauties. So the positive side of salvation is the investiture of the saved man with throbbing health through all his veins, and the strength that comes from a divine life. It is the bestowal upon the delivered man of everything that he needs for blessedness and for duty. All good conferred, and every evil banned back into its dark den, such is the Christian conception of salvation. It is much that the negative should be accomplished, but it is little in comparison with the rich fulness of positive endow-ments, of happiness, and of holiness which make an integral part of the salvation of God.

This, then, being the one side, what about the other?

If this be salvation, its precise opposite is the Scriptural idea of 'perishing.' Utter ruin lies in the word, the entire failure to be what God meant a man to be. That is in it, and no contortions of arbitrary interpretation can knock that solemn significance out of the dreadful expression. If salvation be the cure of the sickness, perishing is the fatal end of the unchecked disease. If salvation be the deliverance from the outstretched claws of the harpy evils that crowd about the trembling soul, then perishing is the fixing of their poisoned talons into their prey, and their rending of it into fragments.

Of course that is metaphor, but no metaphor can be half so dreadful as the plain, prosaic fact that the exact opposite of the salvation, which consists in the healing from sin and the deliverance from danger, and in the endowment with all gifts good and beautiful, is the Christian idea of the alternative 'perishing.' Then it means the disease running its course. It means the dangers laying hold of the man in peril. It means the withdrawal, or the non-bestowal, of all which is good, whether it be good of holiness or good of happiness. It does not mean, as it seems to me, the cessation of conscious existence, any more than salvation means the bestowal of conscious existence. But he who perishes knows that he has perished, even as he knows the process while he is in the process of perishing. Therefore, we have to think of the gradual fading away from consciousness, and dying out of a life, of many things beautiful and sweet and gracious, of the gradual increase of distance from Him, union with whom is the condition of true life, of the gradual sinking into the pit of utter ruin, of the gradual increase of that awful death in life and life in death in which living consciousness makes the conscious subject aware that he is lost; lost to God, lost to himself.

Brethren, it is no part of my business to enlarge upon such awful thoughts, but the brighter the light of salvation, the darker the eclipse of ruin which rings it round. This, then, is the first contrast.

II. Now note, secondly, the progressiveness of both members of the alternative.

All states of heart or mind tend to increase, by the very fact of continuance. Life is a process, and every part of a spiritual being is in living motion and continuous action in a given direction. So the law for the world, and for every man in it, in all regions of his life, quite as much as in the religious, is 'To him that hath shall be given, and he shall have abundance.'

Look, then, at this thought of the process by which these two conditions become more and more confirmed, consolidated, and complete. Salvation is a progressive fact. In the New Testament we have that great idea looked at from three points of view. Sometimes it is spoken of as having been accomplished in the past in the case of every believing soul—'Ye have been saved' is said more than once. Sometimes it is spoken of as being accomplished in the present—'Ye are saved' is said more than once. And sometimes it is relegated to the future—'Now is our salvation nearer than when we believed,' and the like. But there are a number of New Testament passages which coincide with this text in regarding salvation as, not the work of any one moment, but as a continuous operation running through life, not a point either in the past, present, or future, but a continued life. As, for instance, 'The Lord added to the Church daily those that were being saved.' By one offering He hath perfected for ever them that are being sanctified. And in a passage in the Second Epistle to the Corinthians, which, in some respects, is an exact parallel to that of my text, we read of the preaching of the Gospel as being a 'savour of Christ in them that are being saved, and in them that are perishing.'

So the process of being saved is going on as long as a Christian man lives in this world; and every one who professes to be Christ's follower ought, day by day, to be growing more and more saved, more fully filled with that Divine Spirit, more entirely the conqueror of his own lusts and passions and evil, more and more invested with all the gifts of holiness and of blessedness which Jesus Christ is ready to bestow upon him.

Ah, brethren! that notion of a progressive salvation at work in all true Christians has all but faded away out of the beliefs, as it has all but disappeared from the experience, of hosts of you that call yourselves Christ's followers, and are not a bit further on than you were ten years ago; are no more healed of your corruptions (perhaps less so, for relapses are dangerous) than you were then—have not advanced any further into the depths of God than when you first got a glimpse of Him as loving, and your Father, in Jesus Christ—are contented to linger, like some weak band of invaders in a strange land, on the borders and coasts, instead of pressing inwards and making it all your own. Growing Christians—may I venture to say?—are not the majority of professing Christians.

And, on the other side, as certainly, there are progressive deterioration and approximation to disintegration and ruin. How many men there are listening to me now who were far nearer being delivered from their sins when they were lads than they have ever

been since! How many in whom the sensibility to
the message of salvation has disappeared, in whom the
world has ossified their consciences and their hearts,
in whom there is a more entire and unstruggling
submission to low things and selfish things and
worldly things and wicked things, than there used to
be! I am sure that there are not a few among us now
who were far better, and far happier, when they were
poor and young, and could still thrill with generous
emotion and tremble at the Word of God, than they
are to-day. Why! there are some of you that could
no more bring back your former loftier impulses, and
compunction of spirit and throbs of desire towards
Christ and His salvation, than you could bring back the
birds' nests or the snows of your youthful years. You
are perishing, in the very process of going down and
down into the dark.

Now, notice, that the Apostle treats these two classes
as covering the whole ground of the hearers of the
Word, and as alternatives. If not in the one class we
are in the other. Ah, brethren! life is no level plane,
but a steep incline, on which there is no standing still,
and if you try to stand still, down you go. Either up or
down must be the motion. If you are not more of a
Christian than you were a year ago, you are less. If
you are not more saved—for there is a degree of comparison—if you are not more saved, you are less saved.

Now, do not let that go over your head as pulpit
thunder, meaning nothing. It means *you*, and, whether
you feel or think it or not, one or other of these two
solemn developments is at this moment going on in
you. And that is not a thought to be put lightly on
one side.

Further, note what a light such considerations as

these, that salvation and perishing are vital processes—
'going on all the time,' as the Americans say—throw
upon the future.   Clearly the two processes are incomplete here.   You get the direction of the line, but not
its natural termination.   And thus a heaven and a hell
are demanded by the phenomena of growing goodness and of growing badness which we see round about
us. The arc of the circle is partially swept.   Are the
compasses going to stop at the point where the grave
comes in ?   By no means.   Round they will go, and will
complete the circle.   But that is not all.   The necessity
for progress will persist after death; and all through
the duration of immortal being, goodness, blessedness,
holiness, Godlikeness, will, on the one hand, grow in
brighter lustre; and on the other, alienation from God,
loss of the noble elements of the nature, and all the
other doleful darknesses which attend that conception
of a lost man, will increase likewise.   And so, two
people, sitting side by side here now, may start from
the same level, and by the operation of the one principle the one may rise, and rise, and rise, till he is lost
in God, and so finds himself, and the other sink, and
sink, and sink, into the obscurity of woe and evil that
lies beneath every human life as a possibility.

III. And now, lastly, notice the determining attitude
to the Cross which settles the class to which we
belong.

Paul, in my text, is explaining his reason for not
preaching the Gospel with what he calls 'the words of
man's wisdom,' and he says, in effect, 'It would be of
no use if I did, because what settles whether the Cross
shall look " foolishness " to a man or not is the man's
whole moral condition, and what settles whether a man
shall find it to be " the power of God " or not is whether

B

he has passed into the region of those that are being saved.'

So there are two thoughts suggested which sound as if they were illogically combined, but which yet are both true. It is true that men perish, or are saved, because the Cross is to them respectively 'foolishness' or 'the power of God'; and the other thing is also true, that the Cross is to them 'foolishness,' or 'the power of God' because, respectively, they are perishing or being saved. That is not putting the cart before the horse, but both aspects of the truth are true.

If you see nothing in Jesus Christ, and His death for us all, except 'foolishness,' something unfit to do you any good, and unnecessary to be taken into account in your lives—oh, my friends! *that* is the condemnation of your eyes, and not of the thing you look at. If a man, gazing on the sun at twelve o'clock on a June day, says to me, 'It is not bright,' the only thing I have to say to him is, 'Friend, you had better go to an oculist.' And if to us the Cross is 'foolishness,' it is because already a process of 'perishing' has gone so far that it has attacked our capacity of recognising the wisdom and love of God when we see them.

But, on the other hand, if we clasp that Cross in simple trust, we find that it is the power which saves us out of all sins, sorrows, and dangers, and 'shall save us' at last 'into His heavenly kingdom.'

Dear friends, that message leaves no man exactly as it found him. My words, I feel, in this sermon, have been very poor, set by the side of the greatness of the theme; but, poor as they have been, you will not be exactly the same man after them, if you have listened to them, as you were before. The difference may be very imperceptible, but it will be real. One more, almost invisible, film, over the eyeball; one more thin layer of wax in the ear; one more fold of insensibility round heart and conscience—or else some yielding to the love; some finger put out to take the salvation; some lightening of the pressure of the sickness; some removal of the peril and the danger. The same sun hurts diseased eyes, and gladdens sound ones. The same fire melts wax and hardens clay. 'This Child is set for the rise and fall of many in Israel.' 'To the one He is the savour of life unto life; to the other He is the savour of death unto death.' *Which* is He, for He *is* one of them, to you?

THE APOSTLE'S THEME

'I determined not to know anything among you, save Jesus Christ, and Him crucified.'—1 Cor. ii. 2.

MANY of you are aware that to-day I close forty years of ministry in this city—I cannot say to this congregation, for there are very, very few that can go back with me in memory to the beginning of these years. You will bear me witness that I seldom intrude personal references into the pulpit, but perhaps it would be affectation not to do so now. Looking back over these long years, many thoughts arise which cannot be spoken in public. But one thing I may say, and that is, that I am grateful to God and to you, dear friends, for the unbroken harmony, confidence, affection, and forbearance which have brightened and lightened my work. Of its worth I cannot judge; its imperfections I know better than the most unfavourable critic; but I can humbly take the words of this text as expressive, not, indeed, of my attainments, but of my aims. One of my texts, on my first Sunday in Manchester, was 'We preach Christ and Him crucified,' and I look back, and venture to say that the noble words of this text have been, however imperfectly followed, my guiding star.

Now, I wish to say a word or two, less personal perhaps, and yet, as you can well suppose, not without a personal reference in my own consciousness.

I. Note here first, then, the Apostolic theme—Jesus Christ and Him crucified.

Now, the Apostle, in this context, gives us a little autobiographical glimpse which is singularly and interestingly confirmed by some slight incidental notices in the Book of the Acts. He says, in the context, that he was with the Corinthians 'in weakness and in fear and in much trembling,' and, if we turn to the narrative, we find that a singular period of silence, apparent abandonment of his work and dejection, seems to have synchronised with his coming to the great city of Corinth. The reasons were very plain. He had recently come into Europe for the first time and had had to front a new condition of things, very different from what he had found in Palestine or in Asia Minor. His experience had not been encouraging. He had been imprisoned in Philippi; he had been smuggled away by night from Thessalonica; he had been hounded from Berea; he had all but wholly failed to make any impression in Athens, and in his solitude he came to Corinth, and lay quiet, and took stock of his adversaries. He came to the conclusion which he records in my text; he felt that it was not for him to argue with philosophers, or to attempt to vie with Sophists and professional orators, but that his only way to meet

Greek civilisation, Greek philosophy, Greek eloquence, Greek self-conceit, was to preach 'Christ and Him crucified.' The determination was not come to in ignorance of the conditions that were fronting him. He knew Corinth, its wealth, its wickedness, its culture, and knowing these he said, 'I have made up my mind that I will know nothing amongst you save Jesus Christ and Him crucified.'

So, then, this Apostle's conception of his theme was —the biography of a Man, with especial emphasis laid on one act in His history—His death. Christianity is Christ, and Christ is Christianity. His relation to the truth that He proclaimed, and to the truths that may be deducible from the story of His life and death, is altogether different from the relation of any other founder of a religion to the truths that he has proclaimed. For in these you can accept the teaching, and ignore the teacher. But you cannot do that with Christianity; 'I am the Way, and the Truth, and the Life'; and in that revealing biography, which is the preacher's theme, the palpitating heart and centre is the death upon the Cross. So, whatever else Christianity comes to be—and it comes to be a great deal else—the principle of its growth, and the germ which must vitalise the whole, lie in the personality and the death of Jesus Christ.

That is not all. The history of the life and the death want something more to make them a gospel. The fact, I was going to say, is the least part of the fact; as in some vegetable growths, there is far more underground than above. For, unless along with, involved in, and deducible from, but capable of being stated separately from, the external facts, there is a certain commentary or explanation of them: the history is a history, the biography is a biography, the story of the Cross is a touching narrative, but it is no gospel.

And what was Paul's commentary which lifted the bare facts up into the loftier region? This—as for the person, Jesus Christ 'declared to be the son of God with power'—as for the fact of the death, 'died for our sins according to the Scriptures.' Let in these two conceptions into the facts—and they are the necessary explanation and presupposition of the facts —the Incarnation and the Sacrifice, and then you get what Paul calls 'my gospel,' not because it was his invention, but because it was the trust committed to him. That is the Gospel which alone answers to the facts which he deals with; and that is the Gospel which, God helping me, I have for forty years tried to preach.

We hear a great deal at present, or we did a few years ago, about this generation having recovered Jesus Christ, and about the necessity of going 'back to the Christ of the Gospels.' By all means, I say, if in the process you do not lose the Christ of the Epistles, who is the Christ of the Gospels, too. I am free to admit that a past generation has wrapped theological cobwebs round the gracious figure of Christ with disastrous results. For it is perfectly possible to know the things that are said about Him, and not to know Him about whom these things are said. But the mistake into which the present generation is far more likely to fall than that of substituting theology for Christ, is the converse one—that of substituting an undefined Christ for the Christ of the Gospels and the Epistles, the Incarnate Son of God, who died for our salvation. And that is a more disastrous mistake than the other, for you can know nothing about Him and He can be nothing to you, except as you grasp the Apostolic explanation of the bare facts—seeing in Him the Word who became flesh, the Son who died that we might receive the adoption of sons.

I would further point out that a clear conception of what the theme is, goes a long way to determine the method in which it shall be proclaimed. The Apostle says, in the passage which is parallel to the present one, in the previous chapter, 'We preach Christ crucified'; with strong emphasis on the word 'preach.' 'The Jew required a sign'; he wanted a man who would do something. The Greek sought after wisdom; he wanted a man who would perorate and argue and dissertate. Paul says, 'No!' 'We have nothing to *do*. We do not come to philosophise and to argue. We come with a message of fact that has occurred, of a Person that has lived.' And, as most of you know, the word which he uses means in its full signification, 'to proclaim as a herald does.'

Of course, if my business were to establish a set of principles, theological or otherwise, then argumentation would be my weapon, proofs would be my means, and my success would be that I should win your credence, your intellectual consent, and conviction. If I were here to proclaim simply a morality, then the thing that I would aim to secure would be obedience, and the method of securing it would be to enforce the authority and reasonableness of the command. But, seeing that my task is to proclaim a living Person and a historical fact, then the way to do that is to do as the herald does when in the market-place he stands, trumpet in one hand and the King's message in the other—proclaim it loudly, confidently, not 'with bated breath and whispering humbleness,' as if apologising, nor too much concerned to buttress it up with argu-

mentation out of his own head, but to say, 'Thus saith
the Lord,' and to what the Lord saith conscience says,
'Amen.' Brethren, we need far more, in all our pulpits,
of that unhesitating confidence in the plain, simple
proclamation, stripped, as far as possible, of human
additions and accretions, of the great fact and the great
Person on whom all our salvation depends.

II. So let me ask you to notice the exclusiveness
which this theme demands.

'Nothing but,' says Paul. I might venture to say—
though perhaps the tone of the personal allusions
in this sermon may seem to contradict it—that this
exclusiveness is to be manifested in one very difficult
direction, and that that is, the herald shall efface
himself. We have to hold up the picture; and if I
might take such a metaphor, like a man in a gallery
who is displaying some masterpiece to the eyes of
the beholders, we have to keep ourselves well behind
it; and it will be wise if not even a finger-tip is allowed
to steal in front and come into sight. One condition,
I believe, of real power in the ministration of the
Gospel, is that people shall be convinced that the
preacher is thinking not at all about himself, but
altogether about his message. You remember that
wonderfully pathetic utterance from John the Baptist's
stern lips, which derives much additional pathos and
tenderness from the character of the man from whom
it came, when they asked him, 'Who art thou?' and
his answer was, 'I am a Voice.' I am a Voice; that is
all! Ah, that is the example! We preach not ourselves, but Christ Jesus as Lord. We must efface
ourselves if we would proclaim Christ.

But I turn to another direction in which this theme
demands exclusiveness, and I revert to the previous

chapter where in the parallel portion to the words of
my text, we find the Apostle very clearly conscious of
the two great streams of expectation and wish which
he deliberately thwarted and set at nought. 'The
Jews require a sign—but we preach Christ crucified.
The Greeks seek after wisdom,' but again, 'we preach
Christ crucified.' Now, take these two. They are
representations, in a very emphatic way, of two sets
of desires and mental characteristics, which divide the
world between them.

On the one hand, there is the sensuous tendency that
wants something done for it, something to see, something that sense can grasp at; and so, as it fancies,
work itself upwards into a higher region. 'The Jew
requires a sign'—that is, not merely a miracle, but
something to look at. He wants a visible sacrifice; he
wants a priest. He wants religion to consist largely
in the doing of certain acts which may be supposed to
bring, in some magical fashion, spiritual blessings.
And Paul opposes to that, 'We preach Christ crucified.'
Brethren, the tendency is strong to-day, not only in
those parts of the Anglican communion where sacra-
mentarian theories are in favour, but amongst all sections of the Christian Church, in which there is obvious
a drift towards more ornate ritual, and æsthetic services,
as means of attracting to church or chapel, and as more
important than proclaiming Christ. I am free to confess that possibly some of us, with our Puritan up-
bringing and tendency, too much disregard that side
of human nature. Possibly it is so. But for all that
I profoundly believe that if religion is to be strong it
must have a very, very small infusion of these external
aids to spiritual worship, and that few things more
weaken the power of the Gospel that Paul preached

than the lowering of the flag in conformity with the desires of men of sense, and substituting for the simple glory of the preached Word the meretricious, and in time impotent, and always corrupting, attractions of a sensuous worship.

Further, 'The Greeks seek after wisdom.' They wanted demonstration, abstract principles, systematised philosophies, and the like. Paul comes again with his 'We preach Christ and Him crucified.' The wisdom is there, as I shall have to say in a moment, but the form that it takes is directly antagonistic to the wishes of these wisdom-seeking Greeks. The same thing in modern guise besets us to-day. We are called upon, on all sides, to bring into the pulpit what they call an ethical gospel; putting it into plain English, to preach morality, and to leave out Christ. We are called upon, on all sides, to preach an applied Christianity, a social gospel—that is to say, largely to turn the pulpit into a Sunday supplement to the daily newspaper. We are asked to deal with the intellectual difficulties which spring from the collision of science, true or false, with religion, and the like. All that is right enough. But I believe from my heart that the thing to do is to copy Paul's example, and to preach Christ and Him crucified. You may think me right or you may think me wrong, but here and now, at the end of forty years, I should like to say that I have for the most part ignored that class of subjects deliberately, and of set purpose, and with a profound conviction, be it erroneous or not, that a ministry which listens much to the cry for 'wisdom' in its modern forms, has departed from the true perspective of Christian teaching, and will weaken the churches which depend upon it. Let who will turn the pulpit into a professor's chair, or a

lecturer's platform, or a concert-room stage or a poli-
tician's rostrum, I for one determine to know nothing
among you save Jesus Christ and Him crucified.

III. Lastly, observe the all-sufficient comprehensive-
ness which this theme secures.

Paul says 'nothing but'; he might have said 'everything in.' For 'Jesus Christ and Him crucified' covers
all the ground of men's needs. No doubt many of you
will have been saying to yourselves whilst you have
been listening, if you have been listening, to what I
have been saying, 'Ah! old-fashioned narrowness;
quite out of date in this generation.' Brethren, there
are two ways of adapting one's ministry to the times.
One is falling in with the requirements of the times,
and the other is going dead against them, and both of
these methods have to be pursued by us.

But the exclusiveness of which I have been speaking,
is no narrow exclusiveness. Paul felt that, if he was
to give the Corinthians what they needed, he must
refuse to give them what they wanted, and that whilst
he crossed their wishes he was consulting their necessities. That is true yet, for the preaching that bases
itself upon the life and death of Jesus Christ, conceived
as Paul had learned from Jesus Christ to conceive them,
that Gospel, whilst it brushes aside men's superficial
wishes, goes straight to the heart of their deep-lying
universal necessities, for what the Jew needs most is not
a sign, and what the Greek needs most is not wisdom,
but what they both need most is deliverance from the
guilt and power of sin. And we all, scholars and fools,
poets and common-place people, artists and ploughmen,
all of us, in all conditions of life, in all varieties of
culture, in all stages of intellectual development, in all
diversities of occupation and of mental bias, what we

all have in common is that human heart in which sin
abides, and what we all need most to have is that evil
drop squeezed out of it, and our souls delivered from
the burden and the bondage. Therefore, any man that
comes with a sign, and does not deal with the sin of
the human heart, and any man that comes with a
philosophical system of wisdom, and does not deal with
sin, does not bring a Gospel that will meet the necessities even of the people to whose cravings he has been
aiming to adapt his message.

But, beyond that, in this message of Christ and Him
crucified, there lies in germ the satisfaction of all that
is legitimate in these desires that at first sight it seems
to thwart. 'A sign?' Yes, and where is there power
like the power that dwells in Him who is the Incarnate
might of omnipotence? 'Wisdom?' Yes, and where
is there wisdom, except 'in Him in whom are hid all
the treasures of wisdom and knowledge'? Let the
Jew come to the Cross, and in the weak Man hanging
there, he will find a mightier revelation of the power
of God than anywhere else. Let the Greek come to
the Cross, and there he will find wisdom and righteousness, sanctification and redemption. The bases of all
social, economical, political reform and well-being, lie
in the understanding and the application to social and
national life, of the principles that are wrapped in, and
are deduced from, the Incarnation and the Sacrifice of
Jesus Christ. We have not learned them all yet. They
have not all been applied to national and individual
life yet. I plead for no narrow exclusiveness, but for
one consistent with the widest application of Christian
principles to all life. Paul determined to know nothing
but Jesus, and to know everything in Jesus, and Jesus
in everything. Do not begin your building at the

second-floor windows. Put in your foundations first,
and be sure that they are well laid. Let the Sacrifice
of Christ, in its application to the individual and his
sins, be ever the basis of all that you say. And then,
when that foundation is laid, exhibit, to your heart's
content, the applications of Christianity and its social
aspects. But be sure that the beginning of them all is
the work of Christ for the individual sinful soul, and
the acceptance of that work by personal faith.

Dear friends, ours has been a long and happy union
but it is a very solemn one. My responsibilities are
great; yours are not small. Let me beseech you to
ask yourselves if, with all your kindness to the messenger, you have given heed to the message. Have
you passed beyond the voice that speaks, to Him of
whom it speaks? Have you taken the truth—veiled
and weakened as I know it has been by my words, but
yet in them—for what it is, the word of the living God?
My occupancy of this pulpit must in the nature of
things, before long, come to a close, but the message
which I have brought to you will survive all changes
in the voice that speaks here. 'All flesh is grass . . .
the Word of the Lord endureth for ever.' And, closing
these forty years, during a long part of which some of
you have listened most lovingly and most forbearingly,
I leave with you this, which I venture to quote, though
it is my Master's word about Himself, 'I judge you not;
the word which I have spoken unto you, the same
shall judge you in the last day.'

GOD'S FELLOW-WORKERS

' Labourers together with God.'—1 Cor. iii. 9.

THE characteristic Greek tendency to factions was threatening to rend the Corinthian Church, and each faction was swearing by a favourite teacher. Paul and his companion, Apollos, had been taken as the figure-heads of two of these parties, and so he sets himself in the context, first of all to show that neither of the two was of any real importance in regard to the Church's life. They were like a couple of gardeners, one of whom did the planting, and the other the watering; but neither the man that put the little plant into the ground, nor the man that came after him with a watering-pot, had anything to do with originating the mystery of the life by which the plant grew. That was God's work, and the pair that had planted and watered were nothing. So what was the use of fighting which of two nothings was the greater?

But then he bethinks himself that that is not quite all. The man that plants and the man that waters are something after all. They do not communicate life, but they do provide for its nourishment. And more than that, the two operations—that of the man with the dibble and that of the man with the watering-pot —are one in issue; and so they are partners, and in some respects may be regarded as one. Then what is the sense of pitting them against each other?

But even that is not quite all; though united in operation, they are separate in responsibility and activity, and will be separate in reward. And even that is not all; for, being nothing and yet something, being united and yet separate, they are taken into participation and co-operation with God; and as my text puts it, in what is almost a presumptuous phrase, they are 'labourers together with Him.' That partnership of co-operation is not merely a partnership of the two, but it is a partnership of the three—God and the two who, in some senses, are one.

Now whilst this text is primarily spoken in regard to the apostolic and evangelistic work of these early teachers, the principle which it embodies is a very wide one, and it applies in all regions of life and activity, intellectual, scholastic, philanthropic, social. Wherever men are thinking God's thoughts and trying to carry into effect any phase or side of God's manifold purposes of good and blessing to the world, there it is true. We claim no special or exclusive prerogative for the Christian teacher. Every man that is trying to make men understand God's thought, whether it is expressed in creation, or whether it is written in history, or whether it is carven in half-obliterated letters on the constitution of human nature, every man who, in any region of society or life, is seeking to effect the great designs of the universal loving Father—can take to himself, in the measure and according to the manner of his special activity, the great encouragement of my text, and feel that he, too, in his little way, is a fellow-helper to the truth and a fellow-worker with God. But then, of course, according to New Testament teaching, and according to the realities of the case, the highest form in which men thus can co-operate with God, and carry into effect His purposes is that in which men devote themselves, either directly or indirectly, to spreading throughout the whole world the name and the power of the Saviour Jesus Christ, in whom all God's will is gathered, and through whom all God's blessings are communicated to mankind. So

the thought of my text comes appropriately when I
have to bring before you the claims of our missionary
operations.

Now, the first way in which I desire to look at this
great idea expressed in these words, is that we find in it

I. A solemn thought.

'Labourers together with God.' Cannot He do it
all Himself? No. God needs men to carry out His
purposes. True, on the Cross, Jesus spoke the
triumphant word, 'It is finished!' He did not thereby
simply mean that He had completed all His suffering;
but He meant that He had then done all which the
world needed to have done in order that it should be a
redeemed world. But for the distribution and application of that finished work God depends on men. You
all know, in your own daily businesses, how there must
be a middleman between the mill and the consumer.
The question of organising a distributing agency is
quite as important as any other part of the manu-
facturer's business. The great reservoir is full, but
there has to be a system of irrigating-channels by
which the water is carried into every corner of the
field that is to be watered. Christian men individually,
and the Church collectively, supply—may I call it the
missing link?—between a redeeming Saviour and the
world which He has redeemed in act, but which is not
actually redeemed, until it has received the message of
the great Redemption that is wrought. The supernatural is implanted in the very heart of the mass of
leaven by the Incarnation and Sacrifice of Jesus Christ;
but the spreading of that supernatural revelation is
left in the hands of men who work through natural
processes, and who thus become labourers together
with God, and enable Christ to be to single souls, in

blessed reality, what He is potentially to the world, and has been ever since. He died upon the Cross. 'It is finished.' Yes—because it is finished, our work begins.

Let me remind you of the profound symbolism in that incident where our Lord for once appeared conspicuously, and almost ostentatiously, before Israel as its true King. He had need—as He Himself said—of the meek beast on which He rode. He cannot pass, in His coronation procession, through the world unless He has us, by whom He may be carried into every corner of the earth. So 'the Lord has need' of us, and we are 'fellow-labourers with Him.'

But this same thought suggests another point. We have here a solemn call addressed to every Christian man and woman.

Do not let us run away with the idea that, because here the Apostle is speaking in regard to himself and Apollos, he is enunciating a truth which applies only to Apostles and evangelists. It is true of all Christians My knowledge of and faith in Jesus Christ as my own personal Saviour impose upon me the obligation, in so far as my opportunities and capacities extend, thus to co-operate with Him in spreading His great Name. Every Christian man, just because he is a Christian, is invested with the power—and power to its last particle is duty—and is, therefore, burdened with the honourable obligation to work for God. There is such a thing as 'coming to the help of the Lord,' though that phrase seems to reverse altogether the true relation. It is the duty of every Christian, partly because of loyalty to Jesus, and partly because of the responsibility which the very constitution of society lays upon every one of us, to diffuse what he possesses, and to be a distributing

c

agent for the life that he himself enjoys. Brethren! there is no possibility of Christian men or women being fully faithful to the Saviour, unless they recognise that the duty of being a fellow-labourer with God inevitably follows on being a possessor of Christ's salvation; and that no Apostle, no official, no minister, no missionary, has any more necessity laid upon him to preach the Gospel, nor pulls down any heavier woe on himself if he is unfaithful, than has and does each one of Christ's servants.

So 'we are fellow-labourers with God.' Alas! alas! how poorly the average Christian realises—I do not say discharges, but realises—that obligation! Brethren, I do not wish to find fault, but I do beseech you to ask yourselves whether, if you are Christians, you are doing anything the least like what my text contemplates as the duty of all Christians.

May I say a word or two with regard to another aspect of this solemn call? Does not the thought of working along with God prescribe for us the sort of work that we ought to do? We ought to work in God's fashion, and if we wish to know what God's fashion is, we have but to look at Jesus Christ. We ought to work in Jesus Christ's fashion. We all know what that involved of self-sacrifice, of pain, of weariness, of utter self-oblivious devotion, of gentleness, of tenderness, of infinite pity, of love running over. 'The master's eye makes a good servant.' The Master's hand working along with the servant ought to make the servant work after the Master's fashion. 'As My Father hath sent Me, so send I you.' If we felt that side by side with us, like two sailors hauling on one rope, 'the Servant of the Lord' was toiling, do you not think it would burn up all our selfishness, and light up

all our indifference, and make us spend ourselves in
His service? A fellow-labourer with God will surely
never be lazy and selfish. Thus my text has in it, to
begin with, a solemn call.

It suggests

II. A signal honour.

Suppose a great painter, a Raphael or a Turner,
taking a little boy that cleaned his brushes, and saying
to him, 'Come into my studio, and I will let you do a
bit of work upon my picture.' Suppose an aspirant, an
apprentice in any walk of life, honoured by being per-
mitted to work along with some one who was recognised all over the world as being at the very top of that
special profession. Would it not be a feather in the
boy's cap all his life? And would he not think it the
greatest honour that ever had been done him that
he was allowed to co-operate, in however inferior a
fashion, with such an one? Jesus Christ says to us,
'Come and work here side by side with Me.' But
Christian men, plenty of them, answer, 'It is a perpetual nuisance, this continual application for money!
money! money! work! work! work! It is never-end-
ing, and it is a burden!' Yes, it is a burden, just
because it is an honour. Do you know that the Hebrew
word which means 'glory' literally means 'weight'?
There is a great truth in that. You cannot get true
honours unless you are prepared to carry them as
burdens.   And the highest honour that Jesus Christ
gives to men when He says to them, not only 'Go work
to-day in My vineyard,' but 'Come, work here side by
side with Me,' is a heavy weight which can only be
lightened by a cheerful heart.

Is it not the right way to look at all the various
forms of Christian activity which are made imperative

upon Christian people, by their possession of Christianity as being tokens of Christ's love to us? Do you remember that this same Apostle said, 'Unto me who am less than the least of all saints is this grace given, that I should preach the unsearchable riches of Christ?' He could speak about burdens and heavy tasks, and being 'persecuted but not forsaken,' almost crushed down and yet not in despair, and about the weights that came upon him daily, 'the care of all the churches,' but far beneath all the sense of his heavy load lay the thrill of thankful wonder that to him, of all men in the world, knowing as he did better than anybody else could do his own imperfection and insufficiency, this distinguishing honour had been bestowed, that he was made the Apostle to the Gentiles. That is the way in which the true man will always look at what the selfish man, and the half-and-half Christian, look at as being a weight and a weariness, or a disagreeable duty, which is to be done as perfunctorily as possible. One question that a great many who call themselves Christians ask is, 'With how little service can I pass muster?' Ah, it is because we have so little of the Spirit of Christ in us that we feel burdened by His command, 'Go ye into all the world,' as being so heavy; and that so many of us —I leave you to judge if you are in the class—so many of us make it criminally light if we do not ignore it altogether. I believe that, if it were possible to conceive of the duty and privilege of spreading Christ's name in the world being withdrawn from the Church, all His real servants would soon be yearning to have it back again. It is a token of His love; it is a source of infinite blessings to ourselves; 'if the house be not worthy, your peace shall return to you again.'

And now, lastly, we have suggested by this text

III. A strong encouragement.

'Fellow-labourers with God'—then, God is a Fellow-labourer with us. The co-operation works both ways, and no man who is seeking to spread that great salvation, to distribute that great wealth, to irrigate some little corner of the field by some little channel that he has dug, needs to feel that he is labouring alone. If I am working with God, God is working with me. Do you remember that most striking picture which is drawn in the verses appended to Mark's Gospel, which tells how the universe seemed parted into two halves, and up above in the serene the Lord 'sat on the right hand of God,' while below, in the murky and obscure, 'they went everywhere preaching the Word.' The separation seems complete, but the two halves are brought together by the next word—'The Lord also,' sitting up yonder, 'working with them,' the wandering preachers down here, 'confirming the words with signs following.' Ascended on high, entered into His rest, having finished His work, He yet is working with us, if we are labourers together with God. If we turn to the last book of Scripture, which draws back the curtain from the invisible world which is all filled with the glorified Christ, and shows its relations to the earthly militant church, we read no longer of a Christ enthroned in apparent ease, but of a Christ walking amidst the candlesticks, and of a Lamb standing in the midst of the Throne, and opening the seals, launching forth into the world the sequences of the world's history, and of the Word of God charging His enemies on His white horse, and behind Him the armies of God following. The workers who labour with God have the ascended Christ labouring with them.

But if God works with us, success is sure. Then

comes the old question that Gideon asked with bitterness of heart, when he was threshing out his handful of wheat in a corner to avoid the oppressors, 'If the Lord be with us, wherefore is all this come upon us? Will any one say that the progress of the Gospel in the world has been at the rate which its early believers expected, or at the rate which its own powers warranted them to expect? Certainly not. And so it comes to this, that whilst every true labourer has God working with him, and therefore success is certain, the planter and the waterer can delay the growth of the plant by their unfaithfulness, by not expecting success, by not so working as to make it likely, or by neutralising their evangelistic efforts by their worldly lives. When Jesus Christ was on earth, it is recorded, 'He could there do no mighty works because of their unbelief, save that He laid His hands on a few sick folk and healed them.' A faithless Church, a worldly Church, a lazy Church, an unspiritual Church, an un-Christlike Church—which, to a large extent, is the designation of the so-called Church of to-day—can clog His chariot-wheels, can thwart the work, can hamper the Divine Worker. If the Christians of Manchester were revived, they could win Manchester for Jesus. If the Christians of England lived their Christianity, they could make England what it never has been but in name—a Christian country. If the Church universal were revived, it could win the world. If the single labourer, or the community of such, is labouring 'in the Lord,' their labour will not be in vain; and if they thus plant and water, God will give the increase.

THE TESTING FIRE

'Now if any man build upon this foundation gold, silver, precious stones, wood, hay, stubble: 13. Every man's work shall be made manifest: for the day shall declare it, because it shall be revealed by fire; and the fire shall try every man's work of what sort it is.'—1 Cor. iii. 12, 13.

BEFORE I enter upon the ideas which the words suggest, my exegetical conscience binds me to point out that the original application of the text is not exactly that which I purpose to make of it now. The context shows that the Apostle is thinking about the special subject of Christian teachers and their work, and that the builders of whom he speaks are the men in the Corinthian Church, some of them his allies and some of them his rivals, who were superimposing upon the foundation of the preaching of Jesus Christ other doctrines and principles. The 'wood, hay, stubble' are the vapid and trivial doctrines which the false teachers were introducing into the Church. The 'gold, silver, and precious stones' are the solid and substantial verities which Paul and his friends were proclaiming. And it is about these, and not about the Christian life in the general, that the tremendous metaphors of my text are uttered.

But whilst that is true, the principles involved have a much wider range than the one case to which the Apostle applies them. And, though I may be slightly deflecting the text from its original direction, I am not doing violence to it, if I take it as declaring some very plain and solemn truths applicable to all Christian people, in their task of building up a life and character on the foundation of Jesus Christ; truths which are a great deal too much forgotten in our modern popular Christianity, and which it concerns us all very clearly to keep in view. There are three things here that I wish to say a word about—the patchwork building, the testing fire, the fate of the builders.

I. First, the patchwork structure.

'If any man build upon this foundation gold, silver, precious stones, wood, hay, stubble.' In the original application of the metaphor, Paul is thinking of all these teachers in that church at Corinth as being engaged in building the one structure—I venture to deflect here, and to regard each of us as rearing our own structure of life and character on the foundation of the preached and accepted Christ.

Now, what the Apostle says is that these builders were, some of them, laying valuable things like gold and silver and costly stones—by which he does not mean jewels, but marbles, alabasters, polished porphyry or granite, and the like; sumptuous building materials, which were employed in great palaces or temples—and that some of them were bringing timber, hay, stubble, reeds gathered from the marshes or the like, and filling in with such trash as that. That is a picture of what a great many Christian people are doing in their own lives—the same man building one course of squared and solid and precious stones, and topping them with rubbish. You will see in the walls of Jerusalem, at the base, five or six courses of those massive blocks which are the wonders of the world yet; well jointed, well laid, well cemented, and then on the top of them a mass of poor stuff, heaped together anyhow; scamped work—may I use a modern vulgarism?—'jerry-building.' You may go to some modern village, on an ancient historic site, and you will find built into the mud walls of the hovels in which the people are living, a marble slab with fair carving on it, or the drum of a great column of veined marble, and on the top of that, timber and clay mixed together.

That is the type of the sort of life that hosts of Christian people are living. For, mark, all the builders are on the foundation. Paul is not speaking about mere professed Christians who had no faith at all in them, and no real union with Jesus Christ. These builders were ' on the foundation'; they were building on the foundation, there was a principle deep down in their lives—which really lay at the bottom of their lives—and yet had not come to such dominating power as to mould and purify and make harmonious with itself the life that was reared upon it. We all know that that is the condition of many men, that they have what really are the fundamental bases of their lives, in belief and aim and direction; and which yet are not strong enough to master the whole of the life, and to manifest themselves through it. Especially it is the condition of some Christian people. They have a real faith, but it is of the feeblest and most rudimentary kind. They are on the foundation, but their lives are interlaced with the most heterogeneous mixty-maxty of good and evil, of lofty, high, self-sacrificing thoughts and heavenward aspirations, of resolutions never carried out into practice; and side by side with these there shall be meannesses, selfishnesses, tempers, dispositions all contradictory of the former impulses. One moment they are all fire and love, the next moment ice and selfishness. One day they are all for God, the next day all for the world, the flesh, and the devil. Jacob sees the open heavens and the face of God and vows; to-morrow he meets Laban and drops to shifty ways. Peter leaves all and follows his Master, and in a little while the fervour has gone, and the fire has died down into grey ashes, and a flippant servant-girl's tongue leads him to say ' I know not the man.' ' Gold, silver, precious stones,' and topping them, ' wood, hay, stubble!'

The inconsistencies of the Christian life are what my text, in the application that I am venturing to make of it, suggests to us.   Ah, dear friends! we do not need to go to Jacob and Peter; let us look at our own hearts, and if we will honestly examine one day of our lives, I think we shall understand how it is possible for a man, on the foundation, yet to build upon it these worthless and combustible things, ' wood, hay, stubble.'

We are not to suppose that one man builds *only* ' gold, silver, precious stones.' There is none of us that does that. And we are not to suppose that any man who *is* on the foundations has so little grasp of it, as that he builds *only* ' wood, hay, stubble.'

There is none of us who has not intermingled his building, and there is none of us, if we are Christians at all, who has not sometimes laid a course of ' precious stones.' If your faith is doing *nothing* for you except bringing to you a belief that you are not going to hell when you die, then it is no faith at all. ' Faith without works is dead.' So there is a mingling in the best, and—thank God!—there is a mingling of good with evil, in the worst of real Christian people.

II. Note here, the testing fire.

Paul points to two things, the day and the fire.

' The day shall declare it,' that is the day on which Jesus Christ comes to be the Judge; and it, that is ' the day,' ' shall be revealed in fire; and the fire shall test every man's work.' Now, it is to be noticed that here we are moving altogether in the region of lofty symbolism, and that the metaphor of the testing fire is suggested by the previous enumeration of building materials, gold and silver being capable of being assayed by flame; and ' wood, hay, stubble' being combustible, and sure to be destroyed thereby. The fire here is not an emblem of punishment; it is not an emblem of cleansing. There is no reference to anything in the nature of what Roman Catholics call purgatorial fires. The allusion is simply to some stringent and searching means of testing the quality of a man's work, and of revealing that quality.

So then, we come just to this, that for people ' on the foundation,' there is a Day of revelation and testing of their life's work. It is a great misfortune that so-called Evangelical Christianity does not say as much as the New Testament says about the judgment that is to be passed on ' the house of God.' People seem to think that the great doctrine of salvation, ' not by works of righteousness which we have done, but by His mercy,' is, somehow or other, interfered with when we proclaim, as Paul proclaims, speaking to Christian people, ' *We* must be manifested before the judgment seat of Christ,' and declares that ' Every man will receive the things done in his body, according to that he has done, whether it be good or bad.' Paul saw no contradiction, and there is no contradiction. But a great many professing Christians seem to think that the great blessing of their salvation by faith is, that they are exempt from that future revelation and testing and judgment of their acts. That is not the New Testament teaching. But, on the contrary, ' Whatsoever a man soweth that shall he also reap,' was originally said to a church of Christian people. And here we come full front against that solemn truth, that the Lord will ' gather together His saints, those that have made a covenant with Him by sacrifice, that He may judge His people.' Never mind about the drapery, the symbolism, the expression in material forms with which that future judgment is arranged, in order that we may the more easily grasp it. Remember that these pictures in the New Testament of a future judgment are highly symbolical, and not to be interpreted as if they were plain prose; but also remember that the heart of them is this, that there comes for Christian people as for all others, a time when the light will shine down upon their past, and will flash its rays into the dark chambers of memory, and when men will—to themselves if not to others—be revealed 'in the day when the Lord shall judge the secrets of men according to my Gospel.'

We have all experience enough of how but a few years, a change of circumstances, or a growth into another stage of development, give us fresh eyes with which to estimate the moral quality of our past. Many a thing, which we thought to be all right at the time when we did it, looks to us now very questionable and a plain mistake. And when we shift our stations to up yonder, and get rid of all this blinding medium of flesh and sense, and have the issues of our acts in our possession, and before our sight—ah! we shall think very differently of a great many things from what we think of them now. Judgment will begin at the house of God.

And there is the other thought, that the fire which reveals and tests has also in it a power of destruction. Gold and silver will lose no atom of their weight, and will be brightened into greater lustre as they flash back the beams. The timber and the stubble will go up in a flare, and die down into black ashes. That is highly metaphorical, of course. What does it mean?

It means that some men's work will be crumpled up and perish, and be as of none effect, leaving a great, black sorrowful gap in the continuity of the structure, and that other men's work will stand. Everything that we do is, in one sense, immortal, because it is represented in our final character and condition, just as a thin stratum of rock will represent forests of ferns that grew for one summer millenniums ago, or clouds of insects that danced for an hour in the sun. But whilst that is so, and nothing human ever dies, on the other hand, deeds which have been in accordance, as it were, with the great stream that sweeps the universe on its bosom will float on that surface and never sink. Acts which have gone against the rush of God's will through creation will be like a child's go-cart that comes against the engine of an express train—be reduced, first, to stillness, all the motion knocked out of them, and then will be crushed to atoms. Deeds which stand the test will abide in blessed issue for the doer, and deeds which do not will pass away in smoke, and leave only ashes. Some of us, building on the foundation, have built more rubbish than solid work, and that will be

> ' Cast as rubbish to the void
> When God has made the pile complete.'

III. So, lastly, we have here the fate of the two builders.

The one man gets wages. That is not the bare notion of salvation, for both builders are conceived of as on the foundation, and both are saved. He gets wages. Yes, of course ! The architect has to give his certificate before the builder gets his cheque. The weaver, who has been working his hand-loom at his own house, has to take his web to the counting-house and have it overlooked before he gets his pay. And the man who has built 'gold, silver, precious stones,' will have—over and above the initial salvation—in himself the blessed consequences, and unfold the large results, of his faithful service; while the other man, inasmuch as he has not such work, cannot have the consequences of it, and gets no wages; or at least his pay is subject to heavy deductions for the spoiled bits in the cloth, and for the gaps in the wall.

The Apostle employs a tremendous metaphor here, which is masked in our Authorised Version, but is restored in the Revised. 'He shall be saved, yet so as' (not 'by' but) 'through fire'; the picture being that of a man surrounded by a conflagration, and making a rush through the flames to get to a place of safety. Paul says that he will get through, because down *below* all inconsistency and worldliness, there was a little of that which ought to have been *above* all the inconsistency and the worldliness—a true faith in Jesus Christ. But because it was so imperfect, so feeble, so little operative in his life as that it could not keep him from piling up inconsistencies into his wall, therefore his salvation is so as through the fire.

Brethren, I dare not enlarge upon that great metaphor. It is meant for us professing Christians, real and imperfect Christians—it is meant for us; and it just tells us that there are degrees in that future blessedness proportioned to present faithfulness. We begin there where we left off here. That future is not a dead level; and they who have earnestly striven to work out their faith into their lives shall 'summer high upon the hills of God.' One man, like Paul in his shipwreck, shall lose ship and lading, though 'on broken pieces of the ship' he may 'escape safe to land';

and another shall make the harbour with full cargo of
works of faith, to be turned into gold when he lands.
If we build, as we all may, 'on that foundation, gold
and silver and precious stones,' an entrance 'shall be
ministered unto us abundantly into the everlasting
kingdom of our Lord and Saviour Jesus Christ'; whilst
if we bring a preponderance of 'wood, hay, stubble,' we
shall be 'saved, yet so as through the fire.'

TEMPLES OF GOD

'Know ye not that ye are the temple of God?'—1 Cor. iii. 16.

THE great purpose of Christianity is to make men like
Jesus Christ. As He is the image of the invisible God
we are to be the images of the unseen Christ. The
Scripture is very bold and emphatic in attributing to
Christ's followers likeness to Him, in nature, in char-
acter, in relation to the world, in office, and in ultimate
destiny. Is He the anointed of God? We are anointed
—Christs in Him. Is He the Son of God? We in Him re-
ceive the adoption of sons. Is He the Light of the world?
We in Him are lights of the world too. Is He a King?
A Priest? He hath made us to be kings and priests.

Here we have the Apostle making the same solemn
assertion in regard to Christian men, 'Know ye not
that ye are'—as your Master, and because your Master
is—'that ye are the temple of God, and that the Spirit
of God dwelleth in you?'

Of course the allusion in my text is to the whole
aggregate of believers—what we call the Catholic
Church, as being collectively the habitation of God.
But God cannot dwell in an aggregate of men, unless
He dwells in the individuals that compose the aggre-

gate. And God has nothing to do with institutions except through the people who make the institutions. And so, if the Church as a whole is a Temple, it is only because all its members are temples of God.

Therefore, without forgetting the great blessed lesson of the unity of the Church which is taught in these words, I want rather to deal with them in their individual application now; and to try and lay upon your consciences, dear brethren, the solemn obligations and the intense practical power which this Apostle associated with the thought that each Christian man was, in very deed, a temple of God.

It would be very easy to say eloquent things about this text, but that is no part of my purpose.

I. Let me deal, first of all, and only for a moment or two, with the underlying thought that is here—that every Christian is a dwelling-place of God.

Now, do not run away with the idea that that is a metaphor. It was the outward temple that was the metaphor. The reality is that which you and I, if we are God's children in Jesus Christ, experience. There was no real sense in which that Mighty One whom the Heaven of Heavens cannot contain, dwelt in any house made with hands. But the Temple, and all the outward worship, were but symbolical of the facts of the Christian life, and the realities of our inward experience. These are the truths whereof the other is the shadow. We use words to which it is difficult for us to attach any meaning, when we talk about God as being locally present in any material building; but we do not use words to which it is so difficult to attach a meaning, when we talk about the Infinite Spirit as being present and abiding in a spirit shaped to hold Him, and made on purpose to touch Him and be filled by Him.

All creatures have God dwelling in them in the measure of their capacity. The stone that you kick on the road would not be there if there were not a present God. Nothing would happen if there were not abiding in creatures the force, at any rate, which is God. But just as in this great atmosphere in which we all live and move and have our being, the eye discerns undulations which make light, and the ear catches vibrations which make sound, and the nostrils are recipient of motions which bring fragrance, and all these are in the one atmosphere, and the sense that apprehends one is utterly unconscious of the other, so God's creatures, each through some little narrow slit, and in the measure of their capacity, get a straggling beam from Him into their being, and therefore they are.

But high above all other ways in which creatures can lie patent to God, and open for the influx of a Divine Indweller, lies the way of faith and love. Whosoever opens his heart in these divinely-taught emotions, and fixes them upon the Christ in whom God dwells, receives into the very roots of his being— as the water that trickles through the soil to the rootlets of the tree—the very Godhead Himself. 'He that is joined to the Lord is one spirit.'

That God shall dwell in my heart is possible only from the fact that He dwelt in all His fulness in Christ, through whom I touch Him. That Temple consecrates all heart-shrines; and all worshippers that keep near to Him, partake with Him of the Father that dwelt in Him.

Only remember that in Christ God dwelt completely, all 'the fulness of the Godhead bodily' was there, but in us it is but partially; that in Christ, therefore, the divine indwelling was uniform and invariable, but in us it

D

fluctuates, and sometimes is more intimate and blessed, and sometimes He leaves the habitation when we leave Him; that in Christ, therefore, there was no progress in the divine indwelling, but that in us, if there be any true inhabitation of our souls by God, that abiding will become more and more, until every corner of our being is hallowed and filled with the searching efful-gence of the all-pervasive Light. And let us remember that God dwelt in Christ, but that in us it is God in Christ who dwells. So to Him we owe it all, that our poor hearts are made the dwelling-place of God; or, as this Apostle puts it, in other words conveying the same idea, 'Ye are built upon the foundation of the Apostles and prophets, Jesus Christ Himself being the chief Corner-stone; in whom all the building fitly framed together groweth . . . for a habitation of God through the Spirit.'

II. Now then, turning from this underlying idea of the passage, let us look, for a moment, at some of the many applications of which the great thought is sus-ceptible. I remark, then, in the second place, that as temples all Christians are to be manifesters of God.

The meaning of the Temple as of all temples was, that there the indwelling Deity should reveal Himself; and if it be true that we Christian men and women are, in this deep and blessed reality of which I have been speaking, the abiding places and habitations of God, then it follows that we shall stand in the world as the great means by which God is manifested and made known, and that in a two-fold way; *to ourselves* and *to other people.*

The real revelation of God to our hearts must be His abiding in our hearts. We do not learn God until we possess God. He must fill our souls before we know

His sweetness. The answer that our Lord made to one of His disciples is full of the deepest truth. 'How is it,' said one of them in his blundering way, 'how is it that Thou wilt manifest Thyself to us?' And the answer was, 'We will come and make Our abode with him.' You do not know God until, if I might so say, He sits at your fireside and talks with you in your hearts. Just as some wife may have a husband whom the world knows as hero, or sage, or orator, but she knows him as nobody else can; so the outside, and if I may so say, the public character of God is but the surface of the revelation that He makes to us, when in the deepest secrecy of our own hearts He pours Himself into our waiting spirits. O brethren! it is within the curtains of the Holiest of all that the Shekinah flashes; it is within our own hearts, shrined and templed there, that God reveals Himself to us, as He does not unto the world.

And then, further, Christian men, as the temples and habitations of God, are appointed to be the great means of making Him known to the world around. The eye that cannot look at the sun can look at the rosy clouds that lie on either side of it, and herald its rising; their opalescent tints and pearly lights are beautiful to dim vision, to which the sun itself is too bright to be looked upon. Men will believe in a gentle Christ when they see you gentle. They will believe in a righteous love when they see it manifesting itself in you. You are 'the secretaries of God's praise,' as George Herbert has it. He dwells in your hearts that out of your lives He may be revealed. The pictures in a book of travels, or the diagrams in a mathematical work, tell a great deal more in half a dozen lines than can be put into as many pages of dry words. And it is not books of theology nor eloquent sermons, but it is a Church glowing with the glory of God, and manifestly all flushed with His light and majesty, that will have power to draw men to believe in the God whom it reveals. When explorers land upon some untravelled island and meet the gentle inhabitants with armlets of rough gold upon their wrists, they say there must be many a gold-bearing rock of quartz crystal in the interior of the land. And if you present yourselves, Christian men and women, to the world with the likeness of your Master plain upon you, then people will believe in the Christianity that you profess. You have to popularise the Gospel in the fashion in which go-betweens and middlemen between students and the populace popularise science. You have to make it possible for men to believe in the Christ because they see Christ in you. 'Know ye not that ye are the temples of the living God?' Let His light shine from you.

III. I remark again that as temples all Christian lives should be places of sacrifice.

What is the use of a temple without worship? And what kind of worship is that in which the centre point is not an altar? That is the sort of temple that a great many professing Christians are. They have forgotten the altar in their spiritual architecture. Have you got one in your heart? It is but a poor, half-furnished sanctuary that has not. Where is yours? The key and the secret of all noble life is to yield up one's own will, to sacrifice oneself. There never was anything done in this world worth doing, and there never will be till the end of time, of which sacrifice is not the centre and inspiration. And the difference between all other and lesser nobilities of life, and the supreme

beauty of a true Christian life is that the sacrifice of
the Christian is properly a *sacrifice*—that is, an offering
to *God*, done for the sake of the great love wherewith
He has loved us. As Christ is the one true Temple,
and we become so by partaking of Him, so He is the
one Sacrifice for sins for ever, and we become sacrifices only through Him. If there be any lesson which
comes out of this great truth of Christians as temples,
it is not a lesson of pluming ourselves on our dignity,
or losing ourselves in the mysticisms which lie near
this truth, but it is the hard lesson—If a temple, then
an altar; if an altar, then a sacrifice. 'Ye are built up
a spiritual house, a holy priesthood, that ye may offer
spiritual sacrifices, acceptable to God'—sacrifice, priest,
temple, all in one; and all for the sake and by the
might of that dear Lord who has given Himself a
bleeding Sacrifice for the sins of the whole world, that
we might offer a Eucharistic sacrifice of thanks and
praise and self-surrender unto Him, and to His Father
God.

IV. And, lastly, this great truth of my text enforces
the solemn lesson of the necessary sanctity of the
Christian life.

'The temple of God,' says the context, 'the temple of
God is holy, which (holy persons) ye are.' The plain
first idea of the temple is a place set apart and consecrated to God.

Hence, of course, follows the idea of purity, but the
parent idea of 'holiness' is not purity, which is the
consequence, but consecration or separation to God,
which is the root.

And so in very various applications, on which I have
not time to dwell now, this idea of the necessary sanctity of the Temple is put forth in these two letters to

the Corinthian Church. Corinth was a city honey-combed with the grossest immoralities; and hence, perhaps, to some extent the great emphasis and earnest-ness and even severity of the Apostle in dealing with some forms of evil.

But without dwelling on the details, let me just point you to three directions in which this general notion of sanctity is applied. There is that of our context here. 'Know ye not that ye are the temple of God? If any man *destroy* the temple of God, him shall God destroy, for the temple of God is holy, and such ye are.'

He is thinking here mainly, I suppose, about the devastation and destruction of this temple of God, which was caused by schismatical and heretical teach-ing, and by the habit of forming parties, 'one of Paul, one of Apollos, one of Cephas, one of Christ,' which was rending that Corinthian Church into pieces. But we may apply it more widely than that, and say that anything which corrupts and defiles the Christian life and the Christian character assumes a darker tint of evil when we think that it is sacrilege—the profana-tion of the temple, the pollution of that which ought to be pure as He who dwells in it.

Christian men and women, how that thought darkens the blackness of all sin! How solemnly there peals out the warning, 'If any man destroy or impair the temple, by any form of pollution, 'him' with retribution in kind, 'him shall God destroy.' Keep the temple clear; keep it clean. Let Him come with His scourge of small cords and His merciful rebuke. You Man-chester men know what it is to let the money-changers into the sanctuary. Beware lest, beginning with making your hearts 'houses of merchandise,' you should end by making them 'dens of thieves.'

And then, still further, there is another application of this same principle, in the second of these Epistles. 'What agreement hath the temple of God with idols?' 'Ye are the temple of the living God.'

Christianity is intolerant. There is to be one image in the shrine. One of the old Roman Stoic Emperors had a pantheon in his palace with Jesus Christ upon one pedestal and Plato on the one beside Him. And some of us are trying the same kind of thing. Christ there, and somebody else here. Remember, Christ must be everything or nothing! Stars may be sown by millions, but for the earth there is one sun. And you and I are to shrine one dear Guest, and one only, in the inmost recesses of our hearts.

And there is another application of this metaphor also in our letter. 'Know ye not that your body is the temple of the Holy Ghost which is in you?' Christianity despises 'the flesh'; Christianity reverences the body; and would teach us all that, being robed in that most wonderful work of God's hands, which becomes a shrine for God Himself if He dwell in our hearts, all purity, all chastisement and subjugation of animal passion is our duty. Drunkenness, and gluttony, lusts of every kind, impurity of conduct, and impurity of word and look and thought, all these assume a still darker tint when they are thought of as not only crimes against the physical constitution and the moral law of humanity, but insults flung in the face of the God that would inhabit the shrine.

And in regard to sins of this kind, which it is so difficult to speak of in public, and which grow unchecked in secrecy, and are ruining hundreds of young lives, the words of this context are grimly true, 'If any man defile the temple of God, him shall God destroy.'

I speak now mainly in brotherly or fatherly warning to young men—did you ever read this, ' His bones are full of the iniquities of his youth, which shall lie down with him in the dust '? ' Know ye not that ye are the temple of God?'

And so, brethren, our text tells us what we may all be. There is no heart without its deity. Alas! alas! for the many listening to me now whose spirits are like some of those Egyptian temples, which had in the inmost shrine a coiled-up serpent, the mummy of a monkey, or some other form as animal and obscene.

Oh! turn to Christ and cry, ' Arise, O Lord, into Thy rest, Thou and the ark of Thy strength.' Open your hearts and let Christ come in. And before Him, as of old, the bestial Dagon will be found, dejected and truncated, lying on the sill there; and all the vain, cruel, lustful gods that have held riot and carnival in your hearts will flee away into the darkness, like some foul ghosts at cock-crow. ' If any man hear My voice and open the door I will come in.' And the glory of the Lord shall fill the house.

DEATH, THE FRIEND

'. . . All things are yours . . . death.'—1 Cor. iii. 21, 22.

WHAT Jesus Christ is to a man settles what everything else is to Him. Our relation to Jesus determines our relation to the universe. If we belong to Him, everything belongs to us. If we are His servants, all things are our servants. The household of Jesus, which is the whole Creation, is not divided against itself, and the fellow-servants do not beat one another. Two bodies moving in the same direction, and under the impulse of the same force, cannot come into collision, and since 'all things work together,' according to the counsel of His will, 'all things work together for good' to His lovers. The triumphant words of my text are no piece of empty rhetoric, but the plain result of two facts—Christ's rule and the Christian's submission. 'All things are yours, and ye are Christ's,' so the stars in their courses fight against those who fight against Him, and if we are at peace with Him we shall 'make a league with the beasts of the field, and the stones of the field,' which otherwise would be hindrances and stumbling-blocks, 'shall be at peace with' us.

The Apostle carries his confidence in the subservience of all things to Christ's servants very far, and the words of my text, in which he dares to suggest that 'the Shadow feared of man' is, after all, a veiled friend, are hard to believe, when we are brought face to face with death, either when we meditate on our own end, or when our hearts are sore and our hands are empty. Then the question comes, and often is asked with tears of blood, Is it true that this awful force, which we cannot command, does indeed serve us? Did it serve those whom it dragged from our sides; and in serving them, did it serve us? Paul rings out his 'Yes'; and if we have as firm a hold of Paul's Lord as Paul had, our answer will be the same. Let me, then, deal with this great thought that lies here, of the conversion of the last enemy into a friend, the assurance that we may all have that death is ours, though not in the sense that we can command it, yet in the sense that it ministers to our highest good.

That thought may be true about ourselves when it

comes to our turn to die, and, thank God, has been true about all those who have departed in His faith and fear. Some of you may have seen two very striking engravings by a great, though somewhat unknown artist, representing Death as the Destroyer, and Death as the Friend. In the one case he comes into a scene of wild revelry, and there at his feet lie, stark and stiff, corpses in their gay clothing and with garlands on their brows, and feasters and musicians are flying in terror from the cowled Skeleton. In the other he comes into a quiet church belfry, where an aged saint sits with folded arms and closed eyes, and an open Bible by his side, and endless peace upon the wearied face. The window is flung wide to the sunrise, and on its sill perches a bird that gives forth its morning song. The cowled figure has brought rest to the weary, and the glad dawning of a new life to the aged, and is a friend. The two pictures are better than all the poor words that I can say. It depends on the people to whom he comes, whether he comes as a destroyer or as a helper. Of course, for all of us the mere physical facts remain the same, the pangs and the pain, the slow torture of the loosing of the bond, or the sharp agony of its instantaneous rending apart. But we have gone but a very little way into life and its experiences, if we have not learnt that identity of circumstances may cover profound difference of essentials, and that the same experiences may have wholly different messages and meanings to two people who are equally implicated in them. Thus, while the physical fact remains the same for all, the whole bearing of it may so differ that Death to one man will be a Destroyer, while to another it is a Friend.

For, if we come to analyse the thoughts of humanity about the last act in human life on earth, what is

it that makes the dread darkness of death, which all
men know, though they so seldom think of it?   I
suppose, first of all, if we seek to question our feelings, that which makes Death a foe to the ordinary
experience is, that it is like a step off the edge of a
precipice in a fog; a step into a dim condition of which
the imagination can form no conception, because it has
no experience, and all imagination's pictures are painted
with pigments drawn from our past.   Because it is impossible for a man to have any clear vision of what it
is that is coming to meet him, and he cannot tell 'in
that sleep what dreams may come,' he shrinks, as we
all shrink, from a step into the vast Inane, the dim
Unknown.   But the Gospel comes and says, 'It *is* a
land of great darkness,' but 'To the people that sit in
darkness a great light hath shined.'

> ' Our knowledge of that life is small,
>   The eye of faith is dim.'

But faith has an eye, and there is light, and this we can
see—One face whose brightness scatters all the gloom,
One Person who has not ceased to be the Sun of
Righteousness with healing in His beams, even in the
darkness of the grave.   Therefore, one at least of the
repellent features which, to the timorous heart, makes
Death a foe, is gone, when we know that the known
Christ fills the Unknown.

Then, again, another of the elements, as I suppose,
which constitute the hostile aspect that Death assumes
to most of us, is that it apparently hales us away from
all the wholesome activities and occupations of life,
and bans us into a state of apparent inaction.   The
thought that death is rest does sometimes attract the
weary or harassed, or they fancy it does, but that is a

morbid feeling, and much more common in sentimental epitaphs than among the usual thoughts of men. To most of us there is no joy, but a chill, in the anticipation that all the forms of activity which have so occupied, and often enriched, our lives here, are to be cut off at once. 'What am I to do if I have no books?' says the student. 'What am I to do if I have no mill?' says the spinner. 'What am I to do if I have no nursery or kitchen?' say the women. What are you to do? There is only one quieting answer to such questions. It tells us that what we are doing here is learning our trade, and that we are to be moved into another workshop there, to practise it. Nothing can bereave us of the force we made our own, being here; and 'there is nobler work for us to do' when the Master of all the servants stoops from His Throne and says: 'Thou hast been faithful over a few things, I will make thee ruler over many things; have thou authority over ten cities.' Then the faithfulness of the steward will be exchanged for the authority of the ruler, and the toil of the servant for a share in the joy of the Lord.

So another of the elements which make Death an enemy is turned into an element which makes it a friend, and instead of the separation from this earthly body, the organ of our activity and the medium of our connection with the external universe being the condemnation of the naked spirit to inaction, it is the emancipation of the spirit into greater activity. For nothing drops away at death that does not make a man the richer for its loss, and when the dross is purged from the silver, there remains 'a vessel unto honour, fit for the Master's use.' This mightier activity is the contribution to our blessedness, which Death makes to them who use their activities here in Christ's service.

Then, still further, another of the elements which is converted from being a terror into a joy is that Death, the separator, becomes to Christ's servants Death, the uniter. We all know how that function of death is perhaps the one that makes us shrink from it the most, dread it the most, and sometimes hate it the most. But it will be with us as it was with those who were to be initiated into ancient religious rites. Blindfolded, they were led by a hand that grasped theirs but was not seen, through dark, narrow, devious passages, but they were led into a great company in a mighty hall. Seen from this side, the ministry of Death parts a man from dear ones, but, oh ! if we could see round the turn in the corridor, we should see that the solitude is but for a moment, and that the true office of Death is not so much to part from those beloved on earth as to carry to, and unite with, Him that is best Beloved in the heavens, and in Him with all His saints. They that are joined to Christ, as they who pass from earth are joined, are thereby joined to all who, in like manner, are knit to Him. Although other dear bonds are loosed by the bony fingers of the Skeleton, his very loosing of them ties more closely the bond that unites us to Jesus, and when the dull ear of the dying has ceased to hear the voices of earth that used to thrill it in their lowest whisper, I suppose it hears another Voice that says : 'When thou passest through the fire I will be with thee, and through the waters they shall not over-flow thee.' Thus the Separator unites, first to Jesus, and then to 'the general assembly and Church of the first-born,' and leads into the city of the living God, the pilgrims who long have lived, often isolated, in the desert.

There is a last element in Death which is changed for

the Christian, and that is that to men generally, when they think about it, there is an instinctive recoil from Death, because there is an instinctive suspicion that after Death is the Judgment, and that, somehow or other—never mind about the drapery in which the idea may be embodied for our weakness—when a man dies he passes to a state where he will reap the consequences of what he has sown here. But to Christ's servant that last thought is robbed of its sting, and all the poison sucked out of it, for he can say: 'He that died for me makes it possible for me to die undreading, and to pass thither, knowing that I shall meet as my Judge Him whom I have trusted as my Saviour, and so may have boldness before Him in the Day of Judgment.'

Knit these four contrasts together. Death as a step into a dim unknown *versus* Death as a step into a region lighted by Jesus; Death as the cessation of activity *versus* Death as the introduction to nobler opportunities, and the endowment with nobler capacities of service; Death as the separator and isolator *versus* Death as uniting to Jesus and all His lovers; Death as haling us to the judgment-seat of the adversary *versus* Death as bringing us to the tribunal of the Christ; and I think we can understand how Christians can venture to say, ' All things are ours, whether life or death' which leads to a better life.

And now let me add one word more. All this that I have been saying, and all the blessed strength for ourselves and calming in our sorrows which result therefrom, stand or fall with the Resurrection of Jesus Christ. There is nothing else that makes these things certain. There are, of course, instincts, peradventures, hopes, fears, doubts. But in this region, and in regard

to all this cycle of truths, the same thing applies which
applies round the whole horizon of Christian Revelation—if you want not speculations but certainties, you
have to go to Jesus Christ for them.   There were
many men who thought that there were islands of
the sea beyond the setting sun that dyed the western
waves, but Columbus went and came back again, and
brought their products—and then the thought became
a fact.   Unless you believe that Jesus Christ has
come back from 'the bourne from which no traveller
returns,' and has come laden with the gifts of 'happy
isles of Eden' far beyond the sea, there is no certitude
upon which a dying man can lay his head, or by which
a bleeding heart can be staunched.   But when He
draws near, alive from the dead, and says to us, as He
did to the disciples on the evening of the day of
Resurrection, 'Peace be unto you,' and shows us His
hands and His side, then we do not only speculate or
think a future life possible or probable, or hesitate to
deny it, or hope or fear, as the case may be, but we
know, and we can say : 'All things are ours . . . death'
amongst others.   The fact that Jesus Christ has died
changes the whole aspect of death to His servant, inasmuch as in that great solitude he has a companion,
and in the valley of the shadow of death sees footsteps
that tell him of One that went before.

Nor need I do more than remind you how the manner
of our Lord's death shows that He is Lord not only of
the dead but of the Death that makes them dead.   For
His own tremendous assertion, 'I have power to lay
down My life, and I have power to take it again,' was
confirmed by His attitude and His words at the last, as
is hinted at by the very expressions with which the
Evangelists record the fact of His death : 'He yielded up

His spirit,' 'He gave up the ghost,' 'He breathed out His life.' It is confirmed to us by such words as those remarkable ones of the Apocalypse, which speak of Him as 'the Living One,' who, by His own will, 'became dead.' He died because He would, and He would die because He loved you and me. And in dying, He showed Himself to be, not the Victim, but the Conqueror, of the Death to which He submitted. The Jewish king on the fatal field of Gilboa called his sword-bearer, and the servant came, and Saul bade him smite, and when his trembling hand shrank from such an act, the king fell on his own sword. The Lord of life and death summoned His servant Death, and He came obedient, but Jesus died not by Death's stroke, but by His own act. So that Lord of Death, who died because He would, is the Lord who has the keys of death and the grave. In regard to one servant He says, 'I will that he tarry till I come,' and that man lives through a century, and in regard to another He says, 'Follow thou Me,' and that man dies on a cross. The dying Lord is Lord of Death, and the living Lord is for us all the Prince of Life.

Brethren, we have to take His yoke upon us by the act of faith which leads to a love that issues in an obedience which will become more and more complete, as we become more fully Christ's. Then death will be ours, for then we shall count that the highest good for us will be fuller union with, a fuller possession of, and a completer conformity to, Jesus Christ our King, and that whatever brings us these, even though it brings also pain and sorrow and much from which we shrink, is all on our side. It is possible—may it be so with each of us!—that for us Death may be, not an enemy that bans us into darkness and inactivity, or hales us to a judgment-seat, but the Angel who wakes us, at whose touch the chains fall off, and who leads us through 'the iron gate that opens of its own accord,' and brings us into the City.

SERVANTS AND LORDS

'All things are yours; 22. Whether Paul, or Apollos, or Cephas, or the world, or life, or death, or things present, or things to come; all are yours; 23. And ye are Christ's.'—1 Cor. iii. 21-23.

THE Corinthian Christians seem to have carried into the Church some of the worst vices of Greek—and English—political life. They were split up into wrangling factions, each swearing by the name of some person. Paul was the battle-cry of one set; Apollos of another. Paul and Apollos were very good friends, their admirers bitter foes—according to a very common experience. The springs lie close together up in the hills, the rivers may be parted by half a continent.

These feuds were all the more detestable to the Apostle because his name was dragged into them; and so he sets himself, in the first part of this letter, with all his might, to shame and to argue the Corinthian Christians out of their wrangling. This great text is one of the considerations which he adduces with that purpose. In effect he says, 'To pin your faith to any one teacher is a wilful narrowing of the sources of your blessing and your wisdom. You say you are Paul's men. Has Apollos got nothing that he could teach you? and may you not get any good out of brave brother Cephas? Take them all; they were all meant for your good. Let no man glory in individuals.'

That is all that his argument required him to say. But in his impetuous way he goes on into regions far

E

beyond. His thought, like some swiftly revolving wheel, catches fire of its own rapid motion; and he blazes up into this triumphant enumeration of all the things that serve the soul which serves Jesus Christ. 'You are lords of men, of the world of time, of death, of eternity; but you are not lords of yourselves. You belong to Jesus, and in the measure in which you belong to Him do all things belong to you.'

I. I think, then, that I shall best bring out the fulness of these words by simply following them as they lie before us, and asking you to consider, first, how Christ's servants are men's lords.

'All things are yours, Paul, Apollos, Cephas.' These three teachers were all lights kindled at the central Light, and therefore shining. They were fragments of His wisdom, of Him that spoke; varying, but yet harmonious, and mutually complementary aspects of the one infinite Truth had been committed to them. Each was but a part of the mighty whole, a little segment of the circle

> 'They are but broken lights of Thee,
> And Thou, O Lord! art more than they.'

And in the measure, therefore, in which men adhere to Christ, and have taken Him for theirs; in that measure are they delivered from all undue dependence on, still more from all slavish submission to, any single individual teacher or aspect of truth. To have Christ for ours, and to be His, which are only the opposite sides of the same thing, mean, in brief, to take Jesus Christ for the source of all knowledge of moral and religious truth. His Word is the Christian's creed, His Person and the truths that lie in Him, are the fountains of all our knowledge of God and man. To be Christ's

is to take Him as the master who has absolute authority
over conduct and practice. His commandment is the
Christian's duty ; His pattern the Christian's all-
sufficient example; His smile the Christian's reward.
To be Christ's is to take Him for the home of our hearts,
in whose gracious and sweet love we find all sufficiency
and a rest for our seeking affections. And so, if ye are
His, Paul, Apollos, Cephas, all men are yours; in the
sense that you are delivered from all undue dependence
upon them; and in the sense that they subserve your
highest good.

So the true democracy of Christianity, which abjures
swearing by the words of any teacher, is simply the
result of loyal adherence to the teaching of Jesus
Christ. And that proud independence which some of
you seek to cultivate, and on the strength of which
you declare that no man is your master upon earth,
is an unwholesome and dangerous independence, unless
it be conjoined with the bowing down of the whole
nature, in loyal submission, to the absolute authority
of the only lips that ever spoke truth, truth only, and
truth always. If Christ be our Master, if we take our
creed from Him, if we accept His words and His
revelation of the Father as our faith and our objective
religion, then all the slavery to favourite names, all the
taking of truth second-hand from the lips that we
honour, all the partisanship for one against another
which has been the shame and the ruin of the Christian
Church, and is working untold mischiefs in it to-day,
are ended at once. 'One is your Master, even Christ.'
'Call no man Rabbi! upon earth ; but bow before
Him, the Incarnate and the Personal Truth.'

And in like manner they who are Christ's are delivered
from all temptations to make men's maxims and prac-

tices and approbation the law of their conduct.
Society presses upon each of us; what we call public
opinion, which is generally the clatter of the half-
dozen people that happen to stand nearest us, rules us;
and it needs to be said very emphatically to all Christian
men and women—Take your law of conduct from His
lips, and from nobody else's.

'They say. What say they? Let them say.' If we
take Christ's commandment for our absolute law, and
Christ's approbation for our highest aim and all-
sufficient reward, we shall then be able to brush aside
other maxims and other people's opinions of us, safely
and humbly, and to say, 'With me it is a very small
matter to be judged of you, or of man's judgment. He
that judgeth me is the Lord.'

The envoy of some foreign power cares very little
what the inhabitants of the land to which he is
ambassador may think of him and his doings; it is his
sovereign's good opinion that he seeks to secure. The
soldier's reward is his commander's praise, the slave's
joy is the master's smile, and for us it ought to be the
law of our lives, and in the measure in which we really
belong to Christ it will be the law of our lives, that 'we
labour that, whether present or absent, we may be
pleasing to Him.'

So, brethren, as teachers, as patterns, as objects of
love which is only too apt to be exclusive and to master
us, we can only take one another in subordination to
our supreme submission to Christ, and if we are His,
our duty, as our joy, is to count no man necessary to
our wellbeing, but to hang only on the one Man, whom
it is safe and blessed to believe utterly, to obey abjectly,
and to love with all our strength, because He is more
than man, even God manifest in the flesh.

II. And now let us pass to the next idea here, secondly, Christ's servants are the lords of 'the world.'

That phrase is used here, no doubt, as meaning the external material universe. These creatures around us, they belong to us, if we belong to Jesus Christ. That man owns the world who despises it. There are plenty of rich men in Manchester who say they possess so many thousand pounds. Turn the sentence about and it would be a great deal truer—the thousands of pounds possess them. They are the slaves of their own possessions, and every man who counts any material thing as indispensable to his wellbeing, and regards it as the chiefest good, is the slave-servant of that thing. He owns the world who turns it to the highest use of growing his soul by it. All material things are given, and, I was going to say, were created, for the growth of men, or at all events their highest purpose is that men should, by them, grow. And therefore, as the scaffolding is swept away when the building is finished, so God will sweep away this material universe with all its wonders of beauty and of contrivance, when men have been grown by means of it. The material is less than the soul, and he is master of the world, and owns it, who has got thoughts out of it, truth out of it, impulses out of it, visions of God out of it, who has by it been led nearer to his divine Master. If I look out upon a fair landscape, and the man who draws the rents of it is standing by my side, and I suck more sweetness, and deeper impulses, and larger and loftier thoughts out of it than he does, it belongs to me far more than it does to him. The world is his who from it has learned to despise it, to know himself and to know God. He owns the world who uses it as the arena, or wrestling ground, on which, by labour, he may gain strength, and in which he may do service. Antagonism helps to develop muscle, and the best use of the outward frame of things is that we shall take it as the field upon which we can serve God.

And now all these three things—the contempt of earth, the use of earth for growing souls, and the use of earth as the field of service—all these things belong most truly to the man who belongs to Christ. The world is His, and if we live near Him and cultivate fellowship with Him, and see His face gleaming through all the Material, and are led up nearer to Him by everything around us, then we own the world and wring the sweetness to the last drop out of it, though we may have but little of that outward relation to its goods which short-sighted men call possessing them. We may solve the paradox of those who, 'having nothing, yet have all,' if we belong to Christ the Lord of all things, and so have co-possession with Him of all His riches.

III. Further, my text tells us, in the third place, that Christian men, who belong to Jesus Christ, are the lords and masters of 'life and death.'

Both of these words are here used, as it seems to me, in their simple, physical sense, natural life and natural death. You may say, 'Well, everybody is lord of life in that sense.' Yes, of course, in a fashion we all possess it, seeing that we are all alive. But that mysterious gift of personality, that awful gift of conscious existence, only belongs, in the deepest sense, to the men who belong to Jesus Christ. I do not call that man the owner of his own life who is not the lord of his own spirit. I do not see in what, except in the mere animal sense in which a fly, or a spider, or a toad may be called the master of its life, that man owns

himself who has not given up himself to Jesus Christ.
The only way to get a real hold of yourselves is to
yield yourselves to Him who gives you back Himself,
and yourself along with Him. The true ownership of
life depends upon self-control, and self-control depends
upon letting Jesus Christ govern us wholly. So the
measure in which it is true of me that 'I live; yet not
I, but Christ liveth in me,' is the measure in which the
lower life of sense really belongs to us, and ministers
to our highest good.

And then turn to the other member of this wonderful
antithesis, 'whether life or *death*.' Surely if there is
anything over which no man can become lord, except
by sinfully taking his fate into his own hands, it is
death. And yet even death, in which we seem to be
abjectly passive, and by which so many of us are
dragged away reluctantly from everything that we
care to possess, may become a matter of consent and
therefore a moral act. Animals expire; a Christian
man may yield his soul to his Saviour, who is the Lord
both of the dead and of the living. If thus we feel our
dependence upon Him, and yield up our lives to Him,
and can say, 'Living or dying we are the Lord's,' then
we may be quite sure that death, too, will be our
servant, and that our wills will be concerned even in
passing out of life.

Still more, if you and I, dear brethren, belong to
Jesus Christ, then death is our fellow-servant who
comes to call us out of this ill-lighted workshop into
the presence of the King. And at His magic cold touch,
cares and toils and sorrows are stiffened into silence,
like noisy streams bound in white frost; and we are
lifted clean up out of all the hubbub and the toil into
eternal calm. Death is ours because it fulfils our

deepest desires, and comes as a messenger to paupers to tell them they have a great estate. Death is ours if we be Christ's.

IV. And lastly, Christ's servants are the lords of time and eternity, 'things present or things to come.'

Our Apostle's division, in this catalogue of his, is rhetorical rather than logical; and we need not seek to separate the first of this final pair from others which we have already encountered in our study of the words, but still we may draw a distinction. The whole mass of ' things present,' including not only that material universe which we call the world, but all the events and circumstances of our lives, over these we may exercise supreme control. If we are bowing in humble submission to Jesus Christ, they will all subserve our highest good. Every weather will be right; night and day equally desirable; the darkness will be good for eyes that have been tired of brightness and that need repose, the light will be good. The howling tempests of winter and its white snows, the sharp winds of spring and its bursting sunshine; the calm steady heat of June and the mellowing days of August, all serve to ripen the grain. And so all ' things present,' the light and the dark, the hopes fulfilled and the hopes disappointed, the gains and the losses, the prayers answered and the prayers unanswered, they will all be recognised, if we have the wisdom that comes from submission to Jesus Christ's will, as being ours and ministering to our highest blessing.

We shall be their lords too inasmuch as we shall be able to control them. We need not be 'anvils but hammers.' We need not let outward circumstances dominate and tyrannise over us. We need not be like the mosses in the stream, that lie whichever way the

current sets, nor like some poor little sailing boat that
is at the mercy of the winds and the waves, but may
carry an inward impulse like some great ocean-going
steamer, the throb of whose power shall drive us
straight forward on our course, whatever beats against
us.   That we may have this inward power and mastery
over things present, and not be shaped and moulded and
made by them, let us yield ourselves to Christ, and He
will help us to rule them.

And then, all 'things to come,' the dim, vague
future, shall be for each of us like some sunlit ocean
stretching shoreless to the horizon; every little ripple
flashing with its own bright sunshine, and all bearing
us onwards to the great Throne that stands on the sea
of glass mingled with fire.

Then, my brother, ask yourselves what your future
is if you have not Christ for your Friend.

> 'I backward cast mine eye
>   On prospects drear ;
> And forward though I cannot see,
>   I guess and fear.'

So I beseech you, yield yourselves to Jesus Christ.
He died to win us.   He bears our sins that they may
be all forgiven.   If we give ourselves to Him who has
given Himself to us, then we shall be lords of men, of
the world, of life and death, of time and eternity.

In the old days conquerors used to bestow upon their
followers lands and broad dominions on condition of
their doing suit and service, and bringing homage to
them.   Christ, the King of the universe, makes His
subjects kings, and will give us to share in His dominion,
so that to each of us may be fulfilled that boundless
and almost unbelievable promise: 'He that overcometh
shall inherit all things.' 'All are yours if ye are Christ's.'

THE THREE TRIBUNALS

'But with me it is a very small thing that I should be judged of you, or of man's judgment: yea, I judge not mine own self. 4. For I know nothing by myself; yet am I not hereby justified; but he that judgeth me is the Lord.'—1 Cor. iv. 3, 4.

THE Church at Corinth was honeycombed by the characteristic Greek vice of party spirit. The three great teachers, Paul, Peter, Apollos, were pitted against each other, and each was unduly exalted by those who swore by him, and unduly depreciated by the other two factions. But the men whose names were the war-cries of these sections were themselves knit in closest friendship, and felt themselves to be servants in common of one Master, and fellow-workers in one task.

So Paul, in the immediate context, associating Peter and Apollos with himself, bids the Corinthians think of '*us*' as being servants of Christ, and not therefore responsible to men; and as stewards of the mysteries of God, that is, dispensers of truths long hidden but now revealed, and as therefore accountable for correct accounts and faithful dispensation only to the Lord of the household. Being responsible to Him, they heeded very little what others thought about them. Being responsible to Him, they could not accept vindication by their own consciences as being final. There was a judgment beyond these.

So here we have three tribunals—that of man's estimates, that of our own consciences, that of Jesus Christ. An appeal lies from the first to the second, and from the second to the third. It is base to depend on men's judgments; it is well to attend to the decisions of conscience, but it is not well to take it for granted that, if conscience approve, we are absolved. The court

of final appeal is Jesus Christ, and what He thinks
about each of us. So let us look briefly at these three
tribunals.

I. First, the lowest—men's judgment.

'With me it is a very small thing that I should be
judged of you,' enlightened Christians that you are, or
by the outside world. Now, Paul's letters give ample
evidence that he was keenly alive to the hostile and
malevolent criticisms and slanders of his untiring
opponents. Many a flash of sarcasm out of the cloud
like a lightning bolt, many a burst of wounded affection like rain from summer skies, tell us this. But I
need not quote these. Such a character as his could
not but be quick to feel the surrounding atmosphere,
whether it was of love or of suspicion. So, he had to
harden himself against what naturally had a great
effect upon him, the estimate which he felt that people
round him were making of him. There was nothing
brusque, rough, contemptuous in his brushing aside
these popular judgments. He gave them all due
weight, and yet he felt, 'From all that this lowest
tribunal may decide, there are two appeals, one to my
own conscience, and one to my Master in heaven.'

Now, I suppose I need not say a word about the
power which that terrible court which is always sitting,
and which passes judgment upon every one of us,
though we do not always hear the sentences read, has
upon us all. There is a power which it is meant to
have. It is not good for a man to stand constantly in
the attitude of defying whatever anybody else chooses
to say or to think about him. But the danger to which
we are all exposed, far more than that other extreme,
is of deferring too completely and slavishly to, and being
far too subtly influenced in all that we do by, the

thought of what A, B, or C, may have to say or to think
about it. 'The last infirmity of noble minds,' says
Milton about the love of fame. It is an infirmity to
love it, and long for it, and live by it. It is a weakening of humanity, even where men are spurred to great
efforts by the thought of the reverberation of these in
the ear of the world, and of the honour and glory that
may come therefrom.

But not only in these higher forms of seeking after
reputation, but in lower forms, this trembling before,
and seeking to conciliate, the tribunal of what we call
'general opinion,' which means the voices of the half-
dozen people that are beside us and know about us,
besets us all, and weakens us all in a thousand ways.
How many men would lose all the motive that they
have for living reputable lives, if nobody knew anything about it? How many of you, when you go to
London, and are strangers, frequent places that you
would not be seen in in Manchester? How many of us
are hindered, in courses which we know that we ought
to pursue, because we are afraid of this or that man or
woman, and of what they may look or speak? There
is a regard to man's judgment, which is separated by
the very thinnest partition from hypocrisy. There is
a very shadowy distinction between the man who, consciously or unconsciously, does a thing with an eye to
what people may say about it, and the man who pre-
tends to be what he is not for the sake of the reputation
that he may thereby win.

Now, the direct tendency of Christian faith and
principle is to dwindle into wholesome insignificance
the multitudinous voice of men's judgments. For, if I
understand at all what Christianity means, it means
centrally and essentially this, that I am brought into

loving personal relation with Jesus Christ, and draw
from Him the power of my life, and from Him the law
of my life, and from Him the stimulus of my life, and
from Him the reward of my life. If there is a direct
communication between me and Him, and if I am
deriving from Him the life that He gives, which is 'free
from the law of sin and death,' I shall have little need
or desire to heed the judgment that men, who see only
the surface, may pass upon me, and upon my doings,
and I shall refer myself to Him instead of to them.
Those who can go straight to Christ, whose lives are
steeped in Him, who feel that they draw all from Him,
and that their actions and character are moulded by
His touch and His Spirit, are responsible to no other
tribunal.   And the less they think about what men
have to say of them the stronger, the nobler, the more
Christ-like they will be.

There is no need for any contempt or roughness to
blend with such a putting aside of men's judgments.
The velvet glove may be worn upon the iron hand. All
meekness and lowliness may go with this wholesome
independence, and must go with it unless that independence is false and distorted. 'With me it is a very
small thing to be judged of you, or of man's judgment,'
need not be said in such a tone as to mean 'I do not
care a rush what you think about me'; but it must be
said in such a tone as to mean 'I care supremely for
one approbation, and if I have that I can bear anything
besides.'

Let me appeal to you to cultivate more distinctly, as
a plain Christian duty, this wholesome independence
of men's judgment. I suppose there never was a day
when it was more needed that men should be themselves, seeing with their own eyes what God may reveal

to them and they are capable of receiving, and walking
with their own feet on the path that fits them, whatsoever other people may say about it.   For the multi-
plication of daily literature, the way in which we are
all living in glass houses nowadays—everybody knowing everything about everybody else, and delighting in
the gossip which takes the place of literature in so
many quarters—and the tendency of society to a more
democratic form give the many-headed monster and
its many tongues far more power than is wholesome,
in the shaping of the lives and character and conduct
of most men.   The evil of democracy is that it levels
down all to one plane, and that it tends to turn out
millions of people, as like each other as if they had been
made in a machine.   And so we need, I believe, even
more than our fathers did, to lay to heart this lesson,
that the direct result of a deep and strong Christian
faith is the production of intensely individual character.   And if there are plenty of angles in it, perhaps
so much the better.   We are apt to be rounded by being
rubbed against each other, like the stones on the beach,
till there is not a sharp corner or a point that can prick
anywhere.   So society becomes utterly monotonous,
and is insipid and profitless because of that.   You
Christian people, be yourselves, after your own pattern.
And whilst you accept all help from surrounding sug-
gestions and hints, make it 'a very small thing that
you be judged of men.'   And you, young men, in warehouses and shops, and you, students, and you, boys and
girls, that are budding into life, never mind what other
people say.   'Let thine eyes look right onwards,' and
let all the clatter on either side of you go on as it will.
The voices are very loud, but if we go up high enough
on the hill-top, to the secret place of the Most High, we

shall look down and see, but not hear, the bustle and the buzz; and in the great silence Christ will whisper to us, 'Well done! good and faithful servant.' That praise is worth getting, and one way to get it is to put aside the hindrance of anxious seeking to conciliate the good opinion of men.

II. Note the higher court of conscience.

Our Apostle is not to be taken here as contradicting what he says in other places. 'I judge not mine own self,'—yet in one of these same letters to the Corinthians he says, 'If we judged ourselves we should not be judged.' So that he does not mean here that he is entirely without any estimate of his own character or actions. That he did in some sense judge himself is evident from the next clause, because he goes on to say, 'I know nothing against myself.' If he acquitted himself, he must previously have been judging himself. But his acquittal of himself is not to be understood as if it covered the whole ground of his life and character, but it is to be confined to the subject in hand—viz. his faithfulness as a steward of the mysteries of God. But though there is nothing in that region of his life which he can charge against himself as unfaithfulness, he goes on to say, 'Yet am I not hereby justified?'

Our absolution by conscience is not infallible. I suppose that conscience is more reliable when it condemns than when it acquits. It is never safe for a man to neglect it when it says, 'You are wrong!' It is just as unsafe for a man to accept it, without further investigation, when it says, 'You are right!' For the only thing that is infallible about what we call conscience is its sentence, 'It is right to do right.' But when it proceeds to say 'This, that, and the other thing is right; and therefore it is right for you to do it,' there may be errors in the judgment, as everybody's own experience tells them. The inward judge needs to be stimulated, to be enlightened, to be corrected often. I suppose that the growth of Christian character is very largely the discovery that things that we thought innocent are not, for us, so innocent as we thought them.

You only need to go back to history, or to go down into your own histories, to see how, as light has increased, dark corners have been revealed that were invisible in the less brilliant illumination. How long it has taken the Christian Church to find out what Christ's Gospel teaches about slavery, about the relations of sex, about drunkenness, about war, about a hundred other things that you and I do not yet know, but which our successors will wonder that we failed to see! Inquisitor and martyr have equally said, 'We are serving God.' Surely, too, nothing is more clearly witnessed by individual experience, than that we may do a wrong thing, and think that it is right. 'They that kill you will think that they do God service.'

So, Christian people, accept the inward monition when it is stern and prohibitive. Do not be too sure about it when it is placable and permissive. 'Happy is he that condemneth not himself in the thing which he alloweth.' There may be secret faults, lying all unseen beneath the undergrowth in the forest, which yet do prick and sting. The upper floors of the house where we receive company, and where we, the tenants, generally live, may be luxurious, and sweet, and clean. What about the cellars, where ugly things crawl and swarm, and breed, and sting?

Ah, dear brethren! when my conscience says to me, 'You may do it,' it is always well to go to Jesus Christ, and say to Him 'May I?' 'Search me, O God, and ...

see if there be any wicked way in me,' and show it to me, and help me to cast it out. 'I know nothing against myself; yet am I not hereby justified.'

III. Lastly, note the supreme court of final appeal.

'He that judgeth me is the Lord.' Now it is obvious that 'the Lord' here is Christ, both because of the preceding context and because of the next verse, which speaks of His coming. And it is equally obvious, though it is often unnoticed, that the judgment of which the Apostle is here speaking is a present and preliminary judgment. 'He that *judgeth* me'—not, 'will judge,' but *now*, at this very moment. That is to say, whilst people round us are passing their superficial estimates upon me, and whilst my conscience is excusing, or else accusing me—and in neither case with absolute infallibility—there is another judgment, running concurrently with them, and going on in silence. That calm eye is fixed upon me, and sifting me, and knowing me. *That* judgment is not fallible, because before Him 'the hidden things' that the darkness shelters, those creeping things in the cellars that I was speaking about, are all manifest; and to Him the 'counsels of the heart,' that is, the motives from which the actions flow, are all transparent and legible. So His judgment, the continual estimate of me which Jesus Christ, in His supreme knowledge of me, has, at every moment of my life—*that* is uttering the final word about me and my character.

His estimate will dwindle the sentences of the other two tribunals into nothingness. What matter what his fellow-servants say about the steward's accounts, and distribution of provisions, and management of the household? He has to render his books, and to give account of his stewardship, only to his lord.

F

The governor of a Crown Colony may attach some importance to colonial opinion, but he reports home; and it is what the people in Downing Street will say that he thinks about. We have to report home; and it is the King whom we serve, to whom we have to give an account. The gladiator, down in the arena, did not much mind whether the thumbs of the populace were up or down, though the one was the signal for his life and the other for his death. He looked to the place where, between the purple curtains and the flashing axes of the lictors, the emperor sate. Our Emperor once was down on the sand Himself, and although we are 'compassed about with a cloud of witnesses,' we look to the Christ, the supreme Arbiter, and take acquittal or condemnation, life or death, from Him.

That judgment, persistent all through each of our lives, is preliminary to the future tribunal and sentence. The Apostle employs in this context two distinct words, both of which are translated in our version 'judge.' The one which is used in these three clauses, on which I have been commenting, means a preliminary examination, and the one which is used in the next verse means a final decisive trial and sentence. So, dear brethren, Christ is gathering materials for His final sentence; and you and I are writing the depositions which will be adduced in evidence. Oh! how little all that the world may have said about a man will matter then! Think of a man standing before that great white throne, and saying, 'I held a very high place in the estimation of my neighbours. The newspapers and the reviews blew my trumpet assiduously. My name was carved upon the plinth of a marble statue, that my fellow-citizens set up in honour of my many virtues,'—and the name was illegible centuries before the statue was burned in the last fire!

Brother! seek for the praise from Him, which is praise indeed. If He says, 'Well done, good and faithful servant,' it matters little what censures men may pass on us. If He says, 'I never knew you,' all their praises will not avail. 'Wherefore we labour that, whether present or absent, we may be well-pleasing to Him.'

THE FESTAL LIFE.

'Therefore let us keep the feast, not with old leaven . . . but with the unleavened bread of sincerity and truth.'—1 Cor. v. 8.

THERE had been hideous immorality in the Corinthian Church. Paul had struck at it with heat and force, sternly commanding the exclusion of the sinner. He did so on the ground of the diabolical power of infection possessed by evil, and illustrated that by the very obvious metaphor of leaven, a morsel of which, as he says, 'will leaven the whole lump,' or, as we say, 'batch.' But the word 'leaven' drew up from the depths of his memory a host of sacred associations connected with the Jewish Passover. He remembered the sedulous hunting in every Jewish house for every scrap of leavened matter; the slaying of the Paschal Lamb, and the following feast. Carried away by these associations, he forgets the sin in the Corinthian Church for a moment, and turns to set forth, in the words of the text, a very deep and penetrating view of what the Christian life is, how it is sustained, and what it demands. 'Wherefore,' says he, 'let us keep the feast . . . with the unleavened bread of sincerity and truth.'

That 'wherefore' takes us back to the words before it. And what are these? 'Christ our Passover is sacrificed for us'; therefore—because of that sacrifice, to us is granted the power, and on us is laid imperatively the obligation, to make life a festival and to purge ourselves. Now, in the notion of a feast, there are two things included—joy and plentiful sustenance. So there are three points here, which I have already indicated— what the Christian life is, a festival; on what it is sustained, the Paschal Sacrifice; what it demands, scrupulous purging out of the old leaven.

I. The Christian life ought to be a continual festival.

The Christian life a feast? It is more usually represented as a fight, a wrestle, a race; and such metaphors correspond, as it would appear, far more closely to the facts of our environment, and to the experiences of our hearts, than does such a metaphor as this. But the metaphor of the festival goes deeper than that of the fight or race, and it does not ignore the strenuous and militant side of the Christian life. No man ever lived a more strenuous life than Paul; no man had heavier tasks, and did them more cheerily; no man had a sterner fight and fought it more bravely. There is nothing soft, Epicurean, or oblivious of the patent sad facts of humanity in the declaration that after all, beneath all, above all, central to all, the Christian life is a glad festival, when it is the life that it ought to be.

But you say, 'Ah! it is all very well to call it so; but in the first place, continual joy is impossible in the presence of the difficulties, and often sadnesses, that meet us on our life's path; and, in the second place, it is folly to tell us to pump up emotions, or to ignore the occasions for much heaviness and sorrow of heart.'

True; but, still, it is possible to cultivate such a temper as makes life habitually joyful. We can choose the aspect under which we by preference and habitually regard our lives. All emotion follows upon a preceding thought, or sensible experience, and we can pick the objects of our thoughts, and determine what aspect of our lives to look at most.

The sky is often piled with stormy, heaped-up masses of blackness, but between them are lakes of calm blue. We can choose whether we look at the clouds or at the blue. *These* are in the lower ranges; *that* fills infinite spaces, upwards and out to the horizon. These are transient, eating themselves away even whilst we look, and black and thunderous as they may be, they are there but for a moment—that is perennial. If we are wise, we shall fix our gaze much rather on the blue than on the ugly cloud-rack that hides it, and thus shall minister to ourselves occasions for the noble kind of joy which is not noisy and boisterous, 'like the crackling of thorns under a pot,' and does not foam itself away by its very ebullience, but is calm like the grounds of it; still, like the heaven to which it looks; eternal, like the God on whom it is fastened. If we would only steadfastly remember that the one source of worthy and enduring joy is God Himself, and listen to the command, 'Rejoice in the Lord,' we should find it possible to 'rejoice always.' For that thought of Him, His sufficiency, His nearness, His encompassing presence, His prospering eye, His aiding hand, His gentle consolation, His enabling help will take the sting out of even the bitterest of our sorrows, and will brace us to sustain the heaviest, otherwise crushing burdens, and greatly to 'rejoice, though now for a season we are in heaviness through manifold temptations.' The Gulf

Stream rushes into the northern hemisphere, melts the icebergs and warms the Polar seas, and so the joy of the Lord, if we set it before us as we can and should do, will minister to us a gladness which will make our lives a perpetual feast.

But there is another thing that we can do; that is, we can clearly recognise the occasions for sorrow in our experience, and yet interpret them by the truths of the Christian faith. That is to say, we can think of them, not so much as they tend to make us sad or glad, but as they tend to make us more assured of our possession of, more ardent in our love towards, and more submissive in our attitude to, the all-ordering Love which is God. Brethren, if we thought of life, and all its incidents, even when these are darkest and most threatening, as being what it and they indeed are, His training of us into capacity for fuller blessedness, because fuller possession of Himself, we should be less startled at the commandment, 'Rejoice in the Lord always,' and should feel that it was possible, though the figtree did not blossom, and there was no fruit in the vine, though the flocks were cut off from the pastures, and the herds from the stall, yet to rejoice in the God of our salvation. Rightly understood and pondered on, all the darkest passages of life are but like the cloud whose blackness determines the brightness of the rainbow on its front. Rightly understood and reflected on, these will teach us that the paradoxical commandment, 'Count it all joy that ye fall into divers temptations,' is, after all, the voice of true wisdom speaking at the dictation of a clear-eyed faith.

This text, since it is a commandment, implies that obedience to it, and therefore the realisation of this continual festal aspect of life, is very largely in our own power. Dispositions differ, some of us are constitutionally inclined to look at the blacker, and some at the brighter, side of our experiences. But our Christianity is worth little unless it can modify, and to some extent change, our natural tendencies. The joy of the Lord being our strength, the cultivation of joy in the Lord is largely our duty. Christian people do not sufficiently recognise that it is as incumbent on them to seek after this continual fountain of calm and heavenly joy flowing through their lives, as it is to cultivate some of the more recognised virtues and graces of Christian conduct and character.

Secondly, we have here—

II. The Christian life is a continual feeding on a sacrifice.

'Christ our Passover is sacrificed for us. Wherefore let us keep the feast.' It is very remarkable that this is the only place in Paul's writings where he articulately pronounces that the Paschal Lamb is a type of Jesus Christ. There is only one other instance in the New Testament where that is stated with equal clearness and emphasis, and that is in John's account of the Crucifixion, where he recognises the fact that Christ died with limbs unbroken, as being a fulfilment, in the New Testament sense of that word, of what was enjoined in regard to the antitype, 'a bone of him shall not be broken.'

But whilst the definite statement which precedes my text that Christ is 'our Passover,' and 'sacrificed for us' as such, is unique in Paul's writings, the thought to which it gives clear and crystallised expression runs through the whole of the New Testament. It underlies the Lord's Supper. Did you ever think of how great was the self-assertion of Jesus Christ when He laid His hand on that sacredest of Jewish rites, which had been established, as the words of the institution of it say; to be 'a perpetual memorial through all generations,' brushed it on one side, and in effect, said: 'You do not need to remember the Passover any more. I am the true Paschal Lamb, whose blood sprinkled on the door-posts averts the sword of the destroying Angel, whose flesh, partaken of, gives immortal life. Remember Me, and this do in remembrance of Me.' The Lord's Supper witnesses that Jesus thought Himself to be what Paul tells the Corinthians that He is, even our Passover, sacrificed for us. But the point to be observed is this, that just as in that ancient ritual, the lamb slain became the food of the Israelites, so with us the Christ who has died is to be the sustenance of our souls, and of our Christian life. 'Therefore let us keep the feast.'

Feed upon Him; that is the essential central require-ment for all Christian life, and what does feeding on Him mean? 'How can this man give us his flesh to eat?' said the Jews, and the answer is plain now, though so obscure then. The flesh which He gave for the life of the world in His death, must by us be taken for the very nourishment of our souls, by the simple act of faith in Him. That is the feeding which brings not only sustenance but life. Christ's death for us is the basis, but it is only the basis, of Christ's living in us, and His death for me is of no use at all to me unless He that died for me lives in me. We feed on Him by faith, which not only trusts to the Sacrifice as atoning for sin, but feeds on it as communicating and sustaining eternal life—'Christ our Passover is sacrificed for us, wherefore let us keep the Feast.'

Again, we keep the feast when our minds feed upon Christ by contemplation of what He is, what He has done, what He is doing, what He will do; when we take Him as 'the Master-light of all our seeing,' and in Him, His words and works, His Passion, Resurrection, Ascension, Session as Sovereign at the right hand of God, find the perfect revelation of what God is, the perfect discovery of what man is, the perfect disclosure of what sin is, the perfect prophecy of what man may become, the Light of light, the answer to every question that our spirits can put about the loftiest verities of God and man, the universe and the future. We feed on Christ when, with lowly submission, we habitually subject thoughts, purposes, desires, to His authority, and when we let His will flow into, and make plastic and supple, our wills. We nourish our wills by submitting them to Jesus, and we feed on Him when we not only say 'Lord! Lord!' but when we do the things that He says. We feed on Christ, when we let His great, sacred, all-wise, all-giving, all satisfying love flow into our restless hearts and make them still, enter into our vagrant affections and fix them on Himself. Thus when mind and conscience and will and heart all turn to Jesus, and in Him find their sustenance, we shall be filled with the feast of fat things which He has prepared for all people. With that bread we shall be satisfied, and with it only, for the husks of the swine are no food for the Father's son, and we 'spend our money for that which is not bread, and our labour for that which satisfieth not,' if we look anywhere else than to the Paschal Lamb slain for us for the food of our souls.

III. The Christian life is a continual purging out of the old leaven.

I need not remind you how vivid and profoundly significant that emblem of leaven, as applied to all.

manner of evil, is. But let me remind you how, just as in the Jewish Ritual, the cleansing from all that was leavened was the essential pre-requisite to the participation in the feast, feeding on Jesus Christ, as I have tried to describe it, is absolutely impossible unless our leaven is cleansed away. Children spoil their appetites for wholesome food by eating sweetmeats. Men destroy their capacity for feeding on Christ by hungry desires, and gluttonous satisfying of those desires with the delusive sweets of this passing world. But, my brother, your experience, if you are a Christian man at all, will tell you that in the direct measure in which you have been drawn away into paltering with evil, your appetite for Christ and your capacity for gazing upon Him, contemplating Him, feeding on Him, has died out. There comes a kind of constriction in a man's throat when he is hungering after lesser good, especially when there is a tinge of evil in the supposed good that he is hungering after, which incapacitates Him from eating the bread of God, which is Jesus Christ.

But let us remember that absolute cleansing from all sin is not essential, in order to have real participation in Jesus Christ. The Jew had to take every scrap of leaven out of his house before he began the Passover. If that were the condition for us, alas! for us all; but the effort after purity, though it has not entirely attained its aim, is enough. Sin abhorred does not prevent a man from participating in the Bread that came down from heaven.

Then observe, too, that for this power to cleanse ourselves, we must have had some participation in Christ, by which there is given to us that new life that conquers evil. In the words immediately preceding my text, the Apostle bases his injunction to purge out the old leaven on the fact that 'ye are unleavened.' Ideally, in so far as the power possessed by them was concerned, these Corinthians were unleavened, even whilst they were bid to purge out the leaven. That is to say, be what you are; realise your ideal, utilise the power you possess, and since by your faith there has been given to you a new life that can conquer all corruption and sin, see that you use the life that is given. Purge out the old leaven because ye are unleavened.

One last word—this stringent exhortation, which makes Christian effort after absolute purity a Christian duty, and the condition of participation in the Paschal Lamb, is based upon that thought to which I have already referred, of the diabolical power of infection which Evil possesses. Either you must cast it out, or it will choke the better thing in you. It spreads and grows, and propagates itself, and works underground through and through the whole mass. A water-weed got into some of our canals years ago, and it has all but choked some of them. The slime on a pond spreads its green mantle over the whole surface with rapidity. If we do not eject Evil it will eject the good from us. Use the implanted power to cast out this creeping, advancing evil. Sometimes a wine-grower has gone into his cellars, and found in a cask no wine, but a monstrous fungus into which all the wine had, in the darkness, passed unnoticed. I fear some Christian people, though they do not know it, have something like that going on in them.

It is possible for us all to keep this perpetual festival. To live in, on, for, Jesus Christ will give us victory over enemies, burdens, sorrows, sins. We may, if we will, dwell in a calm zone where no tempests rage, hear a perpetual strain of sweet music persisting through thunder peals of sorrow and suffering, and find a table spread for us in the presence of our enemies, at which we shall renew our strength for conflict, and whence we shall rise to fight the good fight a little longer, till we sit with Him at His table in His Kingdom, and 'eat, and live for ever.'

FORMS *VERSUS* CHARACTER

'Circumcision is nothing, and uncircumcision is nothing, but the keeping of the commandments of God.'—1 COR. vii. 19.

'For in Jesus Christ neither circumcision availeth anything, nor uncircumcision, but faith which worketh by love.'—GAL. v. 6.

'For neither is circumcision anything, nor uncircumcision, but a new creature.' —GAL. vi. 15 (R.V.).

THE great controversy which embittered so much of Paul's life, and marred so much of his activity, turned upon the question whether a heathen man could come into the Church simply by the door of faith, or whether he must also go through the gate of circumcision. We all know how Paul answered the question. Time, which settles all controversies, has settled that one so thoroughly that it is impossible to revive any kind of interest in it; and it may seem to be a pure waste of time to talk about it. But the principles that fought then are eternal, though the forms in which they manifest themselves vary with every varying age.

The Ritualist—using that word in its broadest sense— on the one hand, and the Puritan on the other, represent permanent tendencies of human nature; and we find to-day the old foes with new faces. These three passages, which I have read, are Paul's deliverance on the question of the comparative value of external rites and spiritual character. They are remarkable both for the identity in the former part of each and for the variety in the latter. In all the three cases he affirms, almost in the same language, that 'circumcision is nothing, and uncircumcision is nothing,' that the Ritualist's rite and the Puritan's protest are equally insignificant in comparison with higher things. And then he varies the statement of what the higher things are, in a very remarkable and instructive fashion. The 'keeping of the commandments of God,' says one of the texts, is the all-important matter. Then, as it were, he pierces deeper, and in another of the texts (I take the liberty of varying their order) pronounces that 'a new creature' is the all-important thing. And then he pierces still deeper to the bottom of all, in the third text, and says the all-important thing is 'faith which worketh by love.'

I think I shall best bring out the force of these words by dealing first with that emphatic threefold proclamation of the nullity of all externalism; and then with the singular variations in the triple statement of what is essential, viz. spiritual conduct and character.

I. First, the emphatic proclamation of the nullity of outward rites.

'Circumcision is nothing, and uncircumcision is nothing,' say two texts. 'Circumcision availeth nothing, and uncircumcision availeth nothing,' says the other. It neither is anything nor does anything. Did Paul say that because circumcision was a Jewish rite? No. As I believe, he said it because it was *a rite*; and because he had learned that the one thing needful was spiritual character, and that no external ceremonial of any sort could produce that. I think we are perfectly warranted in taking this principle of my text, and in extending it beyond the limits of the Jewish rite about which Paul was speaking. For if you remember, he speaks about baptism, in the first chapter of the First Epistle to the Corinthians, in a precisely similar tone and for precisely the same reason, when he says, in effect, 'I baptized Crispus and Gaius and the household of Stephanas, and I think these are all. I am not quite sure. I do not keep any kind of record of such things; God did not send me to baptize, He sent me to preach the Gospel.'

The thing that produced the spiritual result was not the rite, but the truth, and therefore he felt that his function was to preach the truth and leave the rite to be administered by others. Therefore we can extend the principle here to all externalisms of worship, in all forms, in all churches, and say that in comparison with the essentials of an inward Christianity they are nothing and they do nothing.

They have their value. As long as we are here on earth, living in the flesh, we must have outward forms and symbolical rites. It is in Heaven that the seer 'saw no temple.' Our sense-bound nature requires, and thankfully avails itself of, the help of external rites and ceremonials to lift us up towards the Object of our devotion. A man prays all the better if he bow his head, shut his eyes, and bend his knees. Forms do help us to the realisation of the realities, and the truths which they express and embody. Music may waft our souls to the heavens, and pictures may stir deep thoughts. That is the simple principle on which the value of all external aids to devotion depends. They may be helps towards the appreciation of divine truth, and to the suffusing of the heart with devout emotions which may lead to building up a holy character.

There is a worth, therefore—an auxiliary and sub-ordinate worth—in these things, and in that respect they are *not* nothing, nor do they ' avail nothing.' But then all external rites tend to usurp more than belongs to them, and in our weakness we are apt to cleave to them, and instead of using them as means to lift us higher, to stay in them, and as a great many of us do, to mistake the mere gratification of taste and the excitement of the sensibilities for worship. A bit of stained glass may be glowing with angel-forms and pictured saints, but it always keeps some of the light out, and it always hinders us from seeing through it. And all external worship and form have so strong a tendency to usurp more than belongs to them, and to drag us down to their own level, even whilst we think that we are praying, that I believe the wisest man will try to pare down the externals of his worship to the lowest possible point. If there be as much body as will keep a soul in, as much form as will embody the spirit, that is all that we want. What is more is dangerous.

All form in worship is like fire, it is a good servant but it is a bad master, and it needs to be kept very rigidly in subordination, or else the spirituality of Christian worship vanishes before men know; and they are left with their dead forms which are only evils—crutches that make people limp by the very act of using them.

Now, my dear friends, when that has happened, when men begin to say, as the people in Paul's time were saying about circumcision, and as people are saying in this day about Christian rites, that they are necessary, then it is needful to take up Paul's ground and to say, ' No ! they are nothing !' They are useful in a certain place, but if you make them obligatory, if you make them essential, if you say that grace is miraculously conveyed through them, then it is needful that we should raise a strong note of protestation, and declare their absolute nullity for the highest purpose, that of making that spiritual character which alone is essential.

And I believe that this strange recrudescence—to use a modern word—of ceremonialism and æsthetic worship which we see all round about us, not only in the ranks of the Episcopal Church, but amongst Nonconformists, who are sighing for a less bare service, and here and there are turning their chapels into concert-rooms, and instead of preaching the Gospel are having 'Services of Song' and the like—that all this makes it as needful to-day as ever it was to say to men : 'Forms are not worship.   Rites may crush the spirit.   Men may yield to the sensuous impressions which they produce, and be lapped in an atmosphere of æsthetic emotion, without any real devotion.'

Such externals are only worth anything if they make us grasp more firmly with our understandings and feel more profoundly with our hearts, the great truths of the Gospel.   If they do that, they help ; if they are not doing that, they hinder, and are to be fought against. And so we have again to proclaim to-day, as Paul did, 'Circumcision is nothing,' 'but the keeping of the commandments of God.'

Then notice with what remarkable fairness and boldness and breadth the Apostle here adds that other clause: 'and uncircumcision is nothing.'   It is a very hard thing for a man whose life has been spent in fighting against an error, not to exaggerate the value of his protest.   It is a very hard thing for a man who has been delivered from the dependence upon forms, not to fancy that his formlessness is what the other people think that their forms are. The Puritan who does not believe that a man can be a good man because he is a Ritualist or a Roman Catholic, is committing the very same error as the Ritualist or the Roman Catholic who does not believe that the Puritan can be a Christian unless he has been 'christened.' The two people are exactly the same, only the one has hold of the stick at one end, and the other at the other. There may be as much idolatry in superstitious reliance upon the bare worship as in the advocacy of the ornate; and many a Nonconformist who fancies that he has 'never bowed the knee to Baal' is as true an idol-worshipper in his superstitious abhorrence of the ritualism that he sees in other communities, as are the men who trust in it the most.

It is a large attainment in Christian character to be able to say with Paul, 'Circumcision is nothing, and my own favourite point of uncircumcision is nothing either. Neither the one side nor the other touches the essentials.'

II. Now let us look at the threefold variety of the designation of these essentials here.

In our first text from the Epistle to the Corinthians we read, 'Circumcision is nothing, and uncircumcision is nothing, but the keeping of the commandments of God.' If we finished the sentence it would be, 'but the keeping of the commandments of God is everything.'

And by that 'keeping the commandments,' of course, the Apostle does not mean merely external obedience. He means something far deeper than that, which I put into this plain word, that the one essential of a Christian life is the conformity of the will with God's—not

G

the external obedience merely, but the entire surrender and the submission of my will to the will of my Father in Heaven. That is the all-important thing; that is what God wants; that is the end of all rites and ceremonies; that is the end of all revelation and of all utterances of the divine heart. The Bible, Christ's mission, His passion and death, the gift of His Divine Spirit, and every part of the divine dealings in providence, all converge upon this one aim and goal. For this purpose the Father worketh hitherto, and Christ works, that man's will may yield and bow itself wholly and happily and lovingly to the great infinite will of the Father in heaven.

Brethren! that is the perfection of a man's nature, when his will fits on to God's like one of Euclid's triangles superimposed upon another, and line for line coincides. When his will allows a free passage to the will of God, without resistance or deflection, as light travels through transparent glass; when his will responds to the touch of God's finger upon the keys, like the telegraphic needle to the operator's hand, then man has attained all that God and religion can do for him, all that his nature is capable of; and far beneath his feet may be the ladders of ceremonies and forms and outward acts, by which he climbed to that serene and blessed height, 'Circumcision is nothing, and uncircumcision is nothing, but the keeping of God's commandments is everything.'

That submission of will is the sum and the test of your Christianity. Your Christianity does not consist only in a mere something which you call faith in Jesus Christ. It does not consist in emotions, however deep and blessed and genuine they may be. It does not consist in the acceptance of a creed. All these are

means to an end. They are meant to drive the wheel
of life, to build up character, to make your deepest
wish to be, 'Father! not my will, but Thine, be done.'
In the measure in which that is your heart's desire,
and not one hair's-breadth further, have you a right to
call yourself a Christian.

But, then, I can fancy a man saying: 'It is all very
well to talk about bowing the will in this fashion; how
can I do that?' Well, let us take our second text—the
third in the order of their occurrence—'For neither
circumcision is anything, nor uncircumcision, but a new
creature.' That is to say, if we are ever to keep the
will of God we must be made over again. Ay! we
must! Our own consciences tell us that; the history of
all the efforts that ever we have made—and I suppose
all of us have made some now and then, more or less
earnest and more or less persistent—tells us that there
needs to be a stronger hand than ours to come into the
fight if it is ever to be won by us. There is nothing
more heartless and more impotent than to preach,
'Bow your wills to God, and then you will be happy;
bow your wills to God, and then you will be good.' If
that is all the preacher has to say, his powerless words
will but provoke the answer, 'We cannot. Tell the
leopard to change his spots, or the Ethiopian his skin,
as soon as tell a man to reduce this revolted kingdom
within him to obedience, and to bow his will to the
will of God. We cannot do it.' But, brethren, in that
word, 'a new creature,' lies a promise from God; for a
creature implies a creator. 'It is He that hath made
us, and not we ourselves.' The very heart of what
Christ has to offer us is the gift of His own life to
dwell in our hearts, and by its mighty energy to make
us free from the law of sin and death which binds our

wills. We may have our spirits moulded into His like-ness, and new tastes, and new desires, and new capa-cities infused into us, so as that we shall not be left with our own poor powers to try and force ourselves into obedience to God's will, but that submission and holiness and love that keeps the commandments of God, will spring up in our renewed spirits as their natural product and growth. Oh! you men and women who have been honestly trying, half your life-time, to make yourselves what you know God wants you to be, and who are obliged to confess that you have failed, hearken to the message: 'If any man be in Christ, he is a new creature, old things are passed away.' The one thing needful is keeping the com-mandments of God, and the only way by which we can keep the commandments of God is that we should be formed again into the likeness of Him of whom alone it is true that 'He did always the things that pleased' God.

And so we come to the last of these great texts: 'In Christ Jesus, neither circumcision availeth anything, nor uncircumcision, but faith which worketh by love.' That is to say, if we are to be made over again, we must have faith in Christ Jesus. We have got to the root now, so far as we are concerned. We must keep the commandments of God; if we are to keep the com-mandments we must be made over again, and if our hearts ask how can we receive that new creating power into our lives, the answer is, by 'faith which worketh by love.'

Paul did not believe that external rites could make men partakers of a new nature, but he believed that if a man would trust in Jesus Christ, the life of that Christ would flow into his opened heart, and a new spirit and nature would be born in him. And, therefore, his triple requirements come all down to this one, so far as we are concerned, as the beginning and the condition of the other two. 'Neither circumcision does anything, nor uncircumcision, but faith which worketh by love,' does everything. He that trusts Christ opens his heart to Christ, who comes with His new-creating Spirit, and makes us willing in the day of His power to keep His commandments.

But faith leads us to obedience in yet another fashion, than this opening of the door of the heart for the entrance of the new-creating Spirit. It leads to it in the manner which is expressed by the words of our text, 'worketh by love.' Faith shows itself living, because it leads us to love, and through love it produces its effects upon conduct.

Two things are implied in this designation of faith. If you trust Christ you will love Him. That is plain enough. And you will not love Him unless you trust Him. Though it lies wide of my present purpose, let us take this lesson in passing. You cannot work yourself up into a spasm or paroxysm of religious emotion and love by resolution or by effort. All that you can do is to go and look at the Master and get near Him, and that will warm you up. You can love if you trust. Your trust will make you love; unless you trust you will never love Him.

The second thing implied is, that if you love you will obey. That is plain enough. The keeping of the commandments will be easy where there is love in the heart. The will will bow where there is love in the heart. Love is the only fire that is hot enough to melt the iron obstinacy of a creature's will. The will cannot be driven. Strike it with violence and it stiffens; touch it gently and it yields.   If you try to put an iron collar upon the will, like the demoniac in the Gospels, the touch of the apparent restraint drives it into fury, and it breaks the bands asunder.   Fasten it with the silken leash of love, and a 'little child' can lead it.   So faith works by love, because whom we trust we shall love, and whom we love we shall obey.

Therefore we have got to the root now, and nothing is needful but an operative faith, out of which will come all the blessed possession of a transforming Spirit, and all sublimities and noblenesses of an obedient and submissive will.

My brother! Paul and James shake hands here. There is a 'faith' so called, which does not work. It is dead! Let me beseech you, none of you to rely upon what you choose to call your faith in Jesus Christ, but examine it.   Does it do anything?   Does it help you to be like Him?   Does it open your hearts for His Spirit to come in?   Does it fill them with love to that Master, a love which proves itself by obedience?   Plain questions, questions that any man can answer; questions that go to the root of the whole matter.   If your faith does that, it is genuine; if it does not, it is not.

And do not trust either to forms, or to your freedom from forms.   They will not save your souls, they will not make you more Christ-like.   They will not help you to pardon, purity, holiness, blessedness.   In these respects neither if we have them are we the better, nor if we have them not are we the worse.   If you are trusting to Christ, and by that faith are having your hearts moulded and made over again into all holy obedience, then you have all that you need.   Unless you have, though you partook of all Christian rites, though you believed all Christian truth, though you fought against superstitious reliance on forms, you have not the one thing needful, for 'in Christ Jesus neither circumcision availeth anything, nor uncircumcision, but faith which worketh by love.'

SLAVES AND FREE

'He that is called in the Lord, being a servant, is the Lord's free man: likewise also he that is called, being free, is Christ's servant.'—1 COR. vii. 22.

THIS remarkable saying occurs in a remarkable connection, and is used for a remarkable purpose. The Apostle has been laying down the principle, that the effect of true Christianity is greatly to diminish the importance of outward circumstance. And on that principle he bases an advice, dead in the teeth of all the maxims recognised by worldly prudence. He says, in effect, 'Mind very little about getting on and getting up. Do God's will wherever you are, and let the rest take care of itself.' Now, the world says, 'Struggle, wriggle, fight, do anything to better yourself.' Paul says, 'You will better yourself by getting nearer God, and if you secure that—art thou a slave? care not for it; if thou mayest be free, use it rather; art thou bound to a wife? seek not to be loosed; art thou loosed? seek not to be bound; art thou circumcised? seek not to be uncircumcised; art thou a Gentile? seek not to become in outward form a Jew.' Never mind about externals: the main thing is our relation to Jesus Christ, because in that there is what will be compensation for all the disadvantages of any disadvantageous circumstances, and in that there is what will take the gilt off the gingerbread of any superficial and fleeting good, and will bring a deep-seated and permanent blessing.

Now, I am not going to deal in this sermon with that general principle, nor even to be drawn aside to speak of the tone in which the Apostle here treats the great abomination of slavery, and the singular advice that he gives to its victims; though the consideration of the tone of Christianity to that master-evil of the old world might yield a great many thoughts very relevant to pressing questions of to-day. But my one object is to fix upon the combination which he here brings out in regard to the essence of the Christian life; how that in itself it contains both members of the antithesis, servitude and freedom; so that the Christian man who is free externally is Christ's slave, and the Christian man who is outwardly in bondage is emancipated by his union with Jesus Christ.

There are two thoughts here, the application in diverse directions of the same central idea—viz. the slavery of Christ's free men, and the freedom of Christ's slaves. And I deal briefly with these two now.

I. First, then, note how, according to the one-half of the antithesis, Christ's freed men are slaves.

Now, the way in which the New Testament deals with that awful wickedness of a man held in bondage by a man is extremely remarkable. It might seem as if such a hideous piece of immorality were altogether incapable of yielding any lessons of good. But the Apostles have no hesitation whatever in taking slavery as a clear picture of the relation in which all Christian people stand to Jesus Christ their Lord. He is the owner and we are the slaves. For you must remember that the word most inadequately rendered here, 'servant' does not mean a hired man who has, of his own volition, given himself for a time to do specific work and get wages for it; but it means 'a bond-

slave,' a chattel owned by another. All the ugly
associations which gather round the word are transported bodily into the Christian region, and there,
instead of being hideous, take on a shape of beauty,
and become expressions of the deepest and most blessed
truths, in reference to Christian men's dependence
upon, and submission to, and place in the household
and the heart of, Jesus Christ, their Owner.

And what is the centre idea that lies in this metaphor, if you like to call it so? It is this: absolute
authority, which has for its correlative—for the thing
in us that answers to it—unconditional submission.
Jesus Christ has the perfect right to command each
of us, and we are bound to bow ourselves, unreluctant,
unmurmuring, unhesitating, with complete submission
at His feet. His authority, and our submission, go
far, far deeper than the most despotic sway of the
most tyrannous master, or than the most abject submission of the most downtrodden slave. For no man
can coerce another man's will, and no man can require more, or can ever get more, than that outward
obedience which may be rendered with the most sullen
and fixed rebellion of a hating heart and an obstinate
will. But Jesus Christ demands that if we call ourselves Christians we shall bring, not our members only
as instruments to Him, in outward surrender and
service, but that we shall yield ourselves, with our
capacities of willing and desiring, utterly, absolutely,
constantly to Him.

The founder of the Jesuits laid it down as a rule for
his Order that each member of it was to be at the
master's disposal like a corpse, or a staff in the hand of
a blind man. That was horrible. But the absolute
putting of myself at the disposal of another's will, which

is expressed so tyrannously in Loyola's demand, is the simple duty of every Christian, and as long as we have recalcitrating wills, which recoil at anything which Christ commands or appoints, and perk up their own inclinations in the face of His solemn commandment, or that shrink from doing and suffering whatsoever He imposes and enjoins, we have still to learn what it means to be Christ's disciples.

Dear brethren, absolute submission is not all that makes a disciple, but, depend upon it, there is no discipleship worth calling by the name without it. So I come to each of you with His message to you:— Down on your faces before Him! Bow your obstinate will, surrender yourselves and accept Him as absolute, dominant Lord over your whole being! Are you Christians after that pattern? Being freemen, are you Christ's slaves?

It does not matter what sort of work the owner sets his household of slaves to do. One man is picked out to be his pipe-bearer, or his shoe-cleaner; and, if the master is a sovereign, another one is sent off, perhaps, to be governor of a province, or one of his council. They are all slaves; and the service that each does is equally important.

> 'All service ranks the same with God :
> There is no last nor first.'

What does it matter what you and I are set to do? Nothing. And, so, why need we struggle and wear our hearts out to get into conspicuous places, or to do work that shall bring some revenue of praise and glory to ourselves? 'Play well thy part; there all the honour lies,' the world can say. Serve Christ in anything, and all His servants are alike in His sight.

The slave-owner had absolute power of life and death

over his dependants. He could split up families; he could sell away dear ones; he could part husband and wife, parent and child. The slave was his, and he could do what he liked with his own, according to the cruel logic of ancient law. And Jesus Christ, the Lord of the household, the Lord of providence, can say to this one, 'Go!' and he goes into the mists and the shadows of death. And He can say to those who are most closely united, 'Loose your hands! I have need of one of you yonder. I have need of the other one here.' And if we are wise, if we are His servants in any real deep sense, we shall not kick against the appointments of His supreme, autocratic, and yet most loving Providence, but be content to leave the arbitrament of life and death, of love united or of love parted, in His hands, and say, 'Whether we live we are the Lord's, or whether we die we are the Lord's; living or dying we are His.'

The slave-ower owned all that the slave owned. He gave him a little cottage, with some humble sticks of furniture in it; and a bit of ground on which to grow his vegetables for his family. But he to whom the owner of the vegetables and the stools belonged owned them too. And if we are Christ's servants, our banker's book is Christ's, and our purse is Christ's, and our investments are Christ's; and our mills, and our warehouses, and our shops and our businesses are His. We are not His slaves, if we arrogate to ourselves the right of doing what we like with His possessions.

And, then, still further, there comes into our Apostle's picture here yet another point of resemblance between slaves and the disciples of Jesus. For the hideous abominations of the slave-market are transferred to the Christian relation, and defecated and cleansed of all their abominations and cruelty thereby. For what immediately follows my text is, 'Ye are bought with a price.' Jesus Christ has won us for Himself. There is only one price that can buy a heart, and that is a heart. There is only one way of getting a man to be mine, and that is by giving myself to be his. So we come to the very vital, palpitating centre of all Christianity when we say, 'He gave Himself for us, that He might acquire to Himself a people for His possession.' Thus His purchase of His slave, when we remember that it is the buying of a man in his inmost personality, changes all that might seem harsh in the requirement of absolute submission into the most gracious and blessed privilege. For when I am won by another, because that other has given him or her whole self to me, then the language of love is submission, and the conformity of the two wills is the delight of each loving will. Whoever has truly been wooed into relationship with Jesus, by reflection upon the love with which Jesus grapples him to His heart, finds that there is nothing so blessed as to yield one's self utterly and for ever to His service.

The one bright point in the hideous institution of slavery was, that it bound the master to provide for the slave, and though that was degrading to the inferior, it made his life a careless, child-like, merry life, even amidst the many cruelties and abominations of the system. But what was a good, dashed with a great deal of evil, in that relation of man to man, comes to be a pure blessing and good in our relation to Him. If I am Christ's slave, it is His business to take care of His own property, and I do not need to trouble myself much about it. If I am His slave, He will be quite sure to find me in food and necessaries enough to get His tale of work out of me; and I may cast all my care upon Him, for He careth for me. So, brethren, absolute submission and the devolution of all anxiety on the Master are what is laid upon us, if we are Christ's slaves.

II. Then there is the other side, about which I must say, secondly, a word or two; and that is, the freedom of Christ's slaves.

As the text puts it, 'He that is called, being a servant, is the Lord's freedman.' A freedman was one who was emancipated, and who therefore stood in a relation of gratitude to his emancipator and patron. So in the very word 'freedman' there is contained the idea of submission to Him who has struck off the fetters.

But, apart from that, let me just remind you, in a sentence or two, that whilst there are many other ways by which men have sought, and have partially attained, deliverance from the many fetters and bondages that attach to our earthly life, the one perfect way by which a man can be truly, in the deepest sense of the word and in his inmost being, a free man is by faith in Jesus Christ.

I do not for a moment forget how wisdom and truth, and noble aims and high purposes, and culture of various kinds have, in lower degrees and partially, emancipated men from self and flesh and sin and the world, and all the other fetters that bind us. But sure I am that the process is never so completely and so assuredly effected as by the simple way of absolute submission to Jesus Christ, taking Him for the supreme and unconditional Arbiter and Sovereign of a life.

If we do that, brethren, if we really yield ourselves

to Him, in heart and will, in life and conduct, submitting our understanding to His infallible Word, and our wills to His authority, regulating our conduct by His perfect pattern, and in all things seeking to serve Him and to realise His presence, then be sure of this, that we shall be set free from the one real bondage, and that is the bondage of our own wicked selves. There is no such tyranny as mob tyranny; and there is no such slavery as to be ruled by the mob of our own passions and lusts and inclinations and other meannesses that yelp and clamour within us, and seek to get hold of us and to sway. There is only one way by which the brute domination of the lower part of our nature can be surely and thoroughly put down, and that is by turning to Jesus Christ and saying to Him, 'Lord! do Thou rule this anarchic kingdom within me, for I cannot govern it myself. Do Thou guide and direct and subdue.' You can only govern yourself and be free from the compulsion of your own evil nature when you surrender the control to the Master, and say ever, 'Speak, Lord! for Thy slave hears. Here am I, send me.'

And that is the only way by which a man can be delivered from the bondage of dependence upon outward things. I said at the beginning of these remarks that my text occurred in the course of a discussion in which the Apostle was illustrating the tendency of true Christian faith to set man free from, and to make him largely independent of, the varieties in external circumstances. Christian faith does so, because it brings into a life a sufficient compensation for all losses, limitations, and sorrows, and a good which is the reality of which all earthly goods are but shadows. So the slave may be free in Christ, and the poor man may be rich in Him, and the sad man may be joyful, and the joyful man may be delivered from excess of gladness, and the rich man be kept from the temptations and sins of wealth, and the free man be taught to surrender his liberty to the Lord who makes him free. Thus, if we have the all-sufficient compensation which there is in Jesus Christ, the satisfaction for all our needs and desires, we do not need to trouble ourselves so much as we sometimes do about these changing things round about us. Let them come, let them go; let the darkness veil the light, and the light illuminate the darkness; let summer and winter alternate; let tribulation and prosperity succeed each other; we have a source of blessedness unaffected by these. Ice may skin the surface of the lake, but deep beneath, the water is at the same temperature in winter and in summer. Storms may sweep the face of the deep, but in the abyss there is calm which is not stagnation. So he that cleaves to Christ is delivered from the slavery that binds men to the details and accidents of outward life.

And if we are the servants of Christ, we shall be set free, in the measure in which we are His, from the slavery which daily becomes more oppressive as the means of communication become more complete, the slavery to popular opinion and to men round us. Dare to be singular; take your beliefs at first hand from the Master. Never mind what fellow-slaves say. It is His smile or frown that is of importance. 'Ye are bought with a price; be not servants of men.'

And so, brethren, 'choose you this day whom ye will serve.' You are not made to be independent. You must serve some thing or person. Recognise the narrow limitations within which your choice lies, and the issues which depend upon it. It is not whether you will serve Christ or whether you will be free. It is whether you will serve Christ or your own worst self, the world, men, and I was going to add, the flesh and the devil. Make your choice. He has bought you. You belong to Him by His death. Yield yourselves to Him, it is the only way of breaking your chains. He that doeth sin is the servant of sin. 'If the Son make you free, ye shall be free indeed,' and not only free; for the King's slaves are princes and nobles, and 'all things are yours, and ye are Christ's.' They who say to Him 'O Lord! truly I am Thy servant,' receive from Him the rank of kings and priests to God, and shall reign with Him for ever.

THE CHRISTIAN LIFE

'Brethren, let every man, wherein he is called, therein abide with God.'—2 Cor. vii. 24.

You find that three times within the compass of a very few verses this injunction is repeated. 'As God hath distributed to every man,' says the Apostle in the seventeenth verse, 'as the Lord hath called every one, so let him walk. And so ordain I in all the churches.' Then again in the twentieth verse, 'Let every man abide in the same calling wherein he is called.' And then finally in our text.

The reason for this emphatic reiteration is not difficult to ascertain. There were strong temptations to restlessness besetting the early Christians. The great change from heathenism to Christianity would seem to loosen the joints of all life, and having been swept from their anchorage in religion, all external things would

appear to be adrift. It was most natural that a man
should seek to alter even the circumstances of his outward life, when such a revolution had separated him
from his ancient self. Hence would tend to come the
rupture of family ties, the separation of husband and
wife, the Jewish convert seeking to become like a Gentile, the Gentile seeking to become like a Jew; the
slave trying to be free, the freeman, in some paroxysm
of disgust at his former condition, trying to become a
slave. These three cases are all referred to in the context — marriage, circumcision, slavery. And for all
three the Apostle has the same advice to give—'Stop
where you are.' In whatever condition you were when
God's invitation drew you to Himself—for that, and not
being set to a 'vocation' in life, is the meaning of the
word 'called' here—remain in it.

And then, on the other hand, there was every reason
why the Apostle and his co-workers should set themselves, by all means in their power, to oppose this restlessness. For, if Christianity in those early days had
once degenerated into the mere instrument of social
revolution, its development would have been thrown
back for centuries, and the whole worth and power of
it, for those who first apprehended it, would have been
lost. So you know Paul never said a word to encourage
any precipitate attempts to change externals. He let
slavery—he let war alone; he let the tyranny of the
Roman Empire alone—not because he was a coward, not
because he thought that these things were not worth
meddling with, but because he, like all wise men, believed in making the tree good and then its fruit good.
He believed in the diffusion of the principles which he
proclaimed, and the mighty Name which he served, as
able to girdle the poison-tree, and to take the bark off

it, and the rest, the slow dying, might be left to the
work of time. And the same general idea underlies
the words of my text. 'Do not try to change,' he says,
'do not trouble about external conditions; keep to
your Christian profession; let those alone, they will
right themselves. Art thou a slave? Seek not to be
freed. Art thou circumcised? Seek not to be uncircumcised. Get hold of the central, vivifying, trans-
muting influence, and all the rest is a question of time.'

But, besides this more especial application of the
words of my text to the primitive times, it carries with
it, dear brethren, a large general principle that applies
to all times—a principle, I may say, dead in the teeth of
the maxims upon which life is being ordered by the most
of us. *Our* maxim is, 'Get on!' Paul's is, 'Never mind
about getting *on*, get *up*!' Our notion is—'Try to make
the circumstances what I would like to have them.'
Paul's is—'Leave circumstances to take care of themselves, or rather leave God to take care of the circumstances. You get close to Him, and hold His hand, and
everything else will right itself.' Only he is not preaching stolid acquiescence. His previous injunctions were
—'Let every man abide in the same calling wherein he
was called.' He sees that that may be misconceived
and abused, and so, in his third reiteration of the precept, he puts in a word which throws a flood of light
upon the whole thing—'Let every man wherein he is
called therein abide.' Yes, but that is not all—'therein
abide *with God*!' Ay, that is it! not an impossible
stoicism; not hypocritical, fanatical contempt of the
external. But whilst that gets its due force and weight,
whilst a man yields himself in a measure to the natural
tastes and inclinations which God has given him, and
with the intention that he should find there subordinate

guidance and impulse for his life, still let him abide where he is called with God, and seek to increase his fellowship with Him, as the main thing that he has to do.

I. Thus we are led from the words before us first to the thought that our chief effort in life ought to be union with God.

'Abide with God,' which, being put into other words, means, I think, mainly two things — constant communion, the occupation of all our nature with Him, and, consequently, the recognition of His will in all circumstances.

As to the former, we have the mind and heart and will of God revealed to us for the light, the love, the obedience of our will and heart and mind; and our Apostle's precept is, first, that we should try, moment by moment, in all the bustle and stir of our daily life, to have our whole being consciously directed to and engaged with, fertilised and calmed by contact with, the perfect and infinite nature of our Father in heaven.

As we go to our work again to-morrow morning, what difference would obedience to this precept make upon my life and yours? Before all else, and in the midst of all else, we should think of that Divine Mind that in the heavens is waiting to illumine our darkness; we should feel the glow of that uncreated and perfect Love, which, in the midst of change and treachery, of coldness and of 'greetings where no kindness is,' in the midst of masterful authority and unloving command, is ready to fill our hearts with tenderness and tranquillity: we should bow before that Will which is absolute and supreme indeed, but neither arbitrary nor harsh, which is 'the eternal purpose that He hath purposed in Himself' indeed, but is also 'the good pleasure of His goodness and the counsel of His grace.'

And with such a God near to us ever in our faithful thoughts, in our thankful love, in our lowly obedience, with such a mind revealing itself to us, and such a heart opening its hidden storehouses for us as we approach, like some star that, as one gets nearer to it, expands its disc and glows into rich colour, which at a distance was but pallid silver, and such a will sovereign above all, energising, even through opposition, and making obedience a delight, what room, brethren, would there be in our lives for agitations, and distractions, and regrets, and cares, and fears—what room for earthly hopes or for sad remembrances? They die in the fruition of a present God all-sufficient for mind, and heart, and will—even as the sun when it is risen with a burning heat may scorch and wither the weeds that grow about the base of the fruitful tree, whose deeper roots are but warmed by the rays that ripen the rich clusters which it bears. 'Let every man, wherein he is called, therein abide *with God.*'

And then, as a consequence of such an occupation of the whole being with God, there will follow that second element which is included in the precept, namely, the recognition of God's will as operating in and determining all circumstances. When our whole soul is occupied with Him, we shall see Him everywhere. And this ought to be our honest effort—to connect everything which befalls ourselves and the world with Him. We should see that Omnipotent Will, the silent energy which flows through all being, asserting itself through all secondary causes, marching on towards its destined and certain goal, amidst all the whirl and perturbation of events, bending even the antagonism of rebels and

the unconsciousness of godless men, as well as the play
of material instruments, to its own purposes, and
swinging and swaying the whole set and motion of
things according to its own impulse and by the touch
of its own fingers.

Such a faith does not require us to overlook the visible
occasions for the things which befall us, nor to deny
the stable laws according to which that mighty will
operates in men's lives.   Secondary causes?   Yes.
Men's opposition and crime?   Yes.   Our own follies
and sins?   No doubt.   Blessings and sorrows falling
indiscriminately on a whole community or a whole
world?   Certainly.   And yet the visible agents are not
the sources, but only the vehicles of the power, the
belting and shafting which transmit a mighty impulse
which they had nothing to do in creating.   And the
antagonism subserves the purposes of the rule which
it opposes, as the blow of the surf may consolidate the
sea-wall that it breaks against.   And our own follies and
sins may indeed sorrowfully shadow our lives, and
bring on us pains of body and disasters in fortune, and
stings in spirit for which we alone are responsible, and
which we have no right to regard as inscrutable judgments—yet even these bitter plants of which our own
hands have sowed the seed, spring by His merciful will,
and *are* to be regarded as His loving, fatherly chastise-
ments—sent before to warn us by a premonitory experience that 'the wages of sin is death.'   As a rule,
God does not interpose to pick a man out of the mud
into which he has been plunged by his own faults and
follies, until he has learned the lessons which he can
find in plenty down in the slough, if he will only look
for them !   And the fact that some great calamity or
some great joy affects a wide circle of people, does not

make its having a special lesson and meaning for each of them at all doubtful. *There* is one of the great depths of all-moving wisdom and providence, that in the very self-same act it is in one aspect universal, and in another special and individual. The ordinary notion of a special providence goes perilously near the belief that God's will is less concerned in some parts of a man's life than in others. It is very much like desecrating and secularising a whole land by the very act of focussing the sanctity in some single consecrated shrine. But the true belief is that the whole sweep of a life is under the will of God, and that when, for instance, war ravages a nation, though the sufferers be involved in a common ruin occasioned by murderous ambition and measureless pride, yet for each of the sufferers the common disaster has a special message. Let us believe in a divine will which regards each individual caught up in the skirts of the horrible storm, even as it regards each individual on whom the equal rays of His universal sunshine fall. Let us believe that every single soul has a place in the heart, and is taken into account in the purposes of Him who moves the tempest, and makes His sun to shine upon the unthankful and on the good. Let us, in accordance with the counsel of the Apostle here, first of all try to anchor and rest our own souls fast and firm in God all the day long, that, grasping His hand, we may look out upon all the confused dance of fleeting circumstances and say, 'Thy will is done on earth'—if not yet 'as it is done in heaven,' still done in the issues and events of all—and done with my cheerful obedience and thankful acceptance of its commands and allotments in my own life.

II. The second idea which comes out of these words

is this—Such union with God will lead to contented continuance in our place, whatever it be.

Our text is as if Paul had said, 'You have been "called" in such and such worldly circumstances. The fact proves that these circumstances do not obstruct the highest and richest blessings. The light of God can shine on your souls through them. Since then you have such sacred memorials associated with them, and know by experience that fellowship with God is possible in them, do you remain where you are, and keep hold of the God who has visited you in them.'

If once, in accordance with the thoughts already suggested, our minds have, by God's help, been brought into something like real, living fellowship with Him, and we have attained the wisdom that pierces through the external to the Almighty will that underlies all its mazy whirl, then why should we care about shifting our place? Why should we trouble ourselves about altering these varying events, since each in its turn is a manifestation of His mind and will; each in its turn is a means of discipline for us; and through all their variety a single purpose works, which tends to a single end—'that we should be partakers of His holiness'?

And that is the one point of view from which we can bear to look upon the world and not be utterly bewildered and over-mastered by it. Calmness and central peace are ours ; a true appreciation of all outward good and a charm against the bitterest sting of outward evils are ours; a patient continuance in the place where He has set us is ours—when by fellowship with Him we have learned to look upon our work as primarily doing His will, and upon all our possessions and conditions primarily as means for making us like Himself. Most men seem to think that they have gone to the very bottom of the thing when they have classified the gifts of fortune as good or evil, according as they produce pleasure or pain. But that is a poor, superficial classification. It is like taking and arranging books by their bindings and flowers by their colours. Instead of saying, 'We divide life into two halves, and we put there all the joyful, and here all the sad, for that is the ruling distinction'—let us rather say, 'The whole is one, because it all comes from one purpose, and it all tends towards one end. The only question worth asking in regard to the externals of our life is—How far does each thing help me to be a good man? how far does it open my understanding to apprehend Him? how far does it make my spirit pliable and plastic under His touch? how far does it make me capable of larger reception of greater gifts from Himself? what is its effect in preparing me for that world beyond?' Is there any other greater, more satisfying, more majestic thought of life than this—the scaffolding by which souls are built up into the temple of God? And to care whether a thing is painful or pleasant is as absurd as to care whether the bricklayer's trowel is knocking the sharp corner off a brick, or plastering mortar on the one below it before he lays it carefully on its course. Is the *building* getting on? That is the one question that is worth thinking about.

You and I write our lives as if on one of those manifold writers which you use. A thin filmy sheet *here*, a bit of black paper below it; but the writing goes through upon the next page, and when the blackness that divides two worlds is swept away *there*, the history of each life written by ourselves remains legible in eternity. And the question is—What sort of autobiography are we writing for the revelation of that

day, and how far do our circumstances help us to tran-
scribe fair in our lives the will of our God and the image
of our Redeemer?

If, then, we have once got hold of that principle that
all which is—summer and winter, storm and sunshine,
possession and loss, memory and hope, work and rest,
and all the other antitheses of life—is equally the product of His will, equally the manifestation of His mind,
equally His means for our discipline, then we have the
amulet and talisman which will preserve us from the
fever of desire and the shivering fits of anxiety as to
things which perish. And, as they tell of a Christian
father who, riding by one of the great lakes of Switzer-
land all day long, on his journey to the Church Council
that was absorbing his thoughts, said towards evening
to the deacon who was pacing beside him, 'Where is
the lake?' so you and I, journeying along by the margin
of this great flood of things when wild storms sweep
across it, or when the sunbeams glint upon its blue
waters, 'and birds of peace sit brooding on the charmed
wave,' will be careless of the changeful sea, if the eye
looks beyond the visible and beholds the unseen, the
unchanging real presences that make glory in the
darkest lives, and 'sunshine in the shady place.' 'Let
every man, wherein he is called, therein abide with
God.'

III. Still further, another thought may be suggested
from these words, or rather from the connection in
which they occur, and that is—Such contented continuance in our place is the dictate of the truest wisdom.

There are two or three collateral topics, partly suggested by the various connections in which this commandment occurs in the chapter, from which I draw
the few remarks I have to make now.

And the first point I would suggest is that very old commonplace one, so often forgotten, that after all, though you may change about as much as you like, there is a pretty substantial equipoise and identity in the amount of pain and pleasure in all external conditions. The total length of day and night all the year round is the same at the North Pole and at the Equator —half and half. Only, in the one place, it is half and half for four-and-twenty hours at a time, and in the other, the night lasts through gloomy months of winter, and the day is bright for unbroken weeks of summer. But, when you come to add them up at the year's end, the man who shivers in the ice, and the man who pants beneath the beams from the zenith, have had the same length of sunshine and of darkness. It does not matter much at what degrees between the Equator and the Pole you and I live; when the thing comes to be made up we shall be all pretty much upon an equality. You do not get the happiness of the rich man over the poor one by multiplying twenty shillings a week by as many figures as will suffice to make it up to £10,000 a year. What is the use of such eager desires to change our condition, when every condition has disadvantages attending its advantages as certainly as a shadow; and when all have pretty nearly the same quantity of the raw material of pain and pleasure, and when the amount of either actually experienced by us depends not on where we are, but on *what* we are?

Then, still further, there is another consideration to be kept in mind upon which I do not enlarge, as what I have already said involves it—namely, that whilst the portion of external pain and pleasure summed up comes pretty much to the same in everybody's life, any condition may yield the fruit of devout fellowship with God.

Another very remarkable idea suggested by a part of the context is—What is the need for my troubling myself about outward changes when *in Christ* I can get all the peculiarities which make any given position desirable to me? For instance, hear how Paul talks to slaves eager to be set free: 'For he that is called in the Lord, *being* a servant, is the Lord's freeman: likewise also he that is called, *being* free, is Christ's servant.' If you generalise that principle it comes to this, that in union with Jesus Christ we possess, by our fellowship with Him, the peculiar excellences and blessings that are derivable from external relations of every sort. To take concrete examples—if a man is a slave, he may be free in Christ. If free, he may have the joy of utter submission to an absolute master in Christ. If you and I are lonely, we may feel all the delights of society by union with Him. If surrounded and distracted by companionship, and seeking for seclusion, we may get all the peace of perfect privacy in fellowship with Him. If we are rich, and sometimes think that we were in a position of less temptation if we were poorer, we may find all the blessings for which we sometimes covet poverty in communion with Him. If we are poor, and fancy that, if we had a little more just to lift us above the grinding, carking care of to-day and the anxiety of to-morrow, we should be happier, we may find all tranquillity in Him. And so you may run through all the variety of human conditions, and say to yourself—What is the use of looking for blessings flowing from these from without? Enough for us if we grasp that Lord who is all in all, and will give us in peace the joy of conflict, in conflict the calm of peace, in health the refinement of sickness, in sickness the vigour and glow of health, in memory the

brightness of undying hope, in hope the calming of
holy memory, in wealth the lowliness of poverty, in
poverty the ease of wealth; in life and in death being
all and more than all that dazzles us by the false gleam
of created brightness!

And so, finally—a remark which has no connection
with the text itself, but which I cannot avoid inserting
here—I want you to think, and think seriously, of the
antagonism and diametrical opposition between these
principles of my text and the maxims current in the
world, and nowhere more so than in this city. Our text
is a revolutionary one. It is dead against the watch-
words that you fathers give your children—'push,'
'energy,' 'advancement,' 'get on, whatever you do.'
You have made a philosophy of it, and you say that
this restless discontent with a man's present position
and eager desire to get a little farther ahead in the
scramble, underlies much modern civilisation and
progress, and leads to the diffusion of wealth and
to employment for the working classes, and to
mechanical inventions, and domestic comforts, and I
don't know what besides. You have made a religion of
it; and it is thought to be blasphemy for a man to stand
up and say—'It is idolatry!' My dear brethren, I declare I solemnly believe that, if I were to go on to the
Manchester Exchange next Tuesday, and stand up and
say—'There is no God,' I should not be thought half
such a fool as if I were to go and say—'Poverty is not
an evil *per se*, and men do not come into this world to
get *on* but to get *up*—nearer and liker to God.' If you,
by God's grace, lay hold of this principle of my text,
and honestly resolve to work it out, trusting in that
dear Lord who 'though He was rich yet for our sakes
became poor,' in ninety-nine cases out of a hundred

you will have to make up your minds to let the big
prizes of your trade go into other people's hands, and
be contented to say—'I live by peaceful, high, pure,
Christ-like thoughts.' 'He that needs least,' said an old
heathen, 'is nearest the gods'; but I would rather
modify the statement into, 'He that needs most, and
knows it, is nearest the gods.' For surely Christ is
more than mammon; and a spirit nourished by calm
desires and holy thoughts into growing virtues and
increasing Christlikeness is better than circumstances
ordered to our will, in the whirl of which we have lost
our God. 'In everything by prayer and supplication,
with thanksgiving, let your requests be made known to
God, and the peace of God and the God of peace shall
keep your hearts and minds in Christ Jesus.'

'LOVE BUILDETH UP'

'Now, as touching things offered unto idols, we know that we all have knowledge. Knowledge puffeth up, but charity edifieth. 2. And if any man think
that he knoweth any thing, he knoweth nothing yet as he ought to know. 3. But
if any man love God, the same is known of him. 4. As concerning therefore the
eating of those things that are offered in sacrifice unto idols, we know that an idol
is nothing in the world, and that there is none other God but one. 5. For though
there be that are called gods, whether in heaven or in earth, (as there be gods
many, and lords many,) 6. But to us there is but one God, the Father, of whom
are all things, and we in Him; and one Lord Jesus Christ, by whom are all things,
and we by Him. 7. Howbeit there is not in every man that knowledge: for some,
with conscience of the idol unto this hour, eat it as a thing offered unto an idol;
and their conscience being weak is defiled. 8. But meat commendeth us not to
God: for neither, if we eat, are we the better; neither, if we eat not, are we the
worse. 9. But take heed, lest by any means this liberty of yours become a stumb-
lingblock to them that are weak. 10. For if any man see thee which hast knowledge
sit at meat in the idol's temple, shʳˡˡ not the conscience of him which is weak be
emboldened to eat those things ʷnich are offered to idols; 11. And through thy
knowledge shall the weak brother perish, for whom Christ died? 12. But when
ye sin so against the brethren, and wound their weak conscience, ye sin against
Christ. 13. Wherefore, if meat make my brother to offend, I will eat no flesh while
the world standeth, lest I make my brother to offend.'—1 COR. viii. 1-13.

IT is difficult for us to realise the close connection
which existed between idol-worship and daily life.
Something of the same sort is found in all mission

fields. It was almost impossible for Christians to take any part in society and not seem to sanction idolatry. Would that Christianity were as completely interwoven with our lives as heathen religions are into those of their devotees! Paul seems to have had referred to him a pressing case of conscience, which divided the Corinthian Church, as to whether a Christian could join in the usual feasts or sacrifices. His answer is in this passage.

The longest way round is sometimes the shortest way home. The Apostle begins far away from the subject in hand by running a contrast between knowledge and love, and setting the latter first. But his contrast is very relevant to his purpose. Small questions should be solved on great principles.

The first principle laid down by Paul is the superiority of love over knowledge, the bearing of which on the question in hand will appear presently. We note that there is first a distinct admission of the Corinthians' intelligence, though there is probably a tinge of irony in the language 'We know that we all have knowledge.' 'You Corinthians are fully aware that you are very superior people. Whatever else you know, you know that, and I fully recognise it.'

The admission is followed by a sudden, sharp comment, to which the Corinthians' knowledge that they knew laid them open. Swift as the thrust of a spear comes flashing 'Knowledge puffeth up.' Puffed-up things are swollen by wind only, and the more they are inflated the hollower and emptier they are; and such a sharp point as Paul's saying shrivels them. The statement is not meant as the assertion of a necessary or uniform result of knowledge, but it does put plainly a very usual result of it, if it is unaccompanied by love. It is a strange, sad result of superior intelligence or acquirements, that it so often leads to conceit, to a false estimate of the worth and power of knowing, to a ridiculous over-valuing of certain acquirements, and to an insolent contempt and cruel disregard of those who have them not. Paul's dictum has been only too well confirmed by experience.

'Love builds up,' or 'edifies.' Probably the main direction in which that building up is conceived of as taking effect, is in aiding the progress of our neighbours, especially in the religious life. But the tendency of love to rear a fair fabric of personal character is not to be overlooked. In regard to effect on character, the palm must be given to love, which produces solid excellence far beyond what mere knowledge can effect. Further, that pluming one's self on knowledge is a sure proof of ignorance. The more real our acquirements, the more they disclose our deficiencies. All self-conceit hinders us from growing intellectually or morally, and intellectual conceit is the worst kind of it.

Very significantly, love to God, and not the simple emotion of love without reference to its object, is opposed to knowledge; for love so directed is the foundation of all excellence, and of all real love to men. Love to God is not the antithesis of true knowledge, but it is the only victorious antagonist of the conceit of knowing. Very significantly, too, does Paul vary his conclusion in verse 3 by saying that the man who loves God 'is known of Him,' instead of, as we might have expected, 'knows Him.' The latter is true, but the statement in the verse puts more strongly the thought of the man's being an object of God's care. In regard, then, to their effects on character, in producing consideration and helpfulness to others, and in securing

God's protection, love stands first, and knowledge second.

What has all this to do with the question in hand? This, that if looked at from the standpoint of knowledge, it may be solved in one way, but if from that of love, it will be answered in another. So, in verses 4-6, Paul treats the matter on the ground of knowledge. The fundamental truth of Christianity, that there is one God, who is revealed and works through Jesus Christ, was accepted by all the Corinthians. Paul states it here broadly, denying that there were any objective realities answering to the popular conceptions or poetic fancies or fair artistic presentments of the many gods and lords of the Greek pantheon, and asserting that all Christians recognise one God, the Father, from whom the universe of worlds and living things has origin, and to whom we as Christians specially belong, and one Lord, the channel through whom all divine operations of creation, providence, and grace flow, and by whose redeeming work we Christians are endowed with our best life. If a believer was fully convinced of these truths, he could partake of sacrificial feasts without danger to himself, and without either sanctioning idolatry or being tempted to return to it.

No doubt it was on this ground that an idol was nothing that the laxer party defended their action in eating meat offered to idols; and Paul fully recognises that they had a strong case, and that, if there were no other considerations to come in, the answer to the question of conscience submitted to him would be wholly in favour of the less scrupulous section. But there is something better than knowledge; namely, love. And its decision must be taken before the whole material for a judgment is in evidence.

Therefore, in the remainder of the chapter, Paul
dwells on loving regard for brethren. In verse 7, he
reminds the 'knowing' Corinthians that new convictions
do not obliterate the power of old associations. The
awful fascination of early belief still exercises influence.
The chains are not wholly broken off. Every mission
field shows examples of this. Every man knows
that habits are not so suddenly overcome, that there
is no hankering after them or liability to relapse.
It would be a dangerous thing for a weak believer to
risk sharing in an idol feast; for he would be very
likely to slide down to his old level of belief, and Zeus
or Pallas to seem to him real powers once more.

The considerations in verse 7 would naturally be
followed by the further thoughts in verse 9, etc. But,
before dealing with these, Paul interposes another
thought in verse 8, to the effect that partaking of or
abstinence from any kind of food will not, in itself,
either help or hinder the religious life. The bearing of
that principle on his argument seems to be to reduce
the importance of the whole question, and to suggest
that, since eating of idol sacrifices could not be called a
duty or a means of spiritual progress, the way was
open to take account of others' weakness as determining our action in regard to it. A modern application
may illustrate the point. Suppose that a Christian
does not see total abstinence from intoxicants to be
obligatory on him. Well, he cannot say that drinking
is so, or that it is a religious duty, and so the way is
clear for urging regard to others' weakness as an
element in the case.

That being premised, Paul comes to his final point;
namely, that Christian men are bound to restrict their
liberty so that they shall not tempt weaker brethren

I

on to a path on which they cannot walk without stumbling. He has just shown the danger to such of partaking of the sacrificial feasts. He now completes his position by showing, in verse 10, that the stronger man's example may lead the weaker to do what he cannot do innocently. What is harmless to us may be fatal to others, and, if we have led them to it, their blood is on our heads.

The terrible discordance of such conduct with our Lord's example, which should be our law, is forcibly set forth in verse 11, which has three strongly emphasised thoughts—the man's fate—he perishes; his relation to his slayer—a brother; what Christ did for the man whom a Christian has sent to destruction—died for him. These solemn thoughts are deepened in verse 12, which reminds us of the intimate union between the weakest and Christ, by which He so identifies Himself with them that any blow struck on them touches Him.

There is no greater sin than to tempt weak or ignorant Christians to thoughts or acts which their ignorance or weakness cannot entertain or do without damage to their religion. There is much need for laying that truth to heart in these days. Both in the field of speculation and of conduct, Christians, who think that they know so much better than ignorant believers, need to be reminded of it.

So Paul, in verse 13, at last answers the question. His sudden turning to his own conduct is beautiful. He will not so much command others, as proclaim his own determination. He does so with characteristic vehemence and hyperbole. No doubt the liberal party in Corinth were ready to complain against the proposal to restrict their freedom because of others' weakness;

and they would be disarmed, or at least silenced, and might be stimulated to like noble resolution, by Paul's example.

The principle plainly laid down here is as distinctly applicable to the modern question of abstinence from intoxicants.   No one can doubt that 'moderation' in their use by some tempts others to use which soon becomes 'fatally immoderate.   The Church has been robbed of promising members thereby, over and over again.   How can a Christian man cling to a 'moderate' use of these things, and run the risk of destroying by his example a brother for whom Christ died?

THE SIN OF SILENCE

'For though I preach the Gospel, I have nothing to glory of: for necessity is laid upon me; yea, woe is unto me, if I preach not the Gospel! 17. For if I do this thing willingly, I have a reward.'—1 Cor. ix. 16, 17.

THE original reference of these words is to the Apostle's principle and practice of not receiving for his support money from the churches.   Gifts he did accept; pay he did not.   The exposition of his reason is interesting, ingenuous, and chivalrous.   He strongly asserts his right, even while he as strongly declares that he will waive it.   The reason for his waiving it is that he desires to have somewhat in his service beyond the strict line of his duty.   His preaching itself, with all its toils and miseries, was but part of his day's work, which he was bidden to do, and for doing which he deserved no thanks nor praise.   But he would like to have a little bit of glad service over and above what he is ordered to do, that, as he ingenuously says, he may have 'somewhat to boast of.'

In this exposition of motives we have two great

principles actuating the Apostle—one, his profound
sense of obligation, and the other his desire, if it might
be, to do more than he was bound to do, because he
loved his work so much. And though he is speaking
here as an apostle, and his example is not to be unconditionally transferred to us, yet I think that the motives
which actuated his conduct are capable of unconditional application to ourselves.

There are three things here. There is the obligation
of speech, there is the penalty of silence, and there is
the glad obedience which transcends obligation.

I. First, mark the obligation of speech.

No doubt the Apostle had, in a special sense, a
'necessity laid upon' him, which was first laid upon
him on that road to Damascus, and repeated many a
time in his life. But though he differs from us in the
direct supernatural commission which was given to
him, in the width of the sphere in which he had to
work, and in the splendour of the gifts which were
entrusted to his stewardship, he does not differ from
us in the reality of the obligation which was laid upon
him. Every Christian man is as truly bound as was
Paul to preach the Gospel. The commission does not
depend upon apostolic dignity. Jesus Christ, when He
said, 'Go ye into all the world, and preach the Gospel
to every creature,' was not speaking to the eleven, but
to all generations of His Church. And whilst there
are many other motives on which we may rest the
Christian duty of propagating the Christian faith, I
think that we shall be all the better if we bottom it
upon this, the distinct and definite commandment of
Jesus Christ, the grip of which encloses all who for
themselves have found that the Lord is gracious.

For that commandment is permanent. It is exactly

contemporaneous with the duration of the promise
which is appended to it, and whosoever suns himself
in the light of the latter is bound by the precept of the
former. 'Lo! I am with you alway, even to the end of
the world,' defines the duration of the promise, and it
defines also the duration of the duty. Nay, even the
promise is made conditional upon the discharge of the
duty enjoined. For it is to the Church 'going into all
the world, and preaching the Gospel to every creature,'
that the promise of an abiding presence is made.

Let us remember, too, that, just because this commission is given to the whole Church, it is binding on
every individual member of the Church. There is a
very common fallacy, not confined to this subject, but
extending over the whole field of Christian duty, by
which things that are obligatory on the community
are shuffled off the shoulders of the individual. But
we have to remember that the whole Church is nothing
more than the sum total of all its members, and that
nothing is incumbent upon it which is not in their
measure incumbent upon each of them. Whatsoever
Christ says to all, He says to each, and the community
has no duties which you and I have not.

Of course, there are diversities of forms of obedience to
this commandment; of course, the restrictions of local-
ity and the other obligations of life, come in to modify
it; and it is not every man's duty to wander over the ·
whole world doing this work. But the direct work of
communicating to others who know it not the sweetness and the power of Jesus Christ belongs to every
Christian man. You cannot buy yourselves out of the
ranks, as they used to be able to do out of the militia,
by paying for a substitute. Both forms of service are
obligatory upon each of us. We all, if we know any-

thing of Christ and His love and His power, are bound, by the fact that we do know it, to tell it to those whom we can reach. You have all got congregations if you would look for them. There is not a Christian man or woman in this world who has not somebody that he or she can speak to more efficiently than anybody else can. You have your friends, your relations, the people with whom you are brought into daily contact, if you have no wider congregations. You cannot all stand up and preach in the sense in which I do so. But this is not the meaning of the word in the New Testament. It does not imply a pulpit, nor a set discourse, nor a gathered multitude; it simply implies a herald's task of proclaiming. Everybody who has found Jesus Christ can say, 'I have found the Messiah,' and everybody who knows Him can say, 'Come and hear, and I will tell what the Lord hath done for my soul.' Since you can do it you are bound to do it; and if you are one of 'the dumb dogs, lying down and loving to slumber,' of whom there are such crowds paralysing the energies and weakening the witness of every Church upon earth, then you are criminally and suicidally oblivious of an obligation which is a joy and a privilege as much as a duty.

Oh, brethren! I do want to lay on the consciences of all you Christian people this, that nothing can absolve you from the obligation of personal, direct speech to some one of Christ and His salvation. Unless you can say, 'I have not refrained my lips, O Lord! Thou knowest,' there frowns over against you an unfulfilled duty, the neglect of which is laming your spiritual activity, and drying up the sources of your spiritual strength.

But, then, besides this direct effort, there are the

other indirect methods in which this commandment can be discharged, by sympathy and help of all sorts, about which I need say no more here.

Jesus Christ's ideal of His Church was an active propaganda, an army in which there were no non-combatants, even although some of the combatants might be detailed to remain in the camp and look after the stuff, and others of them might be in the forefront of the battle.   But is that ideal ever fulfilled in any of our churches ?   How many amongst us there are who do absolutely nothing in the shape of Christian work ! Some of us seem to think that the voluntary principle on which our Nonconformist churches are largely organised means, 'I do not need to do anything unless I like.   Inclination is the guide of duty, and if I do not care to take any active part in the work of our church, nobody has anything to say.'   No man can force me, but if Jesus Christ says to me, 'Go!' and I say, 'I had rather not,' Jesus Christ and I have to settle accounts between us.   The less *men* control, the more stringent ought to be the control of Christ.   And if the principle of Christian obedience is a willing heart, then the duty of a Christian is to see that the heart is willing. ·

A stringent obligation, not to be shuffled off by any of the excuses that we make, is laid upon us all.   It makes very short work of a number of excuses.   There is a great deal in the tone of this generation which tends to chill the missionary spirit.   We know more about the heathen world, and familiarity diminishes horror.   We have taken up, many of us, milder and more merciful ideas about the condition of those who die without knowing the name of Jesus Christ.   We have taken to the study of comparative religion as a science, forgetting sometimes that the thing that we are studying as a science is spreading a dark cloud of ignorance and apathy over millions of men. And all these reasons somewhat sap the strength and cool the fervour of a good many Christian people nowadays. Jesus Christ's commandment remains just as it was.

Then some of us say, 'I prefer working at home!' Well, if you are doing all that you can there, and really are enthusiastically devoted to one phase of Christian service, the great principle of division of labour comes in to warrant your not entering upon other fields which others cultivate. But unless you are thus casting all your energies into the work which you say that you prefer, there is no reason in it why you should do nothing in the other direction. Jesus Christ still says, 'Go ye into all the world.'

Then some of you say, 'Well, I do not much believe in your missionary societies. There is a great deal of waste of money about them. A number of things there are that one does not approve of. I have heard stories about missionaries being very idle, very luxurious, and taking too much pay, and doing too little work.' Well, be it so! Very probably it is partly true; though I do not know that the people whose testimony is so willingly accepted, to the detriment of our brethren in foreign lands, are precisely the kind of people that should talk much about self-sacrifice and luxurious living, or whose estimate of Christian work is to be relied upon. I fancy many of them, if they walked about the streets of an English town, would have a somewhat similar report to give, as they have when they walk about the streets of an Indian one. But be that as it may, does that indictment draw a wet sponge across the commandment of Jesus Christ? or can you chisel out of the stones of Sinai one of the words written there, by reason of the imperfections of those who are seeking to obey them? Surely not! Christ still says, 'Go ye into all the world!'

I sometimes venture to think that the day will come when the condition of being received into, and retained in, the communion of a Christian church will be obedience to that commandment. Why, even bees have the sense at a given time of the year to turn the drones out of the hives, and sting them to death. I do not recommend the last part of the process, but I am not sure but that it would be a benefit to us all, both to those ejected and to those retained, that we should get rid of that added weight that clogs every organised community in this and other lands—the dead weight of idlers who say that they are Christ's disciples. Whether it is a condition of church membership or not, sure I am that it is a condition of fellowship with Jesus Christ, and a condition, therefore, of health in the Christian life, that it should be a life of active obedience to this plain, imperative, permanent, and universal command.

II. Secondly, a word as to the penalty of silence.

'Woe is me if I preach not the Gospel.' I suppose Paul is thinking mainly of a future issue, but not exclusively of that. At all events, let me point you, in a word or two, to the plain penalties of silence here, and to the awful penalties of silence hereafter.

'Woe is me if I preach not the Gospel.' If you are a dumb and idle professor of Christ's truth, depend upon it that your dumb idleness will rob you of much communion with Jesus Christ. There are many Christians who would be ever so much happier, more joyous, and more assured Christians if they would go and talk about Christ to other people. Because they have locked up God's word in their hearts it melts away unknown, and they lose more than they suspect of the sweetness and buoyancy and assured confidence that might mark them, for no other reason than because they seek to keep their morsel to themselves. Like that mist that lies white and dull over the ground on a winter's morning, which will be blown away with the least puff of fresh air, there lie doleful dampnesses, in their sooty folds, over many a Christian heart, shutting out the sun from the earth, and a little whiff of wholesome activity in Christ's cause would clear them all away, and the sun would shine down upon men again. If you want to be a happy Christian, work for Jesus Christ. I do not lay that down as a specific by itself. There are other things to be taken in conjunction with it, but yet it remains true that the woe of a languid Christianity attaches to the men who, being professing Christians, are silent when they should speak, and idle when they should work.

There is, further, the woe of the loss of sympathies, and the gain of all the discomforts and miseries of a self-absorbed life. And there is, further, the woe of the loss of one of the best ways of confirming one's own faith in the truth—viz. that of seeking to impart it to others. If you want to learn a thing, teach it. If you want to grasp the principles of any science, try to explain it to somebody who does not understand it. If you want to know where, in these days of jangling and controversy, the true, vital centre of the Gospel is, and what is the essential part of the revelation of God, go and tell sinful men about Jesus Christ who died for them; and you will find out that it is the Cross, and Him who died thereon, as dying for the world, that is the power which can move men's hearts. And so you will cleave with a closer grasp, in days of difficulty and unsettlement, to that which is able to bring light into darkness and to harmonise the discord of a troubled and sinful soul. And, further, there is the woe of having none that can look to you and say, 'I owe myself to thee.' Oh, brethren! there is no greater joy accessible to a man than that of feeling that through his poor words Christ has entered into a brother's heart. And you are throwing away all this because you shut your mouths and neglect the plain commandment of your Lord.

Ay! but that is not all. There is a future to be taken into account, and I think that Christian people do far too little realise the solemn truth that it is not all the same *then* whether a man has kept his Master's commandments or neglected them. I believe that whilst a very imperfect faith saves a man, there is such a thing as being 'saved, yet so as through fire,' and that there is such a thing as having 'an abundant entrance ministered unto us into the everlasting kingdom.' He whose life has been very slightly influenced by Christian principle, and who has neglected plain, imperative duties, will not stand on the same level of blessedness as the man who has more completely yielded himself in life to the constraining power of Christ's love, and has sought to keep all His commandments.

Heaven is not a dead level. Every man there will receive as much blessedness as he is capable of, but capacities will vary, and the principal factor in determining the capacity, which capacity determines the blessedness, will be the thoroughness of obedience to all the ordinances of Christ in the course of the life upon earth. So, though we know, and therefore dare say, little about that future, I do beseech you to take this to heart, that he who there can stand before God, and say, 'Behold! I and the children whom God hath given me' will wear a crown brighter than the starless ones of those who saved themselves, and have brought none with them.

'Some on boards, and some on broken pieces of the ship, they all came safe to land.' But the place where they stand depends on their Christian life, and of that Christian life one main element is obedience to the commandment which makes them the apostles and missionaries of their Lord.

III. Lastly, note the glad obedience which transcends the limits of obligation.

'If I do this thing willingly I have a reward.' Paul desired to bring a little more than was required, in token of his love to his Master, and of his thankful acceptance of the obligation. The artist who loves his work will put more work into his picture than is absolutely needed, and will linger over it, lavishing diligence and care upon it, because he is in love with his task. The servant who seeks to do as little as he can scrape through with without rebuke is actuated by no high motives. The trader who barely puts as much into the scale as will balance the weight in the other is grudging in his dealings; but he who, with liberal hand, gives 'shaken down, pressed together, and running over' measure, gives because he delights in the giving.

And so it is in the Christian life. There are many of us whose question seems to be, 'How little can I get off with? how much can I retain?'—many of us whose effort is to find out how much of the world is consistent with the profession of Christianity, and to find the minimum of effort, of love, of service, of gifts which may free us from obligation.

And what does that mean? It means that we are slaves. It means that if we durst we would give nothing, and do nothing. And what does that mean? It means that we do not care for the Lord, and have no joy in our work. And what does that mean? It means that our work deserves no praise, and will get no reward. If we love Christ we shall be anxious, if it were possible, to do more than He commands us, in token of our loyalty to the King, and of our delight in the service. Of course, in the highest view, nothing can be more than necessary. Of course He has the right to all our work; but yet there are heights of Christian consecration and self-sacrifice which a man will not be blamed if he has not climbed, and will be praised if he has. What we want, if I might venture to say so, is extravagance of service. Judas may say, 'To what purpose is this waste?' but Jesus will say, He 'hath wrought a good work on Me,' and the fragrance of the ointment will smell sweet through the centuries.

So, dear brethren, the upshot of the whole thing is, Do not let us do our Christian work reluctantly, else it is only slave's work, and there is no blessing in it, and no reward will come to us from it. Do not let us ask, 'How little may I do?' but 'How much can I do?' Thus, asking, we shall not offer as burnt offering to the Lord that which doth cost us nothing. On His part He has given the commandment as a sign of His love. The stewardship is a token that He trusts us, the duty is an honour, the burden is a grace. On our parts let us seek for the joy of service which is not contented with the bare amount of the tribute that is demanded, but gives something over, if it were possible, because of our love to Him. They who thus give to Jesus Christ

their all of love and effort and service will receive it
all back a hundredfold, for the Master is not going to
be in debt to any of His servants, and He says to them
all, ' I will repay it, howbeit I say not unto thee how
thou owest unto Me even thine own self besides.'

A SERVANT OF MEN

'For though I be free from all men, yet have I made myself servant unto all,
that I might gain the more. 20. And unto the Jews I became as a Jew, that I
might gain the Jews; to them that are under the law, as under the law, that I
might gain them that are under the law; 21. To them that are without law, as
without law, (being not without law to God, but under the law to Christ,) that I
might gain them that are without law. 22. To the weak became I as weak, that
I might gain the weak : I am made all things to all men, that I might by all means
save some. 23. And this I do for the gospel's sake, that I might be partaker thereof with you.'—1 COR. ix. 19-23.

PAUL speaks much of himself, but he is not an egotist.
When he says, ' I do so and so,' it is a gracious way of
enjoining the same conduct on his readers. He will lay
no burden on them which he does not himself carry.
The leader who can say ' Come ' is not likely to want
followers. So, in this section, the Apostle is really enjoining on the Corinthians the conduct which he
declares is his own.

The great principle incumbent on all Christians,
with a view to the salvation of others, is to go as far
as one can without untruthfulness in the direction of
finding points of resemblance and contact with those
to whom we would commend the Gospel. There is a
base counterfeit of this apostolic example, which slurs
over distinctive beliefs, and weakly tries to please
everybody by differing from nobody. That trimming
to catch all winds never gains any. Mr. Facing-both-
ways is not a powerful evangelist. The motive of
becoming all things to all men must be plainly disin-
terested, and the assimilation must have love for the

souls concerned and eagerness to bring the truth to
them, and them to the truth, legibly stamped upon it, or
it will be regarded, and rightly so, as mere cowardice
or dishonesty.   And there must be no stretching the
assimilation to the length of either concealing truth
or fraternising in evil.   Love to my neighbour can
never lead to my joining him in wrongdoing.

But, while the limits of this assumption of the colour
of our surroundings are plainly marked, there is ample
space within these for the exercise of this eminently
Christian grace.   We must get near people if we would
help them.   Especially must we identify ourselves with
them in sympathy, and seek to multiply points of
assimilation, if we would draw them to Jesus Christ.
He Himself had to become man that He might gain
men, and His servants have to do likewise, in their
degree.   The old story of the Christian teacher who
voluntarily became a slave, that he might tell of Christ
to slaves, has in spirit to be repeated by us all.

We can do no good by standing aloof on a height and
flinging down the Gospel to the people below.   They
must feel that we enter into their circumstances, prejudices, ways of thinking, and the like, if our words are
to have power.   That is true about all Christian
teachers, whether of old or young.   You must be a boy
among boys, and try to show that you enter into the
boy's nature, or you may lecture till doomsday and do
no good.

Paul instances three cases in which he had acted, and
still continued to do so, on this principle.   He was a
Jew, but after his conversion he had to ' become a Jew '
by a distinct act ; that is, he had receded so far from
his old self, that he, if he had had only himself to
think of, would have given up all Jewish observances.

But he felt it his duty to conciliate prejudice as far as he could, and so, though he would have fought to the death rather than given countenance to the belief that circumcision was necessary, he had no scruple about circumcising Timothy; and, though he believed that for Christians the whole ancient ritual was abolished, he was quite willing, if it would smooth away the prejudices of the 'many thousands of Jews who believed,' to show, by his participation in the temple worship, that he 'walked orderly, keeping the law.' If he was told ' You must,' his answer could only be ' I will not'; but if it was a question of conciliating, he was ready to go all lengths for that.

The category which he names next is not composed of different persons from the first, but of the same persons regarded from a somewhat different point of view. 'Them that are under the law' describes Jews, not by their race, but by their religion; and Paul was willing to take his place among them, as we have just observed. But he will not do that so as to be misunderstood, wherefore he protests that in doing so he is voluntarily abridging his freedom for a specific purpose. He is not 'under the law'; for the very pith of his view of the Christian's position is that he has nothing to do with that Mosaic law in any of its parts, because Christ has made him free.

The second class to whom in his wide sympathies he is able to assimilate himself, is the opposite of the former—the Gentiles who are 'without law.' He did not preach on Mars' Hill as he did in the synagogues. The many-sided Gospel had aspects fitted for the Gentiles who had never heard of Moses, and the many-sided Apostle had links of likeness to the Greek and the barbarian. But here, too, his assimilation of himself to those whom he seeks to win is voluntary; wherefore he protests that he is not without law, though he recognises no longer the obligations of Moses' law, for he is 'under [or, rather, "in"] law to Christ.'

'The weak' are those too scrupulous-conscienced-Christians of whom he has been speaking in chapter viii. and whose narrow views he exhorted stronger brethren to respect, and to refrain from doing what they could do without harming their own consciences, lest by doing it they should induce a brother to do the same, whose conscience would prick him for it. That is a lesson needed to-day as much as, or more than, in Paul's time, for the widely different degrees of culture and diversities of condition, training, and associations among Christians now necessarily result in very diverse views of Christian conduct in many matters. The grand principle laid down here should guide us all, both in regard to fellow-Christians and others. Make yourself as like them as you honestly can; restrict yourself of allowable acts, in deference to even narrow prejudices; but let the motive of your assimilating yourself to others be clearly their highest good, that you may 'gain' them, not for yourself but for your Master.

Verse 23 lays down Paul's ruling principle, which both impelled him to become all things to all men, with a view to their salvation, as he has been saying, and urged him to effort and self-discipline, with a view to his own, as he goes on to say. 'For the Gospel's sake' seems to point backward; 'that I may be a joint partaker thereof' points forward. We have not only to preach the Gospel to others, but to live on it and be saved by it ourselves.

K

HOW THE VICTOR RUNS

'So run, that ye may obtain.'—1 Cor. ix. 24.

'*So* run.' Does that mean 'Run so that ye obtain?' Most people, I suppose, superficially reading the words, attach that significance to them, but the 'so' here carries a much greater weight of meaning than that. It is a word of comparison. The Apostle would have the Corinthians recall the picture which he has been putting before them—a picture of a scene that was very familiar to them ; for, as most of us know, one of the most important of the Grecian games was celebrated at intervals in the immediate neighbourhood of Corinth. Many of the Corinthian converts had, no doubt, seen, or even taken part in them. The previous portion of the verse in which our text occurs appeals to the Corinthians' familiar knowledge of the arena and the competitors, 'Know ye not that they which run in a race run all, but one receiveth the prize?' He would have them picture the eager racers, with every muscle strained, and the one victor starting to the front; and then he says, 'Look at that panting conqueror. That is how you should run. *So* run—' meaning thereby not, 'Run so that you may obtain the prize,' but 'Run so' as the victor does, 'in order that you may obtain.' So, then, this victor is to be a lesson to us, and we are to take a leaf out of his book. Let us see what he teaches us.

I. The first thing is, the utmost tension and energy and strenuous effort.

It is very remarkable that Paul should pick out these

146

Grecian games as containing for Christian people
any lesson, for they were honeycombed, through and
through, with idolatry and all sorts of immorality, so
that no Jew ventured to go near them, and it was part
of the discipline of the early Christian Church that
professing Christians should have nothing to do with
them in any shape.

And yet here, as in many other parts of his letters,
Paul takes these foul things as patterns for Christians.
'There is a soul of goodness in things evil, if we would
observantly distil it out.' It is very much as if English
preachers were to refer their people to a racecourse,
and say, 'Even there you may pick out lessons, and
learn something of the way in which Christian people
ought to live.'

On the same principle the New Testament deals with
that diabolical business of fighting. It is taken as an
emblem for the Christian soldier, because, with all its
devilishness, there is in it this, at least, that men give
themselves up absolutely to the will of their commander, and are ready to fling away their lives if he
lifts his finger. That at least is grand and noble, and
to be imitated on a higher plane.

In like manner Paul takes these poor racers as
teaching us a lesson. Though the thing be all full of
sin, we can get one valuable thought out of it, and it is
this—If people would work half as hard to gain the
highest object that a man can set before him, as
hundreds of people are ready to do in order to gain
trivial and paltry objects, there would be fewer stunted
and half-dead Christians amongst us. 'That is the way
to run,' says Paul, 'if you want to obtain.'

Look at the contrast that he hints at, between the
prize that stirs these racers' energies into such tre-

mendous operation and the prize which Christians
profess to be pursuing. 'They do it to obtain a corruptible crown'—a twist of pine branch out of the
neighbouring grove, worth half-a-farthing, and a little
passing glory not worth much more. They do it to
obtain a corruptible crown; we do *not* do it, though we
professedly have an incorruptible one as our aim and
object. If we contrast the relative values of the objects
that men pursue so eagerly, and the objects of the
Christian course, surely we ought to be smitten down
with penitent consciousness of our own unworthiness,
if not of our own hypocrisy.

It is not even there that the lesson stops, because
we Christian people may be patterns and rebukes to
ourselves. For, on the one side of our nature we show
what we can do when we are really in earnest about
getting something; and on the other side we show
with how little work we can be contented, when, at
bottom, we do not much care whether we get the prize
or not. If you and I really believed that that crown of
glory which Paul speaks about might be ours, and would
be all sufficing for us if it were ours, as truly as we believe that money is a good thing, there would not be such
a difference between the way in which we clutch at the
one and the apathy which scarcely cares to put out a
hand for the other. The things that are seen and
temporal do get the larger portion of the energies and
thoughts of the average Christian man, and the things
that are unseen and eternal get only what is left.
Sometimes ninety per cent. of the water of a stream
is taken away to drive a milldam or do work, and only
ten per cent. can be spared to trickle down the half-
dry channel and do nothing but reflect the bright sun
and help the little flowers and the grass to grow. So, the

larger portion of most lives goes to drive the mill-wheels,
and there is very little left, in the case of many of us, in
order to help us towards God, and bring us closer into
communion with our Lord. 'Run' for the crown as
eagerly as you 'run' for your incomes, or for anything
that you really, in your deepest desires, want. Take
yourselves for your own patterns and your own rebukes.
Your own lives may show you how you *can* love, hope,
work, and deny yourselves when you have sufficient
inducement, and their flame should put to shame their
frost, for the warmth is directed towards trifles and
the coldness towards the crown. If you would run for
the incorruptible prize of effort in the fashion in which
others and yourselves run for the corruptible, your
whole lives would be changed. Why! if Christian
people in general really took half—half? ay! a tenth
part of—the honest, persistent pains to improve their
Christian character, and become more like Jesus Christ,
which a violinist will take to master his instrument,
there would be a new life for most of our Christian
communities. Hours and hours of patient practice are
not too much for the one; how many moments do we
give to the other? 'So run, that ye obtain.'

II. The victorious runner sets Christians an example
of rigid self-control.

Every man that is striving for the mastery is
'temperate in all things.' The discipline for runners
and athletes was rigid. They had ten months of spare
diet—no wine—hard gymnastic exercises every day,
until not an ounce of superfluous flesh was upon their
muscles, before they were allowed to run in the arena.
And, says Paul, that is the example for us. They
practise this rigid discipline and abstinence by way of
preparation for the race, and after it was run they

might dispense with the training. You and I have to practise rigid abstinence as part of the race, as a continuous necessity. *They* did not abstain only from bad things, they did not only avoid criminal acts of sensuous indulgence; but they abstained from many perfectly legitimate things. So for us it is not enough to say, 'I draw the line there, at this or that vice, and I will have nothing to do with these.' You will never make a growing Christian if abstinence from palpable sins only is your standard. You must 'lay aside' every sin, of course, but also 'every *weight*.' Many things are 'weights' that are not 'sins'; and if we are to run fast we must run light, and if we are to do any good in this world we have to live by rigid control and abstain from much that is perfectly legitimate, because, if we do not, we shall fail in accomplishing the highest purposes for which we are here. Not only in regard to the gross sensual indulgences which these men had to avoid, but in regard to a great deal of the outgoings of our interests and our hearts, we have to apply the knife very closely and cut to the quick, if we would have leisure and sympathy and affection left for loftier objects. It is a very easy thing to be a Christian in one aspect, inasmuch as a Christian at bottom is a man that is trusting to Jesus Christ, and that is not hard to do. It is a very hard thing to be a Christian in another aspect, because a real Christian is a man who, by reason of his trusting Jesus Christ, has set his heel upon the neck of the animal that is in him, and keeps the flesh well down, and not only the flesh, but the desires of the mind as well as of the flesh, and subordinates them all to the one aim of pleasing Him. 'No man that warreth entangleth himself with the affairs of this life' if his object is to please Him that has called him

to be a soldier. Unless we cut off a great many of the
thorns, so to speak, by which things catch hold of us
as we pass them, we shall not make much advance in
the Christian life. Rigid self-control and abstinence
from else legitimate things that draw us away from
Him are needful, if we are so to run as the poor heathen
racer teaches us.

III. The last grace that is suggested here, the last
leaf to take out of these racers' book, is definiteness
and concentration of aim.

'I, therefore,' says the Apostle, 'so run not as uncertainly.' If the runner is now heading that way and now
this, making all manner of loops upon his path, of course
he will be left hopelessly in the rear. It is the old fable
of the Grecian mythology transplanted into Christian
soil. The runner who turned aside to pick up the golden
apple was disappointed of his hopes of the radiant fair.
The ship, at the helm of which is a steersman who has
either a feeble hand or does not understand his business,
and which therefore keeps yawing from side to side,
with the bows pointing now this way and now that, is
not holding a course that will make the harbour first
in the race. The people that to-day are marching with
their faces towards Zion, and to-morrow making a loop-
line to the world, will be a long time before they reach
their terminus. I believe there are few things more
lacking in the average Christian life of to-day than
resolute, conscious concentration upon an aim which
is clearly and always before us. Do you know what
you are aiming at? That is the first question. Have
you a distinct theory of life's purpose that you can put
into half a dozen words, or have you not? In the one
case, there is some chance of attaining your object; in
the other one, none. Alas! we find many Christian

people who do not set before themselves, with emphasis and constancy, as their aim the doing of God's will, and so sometimes they do it, when it happens to be easy, and sometimes, when temptations are strong, they do not. It needs a strong hand on the tiller to keep it steady when the wind is blowing in puffs and gusts, and sometimes the sail bellies full and sometimes it is almost empty. The various strengths of the temptations that blow us out of our course are such that we shall never keep a straight line of direction, which is the shortest line, and the only one on which we shall 'obtain,' unless we know very distinctly where we want to go, and have a good strong will that has learned to say 'No!' when the temptations come. 'Whom resist steadfast in the faith.' 'I therefore so run, not as uncertainly,' taking one course one day and another the next.

Now, that definite aim is one that can be equally pursued in all varieties of life. 'This one thing I do' said one who did about as many things as most people, but the different kinds of things that Paul did were all, at bottom, one thing. And we, in all the varieties of our circumstances, may keep this one clear aim before us, and whether it be in this way or in that, we may be equally and at all times seeking the better country, and bending all circumstances and all duty to make us more like our Master and bring us closer to Him.

The Psalmist did not offer an impossible prayer when he said: 'One thing have I desired of the Lord, that will I seek after, that I may dwell in the house of the Lord all the days of my life, to behold the beauty of the Lord and to enquire in His temple.' Was David in 'the house of the Lord' when he was with his sheep in the wilderness, and when he was in Saul's palace, and

Psa. 27 : 4

when he was living with wild beasts in dens and caves of the earth, and when he was a fugitive, hunted like a partridge upon the mountains? Was he always in the Lord's house? Yes! At any rate he could be. All that we do may be doing His will, and over a life, crowded with varying circumstances and yet simplified and made blessed by unvarying obedience, we may write, 'This one thing I do.'

But we shall not keep this one aim clear before our eyes, unless we habituate ourselves to the contemplation of the end. The runner, according to Paul's vivid picture in another of his letters, forgets the things that are behind, and stretches out towards the things that are before. And just as a man runs with his body inclining forward, and his eager hand nearer the prize than his body, and his eyesight and his heart travelling ahead of them both to grasp it, so if we want to live with the one worthy aim for ours, and to put all our effort and faith into what deserves it all—the Christian race—we must bring clear before us continually, or at least with the utmost frequency, the prize of our high calling, the crown of righteousness. Then we shall run so that we may, at the last, be able to finish our course with joy, and dying to hope with all humility that there is laid up for us a crown of righteousness.

'CONCERNING THE CROWN'

'They do it to obtain a corruptible crown, but we are incorruptible.'
1 COR. ix. 25.

ONE of the most famous of the Greek athletic festivals was held close by Corinth. Its prize was a pine-wreath from the neighbouring sacred grove. The painful abstinence and training of ten months, and the fierce struggle of ten minutes, had for their result a twist of green leaves, that withered in a week, and a little fading fame that was worth scarcely more, and lasted scarcely longer. The struggle and the discipline were noble; the end was contemptible. And so it is with all lives whose aims are lower than the highest. They are greater in the powers they put forth than in the objects they compass, and the question, 'What is it for?' is like a douche of cold water from the cart that lays the clouds of dust in the ways.

So, says Paul, praising the effort and contemning the prize, 'They do it to obtain a corruptible crown.' And yet there was a soul of goodness in this evil thing. Though these festivals were indissolubly intertwined with idolatry, and besmirched with much sensuous evil, yet he deals with them as he does with war and with slavery; points to the disguised nobility that lay beneath the hideousness, and holds up even these low things as a pattern for Christian men.

But I do not mean here to speak so much about the general bearing of this text as rather to deal with its designation of the aim and reward of Christian energy, that 'incorruptible crown' of which my text speaks. And in doing so I desire to take into account likewise other places in Scripture in which the same metaphor occurs.

I. The crown.

Let me recall the other places where the same metaphor is employed. We find the Apostle, in the immediate prospect of death, rising into a calm rapture in which imprisonment and martyrdom lose their terrors, as he thinks of the 'crown of righteousness' which the Lord will give to him. The Epistle of James,

again, assures the man who endures temptation that
'the Lord will give him the crown of life which he Has
promised to all them that love Him.' The Lord Himself from heaven repeats that promise to the persecuted
Church at Smyrna : ' Be thou faithful unto death, and I
will give thee a crown of life.' The elders cast their
crowns before the feet of Him that sitteth upon the
throne. The Apostle Peter, in his letter, stimulates
the elders upon earth to faithful discharge of their
duty, by the hope that thereby they shall 'receive a
crown of righteousness that fadeth not away.' So all
these instances taken together with this of my text
enable us to gather two or three lessons.

It is extremely unlikely that all these instances of
the occurrence of the emblem carry with them reference, such as that in my text, to the prize at the
athletic festivals. For Peter and James, intense Jews
as they were, had probably never seen, and possibly
never heard of, the struggles at the Isthmus and at
Olympus and elsewhere. The Book of the Revelation
draws its metaphors almost exclusively from the circle
of Jewish practices and things. So that we have to
look in other directions than the arena or the racecourse to explain these other uses of the image. It is
also extremely unlikely that in these other passages
the reference is to a crown as the emblem of sove-
reignty, for that idea is expressed, as a rule, by another
word in Scripture, which we have Anglicised as 'diadem.'
The 'crown' in all these passages is a garland twisted
out of some growth of the field. In ancient usage roses
were twined for revellers ; pine-shoots or olive branches
for the victors in the games ; while the laurel was 'the
meed of mighty conquerors'; and plaited oak leaves
were laid upon the brows of citizens who had deserved

well of their country, and myrtle sprays crowned the fair locks of the bride.

And thus in these directions, and not towards the wrestling ground or the throne of the monarch, must we look for the ideas suggested by the emblem.

Now, if we gather together all these various uses of the word, there emerge two broad ideas, that the 'crown' which is the Christian's aim symbolises a state of triumphant repose and of festal enjoyment. There are other aspects of that great and dim future which correspond to other necessities of our nature, and I suppose some harm has been done and some misconceptions have been induced, and some unreality imported into the idea of the Christian future, by the too exclusive prominence given to these two ideas— victorious rest after the struggle, and abundant satisfaction of all desires. That future is other and more than a festival; it is other and more than repose. There are larger fields there for the operation of powers that have been trained and evolved here. The faithfulness of the steward is exchanged, according to Christ's great words, for the authority of the ruler over many cities. But still, do we not all know enough of the worry and turbulence and strained effort of the conflict here below, to feel that to some of our deepest and not ignoble needs and desires that image appeals? The helmet that pressed upon the brow even whilst it protected the brain, and wore away the hair even whilst it was a defence, is lifted off, and on unruffled locks the garland is intertwined that speaks victory and befits a festival. One of the old prophets puts the same metaphor in words imperfectly represented by the English translation, when he promises 'a crown' or a garland 'for ashes'—instead of the symbol of mourning, strewed grey and gritty upon the dishevelled hair of the weepers, flowers twined into a wreath—'the oil of joy for mourning,' and the festival 'garment of praise' to dress the once heavy spirit. So the satisfaction of all desires, the accompaniments of a feast, in abundance, rejoicing and companionship, and conclusive conquest over all foes, are promised us in this great symbol.

But let us look at the passages separately, and we shall find that they present the one thought with differences, and that if we combine these, as in a stereoscope, the picture gains solidity.

The crown is described in three ways. It is the crown of 'life,' of 'glory,' and of 'righteousness.' And I venture to think that these three epithets describe the material, so to speak, of which the wreath is composed. The everlasting flower of life, the radiant blossoms of glory, the white flower of righteousness; these are its components.

I need not enlarge upon them, nor will your time allow that I should. Here we have the promise of life, that fuller life which men want, 'the life of which our veins are scant,' even in the fullest tide and hey-day of earthly existence. The promise sets that future over against the present, as if then first should men know what it means to live: so buoyant, elastic, unwearied shall be their energies, so manifold the new outlets for activity, and the new inlets for the surrounding glory and beauty; so incorruptible and glorious shall be their new being. Here we live a living death; there we shall live indeed; and that will be the crown, not only in regard to physical, but in regard to spiritual, powers and consciousness.

But remember that all this full tide of life is Christ's

gift. There is no such thing as natural immortality; there is no such thing as independent life. All Being, from the lowest creature up to the loftiest created spirit, exists by one law, the continual impartation to it of life from the fountain of life, according to its capacities. And unless Jesus Christ, all through the eternal ages of the future, imparted to the happy souls that sit garlanded at His board the life by which they live, the wreaths would wither on their brows, and the brows would melt away, and dissolve from beneath the wreaths. 'I will give him a crown of life.'

It is a crown of 'glory,' and that means a lustrousness of character imparted by radiation and reflection from the central light of the glory of God. 'Then shall the righteous blaze out like the sun in the Kingdom of My Father.' Our eyes are dim, but we can at least divine the far-off flashing of that great light, and may ponder upon what hidden depths and miracles of transformed perfectness and unimagined lustre wait for us, dark and limited as we are here, in the assurance that we all shall be changed into the 'likeness of the body of His glory.'

It is a crown of 'righteousness.' Though that phrase may mean the wreath that rewards righteousness, it seems more in accordance with the other similar expressions to which I have referred to regard it, too, as the material of which the crown is composed. It is not enough that there should be festal gladness, not enough that there should be calm repose, not enough that there should be flashing glory, not enough that there should be fulness of life. To accord with the intense moral earnestness of the Christian system there must be, emphatically, in the Christian hope, cessation of all sin and investiture with all purity. The word means the same thing as the ancient promise,

'Thy people shall be all righteous.' It means the same thing as the latest promise of the ascended Christ, 'They shall walk with Me in white.' And it sets, I was going to say, the very climax and culmination on the other hopes, declaring that absolute, stainless, infallible righteousness which one day shall belong to our weak and sinful spirits.

These, then, are the elements, and on them all is stamped the signature of perpetuity. The victor's wreath is tossed on the ashen heap, the reveller's flowers droop as he sits in the heat of the banqueting-hall; the bride's myrtle blossom fades though she lay it away in a safe place. The crown of life is incorruptible. It is twined of amaranth, ever blossoming into new beauty and never fading.

II. Now look, secondly, at the discipline by which the crown is won.

Observe, first of all, that in more than one of the passages to which we have already referred great emphasis is laid upon Christ as *giving* the crown. That is to say, that blessed future is not won by effort, but is bestowed as a free gift. It is given from the hands which have procured it, and, as I may say, twined it for us. Unless His brows had been pierced with the crown of thorns, ours would never have worn the garland of victory. Jesus provides the sole means, by His work, by which any man can enter into that inheritance; and Jesus, as the righteous Judge who bestows the rewards, which are likewise the results, of our life here, gives the crown. It remains for ever the gift of His love. 'The wages of sin is death,' but we rise above the region of retribution and desert when we pass to the next clause—'the gift of God is eternal life,' and that 'through Jesus Christ.'

Whilst, then, this must be laid as the basis of all, there must also, with equal earnestness and clearness, be set forth the other thought that Christ's gift has conditions, which conditions these passages plainly set forth. In the one, which I have read as a text, we have these conditions declared as being twofold—protracted discipline and continuous effort. The same metaphor employed by the same Apostle, in his last dying utterance, associates his consciousness that he had fought the good fight and run his race, like the pugilists and runners of the arena, with the hope that he shall receive the crown of righteousness. James declares that it is given to the man who *endures* temptation, not only in the sense of bearing, but of so bearing as not thereby to be injured in Christian character and growth in Christian life. Peter asserts that it is the reward of self-denying discharge of duty. And the Lord from heaven lays down the condition of faithfulness unto death as the necessary pre-requisite of His gift of the crown of life. In two of the passages there is included, though not precisely on the level of these other requirements, the love of Him and the love of 'His appearing,' as the necessary qualifications for the gift of the crown.

So, to begin with, unless a man has such a love to Jesus Christ as that he is happy in His presence, and longs to have Him near, as parted loving souls do; and, especially, is looking forward to that great judicial coming, and feeling that there is no tremor in his heart at the prospect of meeting the Judge, but an outgoing of desire and love at the hope of seeing his Saviour and his Friend, what right has he to expect the crown? None. And he will never get it. There is a test for us which may well make some of us ask ourselves, Are we Christians, then, at all?

And then, beyond that, there are all these other conditions which I have pointed out, which may be gathered into one—strenuous discharge of daily duty and continual effort after following in Christ's footsteps.

This needs to be as fully and emphatically preached as the other doctrine that eternal life is the gift of God. All manner of mischiefs may come, and have come, from either of these twin thoughts, wrenched apart. But let us weave them as closely together as the stems of the flowers that make the garlands are twined, and feel that there is a perfect consistency of both in theory, and that there must be a continual union of both, in our belief and in our practice. Eternal life is the gift of God, on condition of our diligence and earnestness. It is not all the same whether you are a lazy Christian or not. It does make an eternal difference in our condition whether here we 'run with patience the race that is set before us, looking unto Jesus.' We have to receive the crown as a gift; we have to wrestle and run, as contending for a prize.

III. And now, lastly, note the power of the reward as motive for life.

Paul says roundly in our text that the desire to obtain the incorruptible crown is a legitimate spring of Christian action. Now, I do not need to waste your time and my own in defending Christian morality from the fantastic objection that it is low and selfish, because it encourages itself to efforts by the prospect of the crown. If there are any men who are Christians—if such a contradiction can be even stated in words—only because of what they hope to gain thereby in another world, they will not get what they hope for; and they would not like it if they did. I do not believe that

L

there are any such; and sure I am, if there are, that it is not Christianity that has made them so. But a thought that we must not take as a supreme motive, we may rightly accept as a subsidiary encouragement. We are not Christians unless the dominant motive of our lives be the love of the Lord Jesus Christ; and unless we feel a necessity, because of loving Him, to aim to be like Him. But, that being so, who shall hinder me from quickening my flagging energies, and stimulating my torpid faith, and encouraging my cowardice, by the thought that yonder there remain rest, victory, the fulness of life, the flashing of glory, and the purity of perfect righteousness? If such hopes are low and selfish as motives, would God that more of us were obedient to such low and selfish motives!

Now it seems to me, that this spring of action is not as strong in the Christians of this day as it used to be, and as it should be. You do not hear much about heaven in ordinary preaching. I do not think it occupies a very large place in the average Christian man's mind. We have all got such a notion nowadays of the great good that the Gospel does in society and in the present, and some of us have been so frightened by the nonsense that has been talked about the 'other-worldliness' of Christianity—as if that was a disgrace to it—that it seems to me that the future of glory and blessedness has very largely faded away, as a motive for Christian men's energies, like the fresco off a neglected convent wall.

And I want to say, dear brethren, that I believe, for my part, that we suffer terribly by the comparative neglect into which this side of Christian truth has fallen. Do you not think that it would make a difference to you if you really believed, and carried always with you in your thoughts, the thrilling consciousness that every act of the present was registered, and would tell on the far side yonder?

We do not know much of that future, and these days are intolerant of mere unverifiable hypotheses. But accuracy of knowledge and definiteness of impression do not always go together, nor is there the fulness of the one wanted for the clearness and force of the other. Though the thread which we throw across the abyss is very slender, it is strong enough, like the string of a boy's kite, to bear the messengers of hope and desire that we may send up by it, and strong enough to bear the gifts of grace that will surely come down along it.

We cannot understand to-day unless we look at it with eternity for a background. The landscape lacks its explanation, until the mists lift and we see the white summits of the Himalayas lying behind and glorifying the low sandy plain. Would your life not be different; would not the things in it that look great be wholesomely dwindled and yet be magnified; would not sorrow be calmed, and life become 'a solemn scorn of ills,' and energies be stimulated, and all be different, if you really 'did it to obtain an incorruptible crown?'

Brethren, let us try to keep more clearly before us, as solemn and blessed encouragement in our lives, these great thoughts. The garland hangs on the goal, but 'a man is not crowned unless he strive according to the laws' of the arena. The laws are two—No man can enter for the conflict but by faith in Christ; no man can win in the struggle but by faithful effort. So the first law is, 'Believe on the Lord Jesus Christ,' and the second is, 'Hold fast that thou hast; let no man take thy crown.'

THE LIMITS OF LIBERTY

'All things are lawful for me, but all things are not expedient: all things are lawful for me, but all things edify not. 24. Let no man seek his own, but every man another's wealth. 25. Whatsoever is sold in the shambles, that eat, asking no question for conscience sake. 26. For the earth is the Lord's, and the fulness thereof. 27. If any of them that believe not bid you to a feast, and ye be disposed to go, whatsoever is set before you eat, asking no question for conscience sake. 28. But if any man say unto you, This is offered in sacrifice unto idols, eat not for his sake that shewed it, and for conscience sake : for the earth is the Lord's and the fulness thereof : 29. Conscience, I say, not thine own, but of the other : for why is my liberty judged of another man's conscience ? 30. For if I by grace be a partaker, why am I evil spoken of for that for which I give thanks ? 31. Whether therefore ye eat, or drink, or whatsoever ye do, do all to the glory of God. 32. Give none offence, neither to the Jews, nor to the Gentiles, nor to the church of God : 33. Even as I please all men in all things, not seeking mine own profit, but the profit of many, that they may be saved.'—1 COR. x. 23-33.

THIS passage strikingly illustrates Paul's constant habit of solving questions as to conduct by the largest principles. He did not keep his 'theology' and his ethics in separate water-tight compartments, having no communication with each other. The greatest truths were used to regulate the smallest duties. Like the star that guided the Magi, they burned high in the heavens, but yet directed to the house in Bethlehem.

The question here in hand was one that pressed on the Corinthian Christians, and is very far away from our experience. Idolatry had so inextricably inter-twined itself with daily life that it was hard to keep up any intercourse with non-Christians without falling into constructive idolatry; and one very constantly obtruding difficulty was that much of the animal food served on private tables had been slaughtered as sacrifices or with certain sacrificial rites. What was a Christian to do in such a case? To eat or not to eat? Both views had their vehement supporters in the Corinthian church, and the importance of the question is manifest from the large space devoted to it in this letter.

In chapter viii. we have a weighty paragraph, in which one phase of the difficulty is dealt with—the question whether a Christian ought to attend a feast in an idol temple, where, of course, the viands had been offered as sacrifices. But in chapter x. Paul deals with the case in which the meat had been bought in the flesh-market, and so was not necessarily sacrificial. Paul's manner of handling the point is very instructive. He envelops, as it were, the practical solution in a wrapping of large principles; verses 23, 24 precede the specific answer, and are general principles; verses 25-30 contain the practical answer; verses 31-33 and verse 1 of the next chapter are again general principles, wide and imperative enough to mould all conduct, as well as to settle the matter immediately in hand, which, important as it was at Corinth, has become entirely uninteresting to us.

We need not spend time in elucidating the specific directions given as to the particular question in hand further than to note the immense gift of saving common-sense which Paul had, and how sanely and moderately he dealt with his problem. His advice was—'Don't ask where the joint set before you came from. If you do not know that it was offered, your eating of it does not commit you to idol worship.' No doubt there were Corinthian Christians with inflamed consciences who did ask such questions, and rather prided themselves on their strictness and rigidity; but Paul would have them let sleeping dogs lie. If, however, the meat is known to have been offered to an idol, then Paul is as rigid and strict as they are. That combination of willingness to go as far as possible, and inflexible determination not to go one step farther, of yieldingness wherever principle does not come in, and of iron fixedness wherever it does, is rare indeed, but should be aimed at by all Christians. The morality of the Gospel would make more way in the world if its advocates always copied the 'sweet reasonableness' of Paul, which, as he tells us in this passage, he learned from Jesus.

As to the wrapping of general principles, they may all be reduced to one—the duty of limiting Christian liberty by consideration for others. In the two verses preceding the practical precepts, that duty is stated with reference entirely to the obligations flowing from our relationship to others. We are all bound together by a mystical chain of solidarity. Since every man is my neighbour, I am bound to think of him and not only of myself in deciding what I may do or refrain from doing. I must abstain from lawful things if, by doing them, I should be likely to harm my neighbour's building up of a strong character. I can, or I believe that I can, pursue some course of conduct, engage in some enterprise, follow some line of life, without damage to myself, either in regard to worldly position, or in regard to my religious life. Be it so, but I have to take some one else into account. Will my example call out imitation in others, to whom it may be harmful or fatal to do as I can do with real or supposed impunity? If so, I am guilty of something very like murder if I do not abstain.

'What harm is there in betting a shilling? I can well afford to lose it, and I can keep myself from the feverish wish to risk more.' Yes, and you are thereby helping to hold up that gambling habit which is ruining thousands.

'I can take alcohol in moderation, and it does me no harm, and I can go to a prayer-meeting after my dinner and temperate glass, and I am within my Christian liberty in doing so.' Yes, and you take part thereby in the greatest curse that besets our country, and are, by countenancing the drink habit, guilty of the blood of souls. How any Christian man can read these two verses and not abstain from all intoxicants is a mystery. They cut clean through all the pleas for moderate drinking, and bring into play another set of principles which limit liberty by regard to others' good. Surely, if there was ever a subject to which these words apply, it is the use of alcohol, the proved cause of almost all the crime and poverty on both sides of the Atlantic. To the Christians who plead their 'liberty' we can only say, 'Happy is he that condemneth not himself in that thing which he alloweth.'

The same general considerations reappear in the verses following the specific precept, but with a difference. The neighbour's profit is still put forth as the limiting consideration, but it is elevated to a higher sacredness of obligation by being set in connection with the 'glory of God' and the example of Christ. 'Do all to the glory of God.' To put the thought here into modern English—Could you ask a blessing over a glass of spirits when you think that, though it should do you no harm, your taking it may, as it were, tip some weak brother over the precipice? Can you drink to God's glory when you know that drink is slaying thousands body and soul, and that hopeless drunkards are made by wholesale out of moderate drinkers? 'Give no occasion of stumbling'; do not by your example tempt others into risky courses. And remember that 'neighbour' (verse 24) resolves itself into 'Jews' and 'Greeks' and the 'Church of God'—that is, substantially to

your own race and other races—to men with whom
you have affinities, and to men with whom you have
none.

A Christian man is bound to shape his life so that no
man shall be able to say of him that he was the occasion of that one's fall. He is so bound because every
man is his neighbour. He is so bound because he is
bound to live to the glory of God, which can never be
advanced by laying stumbling-blocks in the way for
feeble feet. He is so bound because, unless Christ had
limited Himself within the bound of manhood, and had
sought not His own profit or pleasure, we should have
had neither life nor hope. For all these reasons, the
duty of thinking of others, and of abstaining, for their
sakes, from what one might do, is laid on all Christians.
How do they discharge that duty who will not forswear
alcohol for their neighbour's sake?

'IN REMEMBRANCE OF ME'

'This do in remembrance of Me.'—1 COR. xi. 24.

THE account of the institution of the Lord's Supper,
contained in this context, is very much the oldest
extant narrative of that event. It dates long before
any of the Gospels, and goes up, probably, to somewhere about five and twenty years after the Crucifixion. It presupposes a previous narrative which had
been orally delivered to the Corinthians, and, as the
Apostle alleges, was derived by him from Christ Himself. It is intended to correct corruptions in the ad-
ministration of the rite which must have taken some
time to develop themselves. And so we are carried

back to a period very close indeed to the first institution of the rite, by the words before us.

No reasonable doubt can exist, then, that within a very few years of our Lord's death, the whole body of Christian people believed that Jesus Christ Himself appointed the Lord's Supper. I do not stay to dwell upon the value of a rite contemporaneous with the fact which it commemorates, and continuously lasting throughout the ages, as a witness of the historical veracity of the alleged fact; but I want to fix upon this thought, that Jesus Christ, who cared very little for rites, who came to establish a religion singularly independent of any outward form, did establish two rites, one of them to be done once in a Christian lifetime, one of them to be repeated with indefinite frequency, and, as it appears, at first repeated daily by the early believers. The reason why these two, and only these two, external ordinances were appointed by Jesus Christ was, that, taken together, they cover the whole ground of revealed fact, and they also cover the whole ground of Christian experience. There is no room for any other rites, because these two, the rite of initiation, which is baptism, and the rite of com- memoration, which is the Lord's Supper, say every- thing about Christianity as a revelation, and about Christianity as a living experience.

Not only so, but in the simple primitive form of the Lord's Supper there is contained a reference to the past, the present and the future. It covers all time as well as all revelation and all Christian experience. For the past, as the text shows us, it is a memorial of one Person, and one fact in that Person's life. For the present, it is the symbol of the Christian life, as that great sixth chapter in John's gospel sets forth; and for the future, it is a prophecy, as our Lord Himself said on that night in the upper chamber, 'Till I drink it new with you in My Father's kingdom,' and as the Apostle in this context says, 'Till He come.' It is to these three aspects of this ordinance, as the embodiment of all essential Christian truth, and as the embodiment of all deep Christian experience, covering the past, the present, and the future, that I wish to turn now. I do not deal so much with the mere words of my text as with this threefold significance of the rite which it appoints.

I. So then, first, we have to think of it as a memorial of the past.

'Do this,' is the true meaning of the words, not 'in remembrance of Me,' but something far more sweet and pathetic—'do this for the *remembering* of Me.' The former expression is equal to 'Do this because you remember.' The real meaning of the words is, 'Do this in case you forget'; do this in order that you may recall to memory what the slippery memory is so apt to lose—the impression of even the sweetest sweetness, of the most loving love, and the most self-abnegating sacrifice, which He offered for us.

There is something to me infinitely pathetic and beautiful in looking at the words not only as the commandment of the Lord, but as the appeal of the Friend, who wished, as we all do, not to be utterly forgotten by those whom He cared for and loved; and who, not only because their remembrance was their salvation, but because their forgetfulness pained His human heart, brings to their hearts the plaintive appeal: 'Do not forget Me when I am gone away from you; and even if you have no better way of remembering Me, take these poor symbols, to which I

am not too proud to entrust the care of My memory,
and do this, lest you forget Me.'

But, dear brethren, there are deeper thoughts than
this, on which I must dwell briefly. 'In remembrance
of Me'—Jesus Christ, then, takes up an altogether
unique and solitary position here, and into the sacredest
hours of devotion and the loftiest moments of communion with God, intrudes His personality, and says,
'When you are most religious, remember Me; and let
the highest act of your devout life be a thought turned
to Myself.'

Now, I want you to ask, is that thought diverted
from God? And if it is not, how comes it not to be?
I want you honestly to ask yourselves this question—
what did *He* think about Himself who, at that moment,
when all illusions were vanishing, and life was almost
at its last ebb, took the most solemn rite of His nation
and laid it solemnly aside and said: 'A greater than
Moses is here; a greater deliverance is being wrought':
'Remember Me.' Is that insisting on His own personality, and making the remembrance of it the very
apex and shining summit of all religious aspiration—
is that the work of one about whom all that we have
to say is, He was the noblest of men? If so, then I
want to know how Jesus Christ, in that upper chamber,
founding the sole continuous rite of the religion which
He established, and making its heart and centre the
remembrance of His own personality, can be cleared
from the charge of diverting to Himself what belongs to
God only, and how you and I, if we obey His commands,
escape the crime of idolatry and man-worship? 'Do
this in remembrance,'—not of God—'in remembrance
of Me,' 'and let memory, with all its tendrils, clasp and
cleave to My person.' What an extraordinary demand!

It is obscuring God, unless the 'Me' *is* God manifest in the flesh.

Then, still further, let me remind you that in the appointment of this solitary rite as His memorial to all generations, Jesus Christ Himself designates one part of His whole manifestation as the part into which all its pathos, significance, and power are concentrated. We who believe that the death of Christ is the life of the world, are told that one formidable objection to our belief is that Jesus Christ Himself said so little during His life about His death. I believe His reticence upon that question is much exaggerated, but apart altogether from that, I believe also that there was a necessity in the order of the evolution of divine truth, for the reticence, such as it is, because, whatsoever might be possible to Moses and Elias, on the Mount of Transfiguration, 'His decease which He should accomplish at Jerusalem,' could not be much spoken about in the plain till it had been accomplished. But, apart from both of these considerations, reflect, that whether He said much about His death or not, He said something very much to the purpose about it when He said 'Do this in remembrance of Me.'

It is not His personality only that we are to remember. The whole of the language of the institution of the ritual, as well as the form of the rite, and its connection with the ancient passover, and its connection with the new covenant into connection with which Christ Himself brings it, all point to the significance in His eyes of His death as the Sacrifice for the world's sin. Wherefore 'the body' and 'the blood' separately remembered, except to indicate death by violence? Wherefore the language 'the body *broken* for you'; 'the blood *shed* for many for the remission of sins?'

Wherefore the association with the Passover sacrifice? Wherefore the declaration that 'this is the blood of the Covenant,' unless all tended to the one thought— His death is the foundation of all loving relationships possible to us with God; and the condition of the remission of sins—the Sacrifice for the whole world?'

This is the point that He desires us to remember; this is that which He would have live for ever in our grateful hearts.

I say nothing about the absolute exclusion of any other purpose of this memorial rite. If it was the mysterious thing that the superstition of later ages has made of it, how, in the name of common-sense, does it come that not one syllable, looking in that direction, dropped from His lips when He established it? Surely He, in that upper chamber, knew best what He meant, and what He was doing when He established the rite; and I, for my part, am contented to be told that I believe in a poor, bald Zwinglianism, when I say with my Master, that the purpose of the Lord's Supper is simply the commemoration, and therein the proclamation, of His death. There is no magic, no mystery, no 'sacrament' about it. It blesses us when it makes us remember Him. It does the same thing for us which any other means of bringing Him to mind does. It does that through a different vehicle. A sermon does it by words, the Communion does it by symbols. That is the difference to be found between them. And away goes the whole fabric of superstitious Christianity, and all its mischiefs and evils, when once you accept the simple 'Remember.' Christ told us what He meant by the rite when He said 'Do this in remembrance of Me.'

II. And now one word or two more about the other

particulars which I have suggested. The past, however
sweet and precious, is not enough for any soul to live
upon.   And so this memorial rite, just because it is
memorial, is a symbol for the present.

That is taught us in the great chapter—the sixth
of John's Gospel—which was spoken long before the
institution of the Lord's Supper, but expresses in words
the same ideas which it expresses by material forms.
The Christ who died is the Christ who lives, and must
be lived upon by the Christian.   If our relation to
Jesus Christ were only that 'Once in the end of the
ages He appeared to put away sin by the sacrifice of
Himself'; and if we had to look back through lengthen-
ing vistas of distance and thickening folds of oblivion,
simply to a historical past, in which He was once
offered, the retrospect would not have the sweetness
in it which it now has.   But when we come to this
thought that the Christ who was for us is also the
Christ in us, and that He is not the Christ for us unless
He is the Christ in us; and His death will never wash
away our sins unless we feed upon Him, here and now,
by faith and meditation, then the retrospect becomes
blessedness.   The Christian life is not merely the remembrance of a historical Christ in the past, but it is
the present participation in a living Christ, with us
now.

He is near each of us that we may make Him the
very food of our spirits.   We are to live upon Him.
He is to be incorporated within us by our own act.
This is no mysticism, it is a piece of simple reality.
There is no Christian life without it.   The true life of
the believer is just the feeding of our souls upon Him,
—our minds accepting, meditating upon, digesting the
truths which are incarnated in Jesus; our hearts feeding

upon the love which is so tender, warm, stooping, and close; our wills feeding upon and nourished by the utterance of His will in commandments which to know is joy and to keep is liberty; our hopes feeding upon Him who is our Hope, and in whom they find no chaff and husks of peradventures, but the pure wheat of 'Verily! verily I say unto you'; the whole nature thus finding its nourishment in Jesus Christ. You are Christians in the measure in which the very strength of your spirits, and sustenance of all your faculties, are found in loving communion with the living Lord.

Remember, too, that all this communion, intimate, sweet, sacred, is possible only, or at all events is in its highest forms and most blessed reality, possible only, to those who approach Him through the gate of His death. The feeding upon the living Christ which will be the strength of our hearts and our portion for ever, must be a feeding upon the whole Christ. We must not only nourish our spirits on the fact that He was incarnated for our salvation, but also on the truth that He was crucified for our acceptance with God. 'He that eateth Me, even he shall live by Me,' has for its deepest explanation, 'He that eateth My flesh and drinketh My blood hath eternal life.'

My friends, what about the hunger of your souls? Where is it satisfied? With the swine's husks, or with the 'Bread of God which came down from Heaven?'

III. Now, lastly, that rite which is a memorial and a symbol is also a prophecy.

In the original words of the institution our Lord Himself makes reference to the future; 'till I drink it new with you in My Father's kingdom.' And in the context here, the Apostle provides for the perpetual continuance, and emphasises the prophetic aspect, of the rite, by that word, 'till He come.' His death necessarily implies His coming again. The Cross and the Throne are linked together by an indissoluble bond. Being what it is, the death cannot be the end. Being what He is, if He has once been offered to bear the sins of many, so He must come the second time without sin unto salvation. The rite, just because it is a rite, is the prophecy of a time when the need for it, arising from weak flesh and an intrusive world, shall cease. 'They shall say no more, The ark of the covenant of the Lord; at that time they shall call Jerusalem the throne of the Lord.' There shall be no temple in that great city, because the Lord God Almighty and the Lamb are the Temple thereof. So all external worship is a prophecy of the coming of the perfect time, when that which is perfect being come, the external helps and ladders to climb to the loftiest shall be done away.

But more than that, the memorial and symbol is a prophecy. That upper chamber, with its troubled thoughts, its unbidden tears, starting to the eyes of the half-understanding listeners, who only felt that He was going away and the sweet companionship was dissolved, may seem to be but a blurred and a poor image of the better communion of heaven. But though on that sad night the Master bore a burdened heart, and the servants had but partial apprehension and a more partial love; though He went forth to agonise and to die, and they went forth to deny and to betray, and to leave Him alone, still it was a prophecy of Christ's table in His kingdom. Heaven is to be a feast. That representation promises society to the solitary, rest to the toilers, the oil of joy for mourning, and the full satisfaction of all desires. That heavenly feast

surpasses indeed the antitype in the upper chamber, in
that there the Master Himself partook not, and yonder
we shall sup with Him and He with us, but is prophetic
in that, as there He took a towel and girded Himself
and washed the disciples' feet, so yonder He will come
forth Himself and serve them. The future is unlike
the prophetic past in that 'we shall go no more out';
there shall be no sequences of sorrow, and struggle,
and distance and ignorance; but like it in that we shall
feast on Christ, for through eternity the glorified Jesus
will be the Bread of our spirits, and the fact of His past
sacrifice the foundation of our hopes.

So, dear brethren, though our external celebration
of this rite be dashed, as it always is, with much
ignorance and with feeble faith; and though we gather
round this table as the first generation of Israelites
did round the passover, of which it is the successor,
with staff in hand and loins girded, and have to eat it
often with bitter herbs mingled, and though there be
at our sides empty places, yet even in our clouded and
partial apprehension, and in the imperfections of this
outward type, we may see a gracious shadow of what
is waiting for us when we shall go no more out, and
all empty places shall be filled, and the bitter herbs
shall be changed for the asphodel of Heaven and the
sweet flowerage round the throne of God, and we shall
feast upon the Christ, and in the loftiest experience of
the utmost glories of the Heavens, shall remember the
bitter Cross and agony as that which has bought it all.
'This do in remembrance of Me.' May it be a symbol
of our inmost life, and the prophecy of the Heaven to
which we each shall come!

M

THE UNIVERSAL GIFT

'The manifestation of the Spirit is given to every man to profit withal.'—1 Cor. xii. 7.

THE great fact which to-day[1] commemorates is too often regarded as if it were a transient gift, limited to those on whom it was first bestowed. We sometimes hear it said that the great need of the Christian world is a second Pentecost, a fresh outpouring of the Spirit of God and the like. Such a way of thinking and speaking misconceives the nature and significance of the first Pentecost, which had a transient element in it, but in essence was permanent. The rushing mighty wind and the cloven tongues of fire, and the strange speech in many languages, were all equally transient. The rushing wind swept on, and the house was no more filled with it. The tongues flickered into invisibility and disappeared from the heads. The hubbub of many languages was quickly silent. But that which these things but symbolised is permanent; and we are not to think of Pentecost as if it were a sudden gush from a great reservoir, and the sluice was let down again after it, but as if it were the entrance into a dry bed, of a rushing stream, whose first outgush was attended with noise, but which thereafter flows continuous and unbroken. If churches or individuals are scant of that gift, it is not because it has not been bestowed, but because it has not been accepted.

My text tells us two things: it unconditionally and broadly asserts that every Christian possesses this great gift—the manifestation is given to every man; and then it asserts that the gift of each is meant to be

[1] Whitsunday.

178

utilised for the good of all. 'The manifestation is given to every man to profit withal.'

I. Let me, then, say a word or two, to begin with, about the universality of this gift.

Now, that is implied in our Lord's own language, as commented upon by the Evangelist. For Jesus Christ declared that this was the standing law of His kingdom, to be universally applied to all its members, that 'He that believeth on Him, out of him shall flow rivers of living water'; and the Evangelist's comment goes on to say, 'This spake He of the Spirit which they that believe on Him should receive.' *There* is the condition and the qualification. Wherever there is faith, there the Spirit of God is bestowed, and bestowed in the measure in which faith is exercised. So, then, in full accordance with such fundamental principles in reference to the gift of the Spirit of God, comes the language of my text, and of many another text to which I cannot do more than refer. But let me just quote one or two of them, in order that I may make more emphatic what I believe a great many Christian people do not realise as they ought—viz. that the gift of God's Holy Spirit is not a thing to be desired, as if it were not possessed or confined to select individuals, or manifested by exceptional and lofty attainments, but is the universal heritage of the whole Christian Church. 'Know ye not that ye are the temple of the Holy Ghost?' 'We have all been made to drink into one Spirit,' says Paul again, in the immediate context. 'If any man have not the Spirit of Christ, he is none of His,' says he, unconditionally. And in many other places the same principle is laid down, a principle which I believe the Christian Church to-day needs to have recalled to its consciousness, that it may be quickened to realise it in its experience far more than is the case at present.

Let me remind you, too, that that universality of the gifts of the Divine Spirit is implied in the very conception of what Christ's work, in its deepest and most precious aspects to us, is. For we are not to limit, as a great many so-called earnest evangelical teachers and believers do—we are not to limit His work to that which is effected when a man first becomes a Christian —viz. pardon and acceptance with God. God forbid that I should ever seem to underrate that great initial gift on which everything else must be built. But I am not underrating it when I say, 'Let us prophesy according to the proportion of faith,' and the 'proportion of faith' has been violated, and the perspective and completeness of Christian truth, and of Christ's gifts, have been, alas! to a very large extent distorted because Christian people, trained in what we call the evangelical school, have laid far too little emphasis on the fact that the essential gift of Christ to His people is not pardon, nor acceptance, nor justification, but *life*; and that forgiveness, and altered relationship to God, and assurance of acceptance with Him, are all preliminaries. They are, if I may recur to a figure that I have already employed, the preparing of the channel, and the taking away of the obstacles that block its mouth, in order to the inrush of the flood of the river of the water of life.

This life that Christ gives is the result of the gift of the Spirit. So 'If any man have not the Spirit of Christ he is none of His.' The life is the gift considered from our side, and the Spirit is the gift considered from the divine side. 'Every man that hath the Son hath life'; because the law of the Spirit of life in Christ has made him free from the law of sin and death. So you see if that is true—and I for my part am sure that it is—then all that vulgar way of looking at the influences of the Holy Spirit upon men, as if they were confined to certain exceptional people, or certain abnormal and extraordinary and elevated acts, is swept away. It is not the spasmodic, the exceptional, the rare, not the lofty or transcendentally Christlike acts or characters that are alone the manifestation of the Spirit.

Nor is this gift a thing that a man can discover as distinct from his own consciousness. The point where the river of the water of life comes into the channel of our spirits lies away far up, near the sources, and long before the stream comes into sight in our own consciousness, the blended waters have been inseparably mingled, and flow on peacefully together. 'The Spirit beareth witness *with* our spirits'; and you are not to expect that you can hear two voices speaking, but it is one voice and one only.

Now, that universality of this divine gift underlies the very constitution of the Christian Church. 'Where the Spirit of the Lord is there is liberty,' said Paul. It is because each Christian man has access to the one Source of illumination and of truth and righteousness and holiness, that no Christian man is to become subject to the dominion of a brother. And it is because on the servants and on the handmaidens has been poured out, in these days, God's Spirit and they prophesy, that all domination of classes or individuals, and all stiffening of the free life of God's Church by man-made creeds, are contrary to the very basis of its existence, and an attack on the dignity of each individual member of the Church. 'Ye have an unction from the Holy

One' is said to all Christian people—and 'ye need not that any man teach you,' still less that any man, or body of men, or document framed by men, should be set up as normal and authoritative over Christ's free people.

Still further, and only one word—Let me remind you of what I have already said, and what is only too sadly true, that this grand universality of the Spirit's gift to all Christian people does not fill, in the mind of the ordinary Christian man, the place that it ought, and it does not fill it, therefore, in his experience. I say no more upon that point.

II. And now let me say a word, secondly, about the many-sidedness of this universal gift.

One of the reasons why Christian people as a whole do not realise the universality as they ought is, as I have already suggested in a somewhat different connection, because they limit their notions far too much of what the gift of God's Spirit is to do to men. We must take a wider view of what that Spirit is meant to effect than we ordinarily take, before we understand how real and how visible its universal manifestations are. Take a leaf out of the Old Testament. The man who made the brass-work for the Tabernacle was 'full of the Spirit of God.' The poets who sung the Psalms, in more than one place, declare of themselves that they, too, were but the harps upon which the divine finger played. Samson was capable of his rude feats of physical strength, because 'the Spirit of God was upon him.' Art, song, counsel, statesmanlike adaptation of means to ends, and discernment of proper courses for a nation, such as were exemplified in Joseph and in Daniel, are, in the Old Testament, ascribed to the Spirit of God, and even

the rude physical strength of the simple-natured and
sensuous athlete is traced up to the same source.

But again, we see another sphere of the Spirit's
working in the manifestations of it in the experience
of the primitive Church. These are, as we all know,
accompanied with miracles, speaking with tongues
and working wonders. The signs of that Spirit in
those days were visible and audible. As I said, when
the river first came into its bed, it came like the tide in
Morecambe Bay, breast-high, with a roar and a rush.
But it was quiet after that. In the context we have a
whole series of manifestations of this Divine Spirit,
some of them miraculous and some being natural
faculties heightened, but all concerned with the
Church as a society, and being for the benefit of the
community.

But there is another class. If you turn to the
Epistle to the Galatians, you will find a wonderful list
there of what the Apostle calls 'the fruit of the
Spirit,' beginning with 'love, joy, peace.' These are all
moral and religious, bearing upon personal experience
and the completeness of the individual character.

Now, let us include all these aspects in our conception of the fruit of the Spirit's working on men—the
secular, if we may use that word, as exhibited in the
Old Testament; the miraculous, as seen in the first
days of the Church; the ecclesiastical, if we may so
designate the endowments mentioned in the context,
and the purely personal, moral, and religious emotions
and acts. The plain fact is that everything in a
Christian's life, except his sin, is the manifestation of
that Divine Spirit, from whom all good thoughts,
counsels, and works do proceed. He is the 'Spirit of
adoption,' and whenever in my heart there rises warm

and blessed the aspiration 'Abba! Father!' it is not my voice only, but the voice of that Divine Spirit. He is the Spirit of intercession; and whenever in my soul there move yearning desires after infinite good, child-like longings to be knit more closely to Him, that, too, is the voice of God's Spirit; and our prayers are then 'sweet, indeed, when He the Spirit gives by which we pray.' In like manner, all the variety of Christian emotions and experiences is to be traced to the conjoint operation of that Divine Spirit as the source, and my own spirit as influenced by, and the organ of, the Spirit of God. If I may take a very rough illustration, there is a story in the Old Testament about a king, to whom were given a bow and arrow, with the command to shoot. The prophet's hand was laid on the king's weak hand, and the weak hand was strengthened by the touch of the other; and with one common pull they drew back the string and the arrow sped. The king drew the bow, but it was the prophet's hand grasping his wrist that gave him strength to do it. And that is how the Spirit of God will work with us if we will.

III. Finally, consider the purpose of all the diverse manifestations of the one universal gift.

'To profit withal'—for his own good who possesses it, and for the good of all the rest of his brethren.

Now, that involves two plain things. There have been people in the Christian Church who have said, 'We have all the Spirit, and therefore we do not need one another.' There may be isolation, and self-sufficiency, and a host of other evils coming in, if we only grasp the thought, 'The manifestation of the Spirit is given to every man,' but they are all corrected if we go on and say, 'to profit withal.' For every one of us has something, and no one of us has everything; so, on the one hand, we want each other, and, on the other hand, we are responsible for the use of what we have.

You get the life, not in order that you may plume yourself on its possession, nor in order that you may ostentatiously display it, still less in order that you may shut it up and do nothing with it; but you get the life in order that it may spread through you to others.

'The least flower with a brimming cup may stand,
And share its dew-drop with another near.'

We each have the life that God's grace may fructify through us to all. Power is duty; capacity prescribes ob-ligation; capacity prescribes work. endowment is obligation. 'The manifestation of the Spirit is given to every man to profit withal.'

You can regulate the flow. You have the sluice; you can shut it or open it. I have said that the condition, and the only condition, of possessing the fulness of God's Spirit is faith in Jesus Christ. Therefore, the more you trust the more you have, and the less you the faith the less the gift. You can get much or little," according to the greatness or the smallness, the fixity or the transiency, of your desires. If you hold the empty cup with a tremulous hand, the precious liquid will not be poured into it—for some of it will be spilt —in the same fulness as it would be if you held it steadily. It is the old story—the miraculous flow of the oil stopped when the widow had no more pots and vessels to bring. The reason why some of us have so little of that Divine Spirit is because we have not held out our vessels to be filled. You can diminish the flow by ignoring it, and that is what a host of so-called Christian people do nowadays. You can diminish it by neglecting to use the little that you have for the purpose for which it was given you. Does anybody profit by your spiritual life? Do you profit much by it yourselves? Has it ever been of the least good to anybody else in the world? 'The manifestation of the Spirit is given to' you, if you are a Christian man or woman, more or less. And if you shut it up, and do never an atom of good with it, either to yourselves or to anybody else, of course it will slip away; and, sometime or other, to your astonishment, you will find that the vessels are empty, and that the Spirit of the Lord has departed from you. 'Grieve not the Holy Spirit of God, whereby ye are sealed unto the day of redemption.'

WHAT LASTS

'Whether there be prophecies, they shall fail; whether there be tongues, they shall cease; whether there be knowledge, it shall vanish away. 13. And now abideth faith, hope, charity, these three. . . .'—1 COR. xiii. 8, 13.

WE discern the run of the Apostle's thought best by thus omitting the intervening verses and connecting these two. The part omitted is but a buttress of what has been stated in the former of our two verses; and when we thus unite them there is disclosed plainly the Apostle's intention of contrasting two sets of things, three in each set. The one set is 'prophecies, tongues, knowledge'; the other, 'faith, hope, charity.' There also comes out distinctly that the point mainly intended by the contrast is the transiency of the one and the permanence of the other. Now, that contrast has been obscured and weakened by two mistakes, about which I must say a word.

With regard to the former statement, 'Whether there

be prophecies, they shall fail; whether there be tongues, they shall cease,' that has been misunderstood as if it amounted to a declaration that the miraculous gifts in the early Church were intended to be of brief duration. However true that may be, it is not what Paul means here. The cessation to which he refers is their cessation in the light of the perfect Future. With regard to the other statement, the abiding of faith, hope, charity, that, too, has been misapprehended as if it indicated that faith and hope belonged to this state of things only, and that love was the greatest of the three, because it was permanent. The reason for that misconception has mainly lain in the misunderstanding of the force of 'Now,' which has been taken to mean 'for the present,' as an implied contrast to an unspoken 'then'; just as in the previous verse we have, 'Now we see through a glass, then face to face.' But the 'now' in this text is not, as the grammarians say, temporal, but logical. That is, it does not refer to time, but to the sequence of the Apostle's thought, and is equivalent to 'so then.' 'So then abideth faith, hope, charity.'

The scope of the whole, then, is to contrast the transient with the permanent, in Christian experience. If we firmly grasped the truth involved, our estimates would be rectified and our practice revolutionised.

I. I ask this question—What will drop away?

Paul answers, 'prophecies, tongues, knowledge.' Now these three were all extraordinary gifts belonging to the present phase of the Christian life. But inasmuch as these gifts were the heightening of natural capacities and faculties, it is perfectly legitimate to enlarge the declaration and to use these three words in their widest signification. So understood, they come to this, that all our present modes of apprehension and of utterance are transient, and will be left behind.

'Knowledge, it shall cease,' and as the Apostle goes on to explain, in the verses which I have passed over for my present purpose, it shall cease because the perfect will absorb into itself the imperfect, as the inrushing tide will obliterate the little pools in the rocks on the seashore. For another reason, the knowledge, the mode of apprehension belonging to the present, will pass—because here it is indirect, and there it will be immediate. 'We shall know face to face,' which is what philosophers mean by intuition. Here our knowledge 'creeps from point to point,' painfully amassing facts, and thence, with many hesitations and errors, groping its way towards principles and laws. Here it is imperfect, with many a gap in the circumference; or like the thin red line on a map which shows the traveller's route across a prairie, or like the spider's thread in the telescope, stretched athwart the blazing disc of the sun—'but then face to face.' Incomplete knowledge shall be done away; and many of its objects will drop, and much of what makes the science of earth will be antiquated and effete. What would the handloom weaver's knowledge of how to throw his shuttle be worth in a weaving-shed with a thousand looms? Just so much will the knowledges of earth be when we get yonder.

Modes of utterance will cease. With new experiences will come new methods of communication. As a man can speak, and a beast can only growl or bark, so a man in heaven, with new experiences, will have new methods of communication. The comparison between that mode of utterance which we now have, and that which we shall then possess, will be like the difference

between the old-fashioned semaphore, that used to wave about clumsy wooden arms in order to convey intelligence, and the telegraph.

Think, then, of a man going into that future life, and saying 'I knew more about Sanscrit than anybody that ever lived in Europe'; 'I sang sweet songs'; 'I was a past master in philology, grammars, and lexicons'; 'I was a great orator.' 'Tongues shall cease'; and the modes of utterance that belonged to earth, and all that holds of them, will drop away, and be of no more use.

If these things are true, brethren, with regard even to the highest form of these high and noble things, how much more and more solemnly true are they with regard to the aims and objects which most of us have in view? They will all drop away, and we shall be left, stripped of what, for most of us, has made the whole interest and activity of our lives.

II. What will last?

'So then, abideth these three, faith, hope, love.' When Paul takes three nouns and couples them with a verb in the singular, he is not making a slip of the pen, or committing a grammatical blunder which a child could correct. But there is a great truth in that piece of apparent grammatical irregularity; for the faith, the hope, and the love, for which he can only afford a singular verb, are thereby declared to be in their depth and essence one thing, and it, the triple star, abides, and continues to shine. The three primitive colours are unified in the white beam of light. Do not correct the grammar, and spoil the sense, but discern what he means when he says, 'Now, abideth faith, hope, love.' For this is what he means, that the two latter come out of the former, and that without it they are nought, and that it without them is dead.

Faith breeds Hope. *There* is the difference between earthly hopes and Christian people's hopes. Our hopes, apart from the revelation of God in Jesus Christ, are but the balancing of probabilities, and the scale is often dragged down by the clutch of eager desires. But all is baseless and uncertain, unless our hopes are the outcome of our faith. Which, being translated into other words, is just this, that the one basis on which men can rest—ay! even for the immediate future, and the contingencies of life, as well as for the solemnities and certainties of heaven—any legitimate and substantial hope is trust in Jesus Christ, His word, His love, His power, and for the heavenly future, in His Resurrection and present glory. A man who believes these things, and only that man, has a rock foundation on which he can build his hope.

Faith, in like manner, is the parent of Love. Paul and John, diverse as they are in the whole cast of their minds, the one being speculative and the other mystical, the one argumentative and the other simply gazing and telling what he sees, are precisely agreed in regard to this matter. For, to the Apostle of Love, the foundation of all human love towards God is, 'We have known and believed the love that God hath to us,' and 'We love Him because He first loved us,' and to Paul the first step is the trusting reception of the love of God, 'commended to us' by the fact that 'whilst we were yet sinners Christ died for us,' and from that necessarily flows, if the faith be genuine, the love that answers the sacrifice and obeys the Beloved. So faith, hope, love, these three are a trinity in unity, and it abideth. That is the main point of our last text. Let me say a word or two about it.

I have said that the words have often been misunder-

stood as if the 'now' referred only to the present order
of things, in which faith and hope are supposed to find
their only appropriate sphere. But that is clearly not
the Apostle's meaning here, for many reasons with
which I need not trouble you. The abiding of all three
is eternal abiding, and there is a heavenly as well as an
earthly form of faith and hope as well as of love. Just
look at these points for a moment.

'Faith abides,' says Paul, yonder, as here. Now,
there is a common saying, which I suppose ninety out
of a hundred people think comes out of the Bible, about
faith being lost in sight. There is no such teaching in
Scripture. True, in one aspect, faith is the antithesis
of sight. True, Paul does say 'We walk by faith, not
by sight.' But that antithesis refers only to part of
faith's significance. In so far as it is the opposite of
sight, of course it will cease to be in operation when
'we shall know even as we are known,' and 'see Him
as He is.' But the essence of faith is not in the absence
of the person trusted, but the emotion of trust which
goes out to the person, present or absent. And in its
deepest meaning of absolute dependence and happy
confidence, faith abides through all the glories and the
lustres of the heavens, as it burns amidst the dimnesses
and the darknesses of earth. For ever and ever, on
through the irrevoluble ages of eternity, dependence
on God in Christ will be the life of the glorified, as it
was the life of the militant, Church. No millenniums
of possession, and no imaginable increases in beauty
and perfectness and enrichment with the wealth of
God, will bring us one inch nearer to casting off the
state of filial dependence which is, and ever will be, the
condition of our receiving them all. Faith 'abides.'

Hope 'abides.' For it is no more a Scriptural idea

that hope is lost in fruition, than it is that faith is lost in sight.   Rather that Future presents itself to us as the continual communication of an inexhaustible God to our progressively capacious and capable spirits.   In that continual communication there is continual progress.   Wherever there is progress there must be hope. And thus the fair form, which has so often danced before us elusive, and has led us into bogs and miry places and then faded away, will move before us through all the long avenues of an endless progress, and will ever and anon come back to tell us of the unseen glories that lie beyond the next turn, and to woo us further into the depths of heaven and the fulness of God. Hope ' abides.'

Love ' abides.'   I need not, I suppose, enlarge upon that thought which nobody denies, that love is the eternal form of the human relation to God.   It, too, like the mercy which it clasps, ' endureth for ever.'

But I may remind you of what the Apostle does not explain in our text, that it is greater than its linked sisters, because whilst faith and hope belong only to a creature, and are dependent and expectant of some good to come to themselves, and correspond to something which is in God in Christ, the love which springs from faith and hope not only corresponds to, but resembles, that from which it comes and by which it lives.   The fire kindled is cognate with the fire that kindles; and the love that is in man is like the love that is in God.   It is the climax of his nature; it is the fulfilling of all duty; it is the crown and jewelled clasp of all perfection.   And so ' abideth faith, hope, love, and the greatest of these is love.'

III. Lastly, what follows from all this ?

First, let us be quite sure that we understand what

this abiding love is. I dare say you have heard people
say 'Ah! I do not care much about Paul's theology.
Give me the thirteenth chapter of the first Epistle to
the Corinthians. That is beautiful; that praise of
Love; *that* comes home to men.' Yes, very beautiful.
Are you quite sure that you know what Paul means by
'love'? I do not use the word charity, because that
lovely word, like a glistening meteor that falls upon
the earth, has a rust, as it were, upon its surface that
dims its brightness very quickly. Charity has come to
mean an indulgent estimate of other people's faults;
or, still more degradingly, the giving of money out of
your pockets to other people's necessities. These are
what the people who do not care much about Paul's
theology generally suppose that he means here. But
these do not exhaust his meaning. Paul's notion of
love is the response of the human love to the divine,
which divine is received into the heart by simple faith
in Jesus Christ. And his notion of love which never
faileth, and endureth all things, and hopeth all things,
is love to men, which is but one stream of the great
river of love to God. If we rightly understand what
he means by love, we shall find that his praise of love
is as theological as anything that he ever wrote. We
shall never get further than barren admiration of a
beautiful piece of writing, unless our love to men has
the source and root to which Paul points us.

Again, let us take this great thought of the permanence of faith, hope, and love as being the highest
conception that we can form of our future condition.
It is very easy to bewilder ourselves with speculations
and theories of another life. I do not care much about
them. The great gates keep their secret well. Few
stray beams of light find their way through their

crevices. The less we say the less likely we are to err. It is easy to let ourselves be led away, by turning rhetoric into revelation, and accepting the symbols of the New Testament as if they carried anything more than images of the realities. But far beyond golden pavements, and harps, and crowns, and white robes, lies this one great thought that the elements of the imperfect, Christlike life of earth are the essence of the perfect, Godlike life in heaven. 'Now abide these three, faith, hope, love.'

Last of all, let us shape our lives in accordance with these certainties. The dropping away of the transient things is no argument for neglecting or despising them; for our handling of them makes our characters, and our characters abide. But it is a very excellent argument for shaping our lives so as to seek first the first things, and to secure the permanent qualities, and so to use the transient as that it shall all help us towards that which does not pass.

What will a Manchester man that knows nothing except goods and office work, and knows these only in their superficial aspect, and not as related to God, what, in the name of common-sense, will he do with himself when he gets into a world where there is not a single ledger, nor a desk, nor a yard of cloth of any sort? What will some of us do when, in like manner, we are stripped of all the things that we have cared about, and worked for, and have made our aims down here? Suppose that you knew that you were under sailing orders to go somewhere or other, and that at any moment a breathless messenger might appear and say, 'Come along! we are all waiting for you'; and suppose that you never did a single thing towards getting your outfit ready, or preparing yourself in any way for that which might come at any moment, and could not but come before very long. Would you be a wise man? But that is what a great many of us are doing; doing every day, and all day long, and doing that only. 'He shall leave them in the midst of his days,' says a grim text, 'and at his latter end shall be a fool.'

What will drop? Modes of apprehension, modes of utterance, occupations, duties, relationships, loves; and we shall be left standing naked, stripped, as it were, to the very quick, and only as much left as will keep our souls alive. But if we are clothed with faith, hope, love, we shall not be found naked. Cultivate the high things, the permanent things; then death will not wrench you violently from all that you have been and cared for; but it will usher you into the perfect form of all that you have been and done upon earth. All these things will pass, but faith, hope, love, 'stay not behind nor in the grave are trod,' but will last as long as Christ, their Object, lives, and as long as we in Him live also.

THE POWER OF THE RESURRECTION

'I delivered unto you first of all that which I also received, how that Christ died for our sins according to the Scriptures; 4. And that He was buried, and that He rose again the third day according to the Scriptures.'—1 COR. xv. 3, 4.

CHRISTMAS DAY is probably not the true anniversary of the Nativity, but Easter is certainly that of the Resurrection. The season is appropriate. In the climate of Palestine the first fruits of the harvest were ready at the Passover for presentation in the Temple. It was an agricultural as well as a historical festival;

and the connection between that aspect of the feast and the Resurrection of our Lord is in the Apostle's mind when he says, in a subsequent part of this chapter, that Christ is ' risen from the dead and become the first fruits of them that slept.'

In our colder climate the season is no less appropriate. The 'life re-orient out of dust' which shows itself to-day in every bursting leaf-bud and springing flower is Nature's parable of the spring that awaits man after the winter of death. No doubt, apart from the Resurrection of Jesus, the yearly miracle kindles sad thoughts in mourning hearts, and suggests bitter contrasts to those who sorrow, having no hope, but the grave in the garden has turned every blossom into a smiling prophet of the Resurrection.

And so the season, illuminated by the event, teaches us lessons of hope that 'we shall not all die.' Let us turn, then, to the thoughts naturally suggested by the day, and the great fact which it brings to each mind, and confirmed thereafter by the miracle that is being wrought round about us.

I. First, then, in my text, I would have you note the facts of Paul's gospel.

'First of all . . . I delivered' these things. And the 'first' not only points to the order of time in the proclamation, but to the order of importance as well. For these initial facts are the fundamental facts, on which all that may follow thereafter is certainly built. Now the first thing that strikes me here is that, whatever else the system unfolded in the New Testament is, it is to begin with a simple record of historical fact. It becomes a philosophy, it becomes a religious system; it is a revelation of God; it is an unveiling of man; it is a body of ethical precepts. It is morals and philosophy and religion all in one; but it is first of all a story of something that took place in the world.

If that be so, there is a lesson for men whose work it is to preach it. Let them never forget that their business is to insist upon the truth of these great, supernatural, all-important, and fundamental facts, the death and the Resurrection of Jesus Christ. They must evolve all the deep meanings that lie in them; and the deeper they dig for their meanings the better. They must open out the endless treasures of consolation and enforce the omnipotent motives of action which are wrapped up in the facts; but howsoever far they may carry their evolving and their application of them, they will neither be faithful to their Lord nor true stewards of their message unless, clear above all other aspects of their work, and underlying all other forms of their ministry, there be the unfaltering proclamation—'first of all,' midst of all, last of all—'how that Christ died for our sins according to the Scriptures,' and 'that He was raised again according to the Scriptures.'

Note, too, how this fundamental and original character of the gospel which Paul preached, as a record of facts, makes short work of a great deal that calls itself 'liberal Christianity' in these days. We are told that it is quite possible to be a very good Christian man, and reject the supernatural, and turn away with incredulity from the story of the Resurrection. It may be so, but I confess that it puzzles me to understand how, if the fundamental character of Christian teaching be the proclamation of certain facts, a man who does not believe those facts has the right to call himself a Christian.

Note, further, how there is an element of explanation

involved in the proclamation of the facts which turns them into a gospel. Mark how 'that *Christ* died,' not *Jesus*. It is a great truth, that the man, our Brother, Jesus, passed through the common lot, but that is not what Paul says here, though he often says it. What he says is that ' *Christ* died.' Christ is the name of an office, into which is condensed a whole system of truth, declaring that it is He who is the Apex, the Seal, and ultimate Word of all divine revelation. It was the *Christ* who died; unless it was so, the death of Jesus is no gospel.

'He died for our sins.' Now, if the Apostle had only said 'He died for us,' that might conceivably have meant that, in a multitude of different ways of example, appeal to our pity and compassion and the like, His death was of use to mankind. But when he says 'He died *for our sins*,' I take leave to think that that expression has no meaning, unless it means that He died as the expiation and sacrifice for men's sins. I ask you, in what intelligible sense could Christ 'die for our sins' unless He died as bearing their punishment and as bearing it for us? And then, finally, 'He died and rose . . . according to the Scriptures,' and so fulfilled the divine purposes revealed from of old.

To the fact that a man was crucified outside the gates of Jerusalem, 'and rose again the third day,' which is the narrative, there are added these three things—the dignity of the Person, the purpose of His death, the fulfilment of the divine intention manifested from of old. And these three things, as I said, turn the narrative into a Gospel.

So, brethren, let us remember that, without all three of them, the death of Jesus Christ is nothing to us, any more than the death of thousands of sweet and saintly

men in the past has been, who may have seen a little
more of the supreme goodness and greatness than their
fellows, and tried in vain to make purblind eyes
participate in their vision. Do you think that these
twelve fishermen would ever have shaken the world if
they had gone out with the story of the Cross, unless
they had carried along with it the commentary which
is included in the words which I have emphasised?
And do you suppose that the type of Christianity
which slurs over the explanation, and so does not know
what to do with the facts, will ever do much in the
world, or will ever touch men? Let us liberalise our
Christianity by all means, but do not let us evaporate
it; and evaporate it we surely shall if we falter in
saying with Paul, 'I declare, first of all, that which
received,' how that the death and resurrection were
the death and resurrection of the Christ, 'for our
sins, according to the Scriptures.' These are the
facts which make Paul's gospel.

II. Now I ask you to look, in the second place, at
what establishes the facts.

We have here, in this chapter, a statement very much
older than our existing written gospels. This epistle
is one of the four letters of Paul which nobody that I
know of—with some quite insignificant exceptions in
modern times—has ever ventured to dispute. It is
admittedly the writing of the Apostle, written before
the gospels, and in all probability within five-and-
twenty years of the date of the Crucifixion. And what
do we find alleged by it as the state of things at its
date? That the belief in the Resurrection of Jesus
Christ was the subject of universal Christian teaching,
and was accepted by all the Christian communities.
Its evidence to that fact is undeniable; because there

was in the early Christian Church a very formidable and large body of bitter antagonists of Paul's, who would have been only too glad to have convicted him, if they could, of any misrepresentation of the usual notions, or divergence from the usual type of teaching. So we may take it as undeniable that the representation of this chapter is historically true; and that within five-and-twenty years of the death of Jesus Christ every Christian community and every Christian teacher believed in and proclaimed the fact of the Resurrection.

But if that be so, we necessarily are carried a great deal nearer the Cross than five-and-twenty years; and, in fact, there is not, between the moment when Paul penned these words and the day of Pentecost, a single chink in the history where you can insert such a tremendous innovation as the full-fledged belief in a resurrection coming in as something new.

I do not need to dwell at all upon this other thought, that, unless the belief that Jesus Christ had risen from the dead originated at the time of His death, there would never have been a Church at all. Why was it that they did not tumble to pieces? Take the nave out of the wheel and what becomes of the spokes? A dead Christ could never have been the basis of a living Church. If He had not risen from the dead, the story of His disciples would have been the same as that which Gamaliel told the Sanhedrim was the story of all former pseudo-Messiahs such as that man Theudas. 'He was slain, and as many as followed him were dispersed and came to naught.' Of course! The existence of the Church demands, as a pre-requisite, the initial belief in the Resurrection. I think, then, that the contemporaneousness of the evidence is sufficiently established.

What about its good faith? I suppose that nobody, nowadays, doubts the veracity of these witnesses. Anybody that knows an honest man when he sees him, anybody that has the least ear for the tone of sincerity and the accent of conviction, must say that they may have been fanatics, they may have been mistaken, but one thing is clear as sunlight, they were not false witnesses for God.

What, then, about their competency? Their simplicity, their ignorance, their slowness to believe, their stupor of surprise when the fact first dawned upon them, which they tell not with any idea of manufacturing evidence in their own favour, but simply as a piece of history, all tend to make us certain that there was no play of a morbid imagination, no hysterical turning of a wish into a fact, on the part of these men. The sort of things which they say that they saw and experienced are such as to make any such supposition altogether absurd. There are long conversations, appearances appealing to more than one sense, appearances followed by withdrawals, sometimes in the morning sometimes in the evening, sometimes at a distance, as on the mountain, sometimes close by, as in the chamber, to single souls and to multitudes. Fancy five hundred people all at once smitten with the same mistake, imagining that they saw what they did not see! Miracles may be difficult to believe, they are not half so difficult to believe as absurdities. And this modern explanation of the faith in the Resurrection I venture respectfully to designate as absurd.

But there is one other point to which I would like to turn for a moment; and that is that little clause in my text that 'He was buried.' Why does Paul introduce that amongst his facts? Possibly in order to affirm the reality of Christ's death; but I think for another reason. If it be true that Jesus Christ was laid in that sepulchre, a stone's throw outside the city gate, do you not see what a difficulty that fact puts in the way of disbelief or denial of His Resurrection? If the grave —and it was not a grave, remember, like ours, but a cave, with a stone at the door of it, that anybody could roll away for entrance—if the grave was there, why, in the name of common-sense, did not the rulers put an end to the pestilent heresy by saying, 'Let us go and see if the body is there'?

Modern deniers of the Resurrection may fairly be asked to front this thought—If Jesus Christ's body was in the sepulchre, how was it possible for belief in the Resurrection to have been originated, or maintained? If His body was not in the grave, what had become of it? If His friends stole it away then they were deceivers of the worst type in preaching a resurrection; and we have already seen that that hypothesis is ridiculous. If His enemies took it away, for which they had no motive, why did they not produce it and say, 'There is an answer to your nonsense. There is the dead man. Let us hear no more of this absurdity of His having risen from the dead'?

'He died . . . according to the Scriptures, and He was buried.' And the angels' word carries the only explanation of the fact which it proclaims, 'He is not here—He is risen.'

I take leave to say that the Resurrection of Jesus Christ is established by evidence which nobody would ever have thought of doubting unless for the theory that miracles were impossible. The reason for disbelief is not the deficiency of the evidence, but the bias of the judge.

III. And now I have no time to do more than touch the last thought. I have tried to show what establishes the facts. Let me remind you, in a sentence or two, what the facts establish.

I by no means desire to suspend the whole of the evidence for Christianity on the testimony of the eye-witnesses to the Resurrection. There are a great many other ways of establishing the truth of the Gospel besides that, upon which I do not need to dwell now. But, taking this one specific ground which my text suggests, what do the facts thus established prove?

Well, the first point to which I would refer, and on which I should like to enlarge, if I had time, is the bearing of Christ's Resurrection on the acceptance of the miraculous. We hear a great deal about the impossibility of miracle and the like. It upsets the certainty and fixedness of the order of things, and so forth, and so forth. Jesus Christ has risen from the dead; and that opens a door wide enough to admit all the rest of the Gospel miracles. It is of no use paring down the supernatural in Christianity, in order to meet the prejudices of a quasi-scientific scepticism, unless you are prepared to go the whole length, and give up the Resurrection. There is the turning point. The question is, Do you believe that Jesus Christ rose from the dead, or do you not? If your objections to the supernatural are valid, then Christ is not risen from the dead; and you must face the consequences of that. If He is risen from the dead, then you must cease all your talk about the impossibility of miracle, and be willing to accept a supernatural revelation as God's way of making Himself known to man.

But, further, let me remind you of the bearing of the

Resurrection upon Christ's work and claims. If He be lying in some forgotten grave, and if all that fair thought of His having burst the bands of death is a blunder, then there was nothing in His death that had the least bearing upon men's sin, and it is no more to me than the deaths of thousands in the past. But if He is risen from the dead, then the Resurrection casts back a light upon the Cross, and we understand that His death is the life of the world, and that 'by His stripes we are healed.'

But, further, remember what He said about Himself when He was in the world—how He claimed to be the Son of God; how He demanded absolute obedience, implicit trust, supreme love, how He identified faith in Himself with faith in God—and consider the Resurrection as bearing on the reception or rejection of these tremendous claims. It seems to me that we are brought sharp up to this alternative—Jesus Christ rose from the dead, and was declared by the Resurrection to be the Son of God with power; or Jesus Christ has *not* risen from the dead—and what then? Then He was either deceiver or deceived, and in either case has no right to my reverence and my love. We may be thankful that men are illogical, and that many who reject the Resurrection retain reverence, genuine and deep, for Jesus Christ. But whether they have any right to do so is another matter. I confess for myself that, if I did not believe that Jesus Christ had risen from the dead, I should find it very hard to accept, as an example of conduct, or as religious teacher, a man who had made such great claims as He did, and had asked from me what He asked. It seems to me that He is either a great deal more, or a great deal less, than a beautiful saintly soul. If He rose from the dead

He is much more; if He did not, I am afraid to say how much less He is.

And, finally, the bearing of the Resurrection of Jesus Christ upon our own hopes of the future may be suggested. It teaches us that life has nothing to do with organisation, but persists apart from the body. It teaches us that a man may pass from death and be unaltered in the substance of his being; and it teaches us that the earthly house of our tabernacle may be fashioned like unto the glorious house in which He dwells now at the right hand of God. There is no other absolute proof of immortality than the Resurrection of Jesus Christ.

If we accept with all our hearts and minds Paul's Gospel in its fundamental facts, we need not fear to die, because He has died, and by dying has been the death of death. We need not doubt that we shall live again, because He was dead and is alive for ever more. This Samson has carried away the gates on His strong shoulders, and death is no more a dungeon but a passage. If we rest ourselves upon Him, then we can take up, for ourselves and for all that are dear to us and have gone before us, the triumphant song, 'O Death, where is thy sting?' 'Thanks be to God, which giveth us the victory through our Lord Jesus Christ.'

REMAINING AND FALLING ASLEEP

'After that He was seen of above five hundred brethren at once; of whom the greater part remain unto this present, but some are fallen asleep.'—1 COR. xv. 6.

THERE were, then, some five-and-twenty years after the Resurrection, several hundred disciples who were

known amongst the churches as having been eye-
witnesses of the risen Saviour. The greater part
survived; some, evidently a very few, had died. The
proportion of the living to the dead, after five-and-
twenty years, is generally the opposite. The greater
part have 'fallen asleep'; some, a comparatively few,
remain 'unto this present.' Possibly there was some
divine intervention which supernaturally prolonged
the lives of these witnesses, in order that their testimony might be the more lasting. But, be that as it
may, they evidently were men of mark, and some kind
of honour and observance surrounded them, as was
very natural, and as appears from the fact that Paul
here knows so accurately (and can appeal to His fellow-
Christians' accurate knowledge) the proportion between
the survivors and the departed. We read of one of
them in the Acts of the Apostles at a later date than
this, one Mnason, an 'original disciple.'

So we get a glimpse into the conditions of life
in the early Church, interesting and of value in an
evidential point of view. But my purpose at present
is to draw your attention to the remarkable language
in which the Apostle here speaks of the living and the
dead amongst these witnesses. In neither case does
he use the simple, common words 'living' or 'dead';
but in the one clause he speaks of their 'remaining,'
and in the other of their 'falling asleep'; both phrases
being significant, and, as I take it, both being traced
up to the fact of their having seen the risen Lord as
the cause why their life could be described as a 'remaining,' and their death as a 'falling asleep.' In other
words, we have here brought before us, by these two
striking expressions, the transforming effect upon life
and upon death of the faith in a risen Lord, whether

grounded on sight or not.   And it is simply to these
two points that I desire to turn now.

I. First, then, we have to consider what life may
become to those who see the risen Christ.

'The greater part remain until this present.' Now
the word *remain* is no mere synonym for living or surviving. It not only tells us the fact that the survivors
were living, but the kind of life that they did live. It
is very significant that it is the same expression as
our Lord used in the profound prophetic words, 'If I
will that he tarry till I come, what is that to thee?'
Now we are told in John's Gospel that 'that saying
went abroad amongst the brethren,' and inasmuch as
it was a matter of common notoriety in the early
Church, it is by no means a violent supposition that
it may be floating in Paul's memory here, and may
determine his selection of this remarkable expression
'they remain,' or 'they tarry,' and they were tarrying
till the Master came. So, then, I think if we give due
weight to the significance of the phrase, we get two or
three thoughts worth pondering.

One of them is that the sight of a risen Christ will
make life calm and tranquil. Fancy one of these 500
brethren, after that vision, going back to his quiet
rural home in some little village amongst the hills of
Galilee. How small and remote from Him, and unworthy to ruffle or disturb the heart in which the
memory of that vision was burning, would seem the
things that otherwise would have been important and
distracting! The faith which we have in the risen
Christ ought to do the same thing for us, and will do
it in the measure in which there shines clearly before
that inward eye, which is our true means of apprehending Him, the vision which shone before the

outward gaze of that company of wondering witnesses. If we build our nests amidst the tossing branches of the world's trees, they will sway with every wind, and perhaps be blown from their hold altogether by such a storm as we all have sometimes to meet. But we may build our nests in the clefts of the rock, like the doves, and be quiet, as they are. Distractions will cease to distract, and troubles will cease to agitate, and across the heaving surface of the great ocean there will come a Form beneath whose feet the waves smooth themselves, and at whose voice the winds are still. They who see Christ need not be troubled. The ship that is empty is tossed upon the ocean, that which is well laden is steady. The heart that has Christ for a passenger need not fear being rocked by any storm. Calmness will come with the vision of the Lord, and we shall abide or 'remain,' for there will be no need for us to flee from this Refuge to that, nor shall we be driven from our secure abode by any contingencies. 'He that believeth shall not make haste.'

It is a good thing to cultivate the disposition that says about most of the trifles of this life, 'It does not much matter'; but the only way to prevent wholesome contempt of the world's trivialities from degenerating into supercilious indifference is, to base it upon Christ, discerned as near us and bestowing upon us the calmness of His risen life. Make Him your scale of importance, and nothing will be too small to demand and be worthy of the best efforts of your work, but nothing will be too great to sweep you away from the serenity of your faith.

Again, the vision of the risen Christ will also lead to patient persistence in duty. If we have Him before us, the distasteful duty which He sets us will not be

distasteful, and the small tasks, in which great faithfulness may be manifested, will cease to be small. If we have Him before us we have in that risen Christ the great and lasting Example of how patient continuance in well-doing triumphs over the sorrows that it bears, by and in patiently bearing them, and is crowned at last with glory and honour. The risen Christ is the Pattern for the men who will not be turned aside from the path of duty by any obstacles, dangers, or threats. The risen Christ is the signal Example of glory following upon faithfulness, and of the crown being the result of the Cross. The risen Christ is the manifest Helper of them that put their trust in Him; and one of the plainest lessons and of the most imperative commands which come from the believing gaze upon that Lord who died because He would do the will of the Father, and is throned and crowned in the heavens because He died, is—By patient continuance in well-doing let us commit the keeping of our souls to Him: and abide in the calling wherewith we are called.

And, again, the sight of the risen Christ leads to a life of calm expectancy. 'If I will that He *tarry* till I come' conveys that shade of meaning. The Apostle was to wait for the Lord from Heaven, and that vision which was given to these 500 men sent them home to their abodes to make all the rest of their lives one calm aspiration for, and patient expectation of, the return of the Lord. These primitive Christians expected that Jesus Christ would come speedily. That expectation was disappointed in so far as the date was concerned, but after nineteen centuries it still remains true that all vigorous and vital Christian life must have in it, as a very important element of its

o

vitality, the onward look which ever is anticipating, which often is desiring, and which constantly is confident of, the coming of the Lord from Heaven. The Resurrection has for its consequences, its sequel and corollary, first the Ascension; then the long tract of time during which Jesus Christ is absent, but still in divine presence rules the world; and, finally, His coming again in that same body in which the disciples saw Him depart from them. And no Christian life is up to the level of its privileges, nor has any Christian faith grasped the whole articles of its creed, except that which sets in the very centre of all its visions of the future that great thought—He shall come again.

Questions of chronology have nothing to do with that. It stands there before us, the certain fact, made certain and inevitable by the past facts of the Cross and the Grave and Olivet. He has come, He will come; He has gone, He will come back. And for us the life that we live in the flesh ought to be a life of waiting for God's Son from Heaven, and of patient, confident expectancy that when He shall be manifested we also shall be manifested with Him in glory.

So much, then, for life—calm, persistent in every duty, and animated by that blessed and far-off, but certain, hope, and all of these founded upon the vision and the faith of a risen Lord. What have fears and cares and distractions and faint-heartedness and gloomy sorrow to do with the eyes that have beheld the Christ, and with the lives that are based on faith in the risen Lord?

II. So, secondly, consider what death becomes to those who have seen Christ risen from the dead.

'Some are fallen asleep.' Now that most natural and obvious metaphor for death is not only a Christian idea, but is found, as would be expected, in many tongues, but yet with a great and significant difference. The Christian reason for calling death a sleep embraces a great deal more than the heathen reason for doing so, and in some respects is precisely the opposite of that, inasmuch as to most others who have used the word, death has been a sleep that knew no waking, whereas the very pith and centre of the Christian reason for employing the symbol are that it makes our waking sure. We have here what the act of dying and the condition of the dead become by virtue of faith in the Resurrection of Jesus Christ.

They have 'fallen asleep.' The act of dying is but a laying one's self down to rest, and a dropping out of consciousness of the surrounding world. It is very remarkable and very beautiful that the new Testament scarcely ever employs the words *dying* and *death* for the act of separating body and spirit, or for the condition either of the spirit parted from the body, or of the body parted from the spirit. It keeps those grim words for the reality, the separation of the soul from God; and it only exceptionally uses them for the shadow and the symbol, the physical fact of the parting of the man from the house which here he has dwelt in. But the reason why Christianity uses these periphrases or metaphors, these euphemisms for death, is the opposite of the reason why the world uses them. The world is so afraid of dying that it durst not name the grim, ugly thing. The Christian, or at least the Christian faith, is so little afraid of death that it does not think such a trivial matter worth calling by the name, but only names it 'falling asleep.'

Even when the circumstances of that dropping off

to slumber are painful and violent, the Bible still employs the term. Is it not striking that the first martyr, kneeling outside the city, bruised by stones and dying a bloody death, should have been said to fall asleep? If ever there was an instance in which the gentle metaphor seemed all inappropriate it was that cruel death, amidst a howling crowd, and with fatal bruises, and bleeding limbs mangled by the heavy rocks that lay upon them. But yet, ' when he had said this he fell asleep.' If that be true of such a death, no physical pains of any kind make the sweet word inappropriate for any.

We have here not only the designation of the act of dying, but that of the condition of the dead. They are fallen asleep, and they continue asleep. How many great thoughts gather round that metaphor on which it is needless for me to try to dilate! They will suggest themselves without many words to you all.

There lies in it the idea of repose. ' They rest from their labours.' Sleep restores strength, and withdraws a man at once from effort on the outer world, and from communication from it. We may carry the analogy into that unseen world. We know nothing about the relations to an external universe of the departed who sleep in Jesus. It may be that, if they sleep in Him, since He knows all, they, through Him, may know, too, something—so much as He pleases to impart to them—of what is happening here. · And it may even be that, if they sleep in Him, and He wields the energies of Omnipotence, they, through Him, may have some service to do, even while they wait for their house which is from heaven. But there is no need for, nor profit in, such speculations. It is enough that the sweet emblem suggests repose, and that in that sleep

there are folded around the sleepers the arms of the
Christ on whose bosom they rest, as an infant does on
its first and happiest home—its mother's breast.

But then, besides that, the emblem suggests the idea
of continuous and conscious existence. A man asleep
does not cease to be a man; a dead man does not cease
to live. It has often been argued from this metaphor
that we are to conceive of the space between death
and the resurrection as being a period of unconsciousness, but the analogies seem to me to be in the opposite
direction. A sleeping man does not cease to know
himself to be, and he does not cease to know himself
to be himself. That mysterious consciousness of personal identity survives the passage from waking to
sleep, as dreams sufficiently show us. And, therefore,
they that sleep know themselves to be.

And, finally, the emblem suggests the idea of waking.
Sleep is a parenthesis. If the night comes, the morning
comes. 'If winter comes, can spring be far behind?'
They that sleep will awake, and be satisfied when they
' awake with Thy likeness.' And so these three things
—repose, conscious, continuous existence, and the
certainty of awaking—all lie in that metaphor.

Now, then, the risen Christ is the only ground of
such hope, and faith in Him is the only state of mind
which is entitled to cherish it. Nothing proves immortality except that open grave. Every other foundation
is too weak to bear the weight of such a superstructure.
The current of present opinion shows, I think, that
neither metaphysical nor ethical arguments for the
future life will stand the force of the disintegrating
criticism which is brought to bear upon that hope by
the fashionable materialism of this generation. There
is one barrier that will resist that force, and only one,

and that is the historical facts that Jesus Christ died, and that Jesus Christ has risen again. He rose; therefore death is not the end of individual existence. He rose; therefore life beyond the grave is possible for humanity. He rose; therefore His sacrifice for the world's sin is accepted, and I may be delivered from my guilt and my burden. He rose; therefore He is declared to be the Son of God with power. He rose; therefore we, if we trust Him, may partake in His Resurrection and in some reflection of His glory. The old Greek architects were often careless of the solidity of the soil on which they built their temples, and so, many of them have fallen in ruins. The Temple of Immortality can be built only upon the rock of that proclamation — Jesus Christ is risen from the dead. And we, dear brethren, should have all our hopes founded upon that one fact.

So then, for us, the calm, peaceful passage from life into what else is the great darkness is possible on condition of our having beheld the risen Lord. These witnesses of whom my text speaks, Paul would suggest to us, laid themselves quietly down to sleep, because before them there still hovered the memory of the vision which they had beheld. Faith in the risen Christ is the anchor of the soul in death, and there is nothing else by which we can hold then.

As the same Apostle, in one of his other letters, puts it, the belief that Christ is risen is not only the irrefragable ground of our hope that we, too, shall rise, but has the power to change the whole aspect of our death. Did you ever observe the emphasis with which He says, 'If we believe that Jesus *died* and rose again, even so them also which *sleep* in Jesus will God bring with Him?' His death was death indeed, and faith in it softens ours to sleep. He bore the reality that we might never need to know it, and if our poor hearts are resting upon that dear Lord, then the flames are but painted ones and will not burn, and we shall pass through them, and no smell of fire will be upon us, and all that will be consumed will be the bonds which bind us. He has abolished death. The physical fact remains, but all which to men makes the idea of death is gone if we trust the risen Lord. So that, between two men dying under precisely the same circumstances, of the same disease, in adjacent beds in the same hospital, there may be such a difference as that the same word cannot be applied to the experiences of both.

My dear friends, we have each of us to pass through that last struggle; but we may make it either a quiet going to sleep with a loved Face bending over our closing eyes, like a mother's over her child's cradle, and the same Face meeting us when we open them in the morning of heaven; or we may make it a reluctant departure from all that we care for, and a trembling advance into all from which conscience and heart shrink.

Which is it going to be to you? The answer depends upon that to another question. Are you looking to that Christ that died and is alive for evermore as your life and your salvation? Do you hold fast that Gospel which Paul preached, 'how that Christ died for our sins according to the Scriptures, and that He was buried, and that He rose again the third day, according to the Scriptures'? If you do, life will be a calm, persevering, expectant waiting upon Him, and death will be nothing more terrible than falling asleep.

PAUL'S ESTIMATE OF HIMSELF

'By the grace of God I am what I am: and His grace which was bestowed upon me was not in vain.'—1 Cor. xv. 10.

THE Apostle was, all his life, under the hateful necessity of vindicating his character and Apostleship. Thus here, though his main purpose in the context is simply to declare the Gospel which he preached, he is obliged to turn aside in order to assert, and to back up his assertion, that there was no sort of difference between him and the other recognised teachers of Christian truth. He was forced to do this by persistent endeavours in the Corinthian Church to deny his Apostleship, and the faithfulness of his representation of the Christian verities. The way in which he does it is eminently beautiful and remarkable. He fires up in vindication of himself; and then he checks himself. 'By the grace of God I am'—and he is going to say what he is, but he bethinks himself, as if he had reflected; 'No! I will leave other people to say what that is. By the grace of God I am—what I am, whatever that be. And all that I have to say is that God made me, and that I helped Him. For the grace of God which was bestowed upon me was not in vain. You Corinthians may judge what the product is. I tell you how it has come about.' So there are thoughts here, I think, well worth our pondering and taking into our hearts and lives.

I. First, as to the one power that makes men.

'By the grace of God I am what I am.' Now that word 'grace' has got to be worn threadbare, and to mean next door to nothing, in the ears and minds of a great many continual hearers of the Gospel. But

Paul had a very definite idea of what he meant by it; and what he meant by it was a very large thing, which we may well ponder for a moment as being the only thing which will transform and ennoble character and will produce fruit that a man need not be ashamed of. The grace of God, in Paul's use of the words, which is the scriptural use of them generally, implies these two things which are connected as root and product—the active love of God, in exercise towards us low and sinful creatures, and the gifts with which that love comes full charged to men. These two things, which at bottom are one, love and its gifts, are all, in the Apostle's judgment, gathered up and stored, as in a great storehouse, in Jesus Christ Himself, and through Him are made accessible to us, and brought to bear upon us for the ennobling of our natures, and the investing of us with graces and beauties of character, all strange to us apart from these.

Now it seems to me that these two things, which come from one root, are the precise things which you and I need in order to make us nobler and purer and more Godlike men than otherwise we could ever become. For what is it that men need most for noble and pure living? These two things precisely—motive and power to carry out the dictates of conscience.

Every man in the world knows enough of duty and of right to be a far nobler man than any man in the world is. And it is not for want of clear convictions of duty, it is not for want of recognised models and patterns of life, that men go wrong; but it is because there are these two things lacking, motives for nobler service, and power to do and be what they know they ought to be. And precisely here Paul's gospel comes in, 'By the grace of God I am what I am.' That grace, considered in its two sides of love and of giving, supplies all that we want.

It supplies motives. There is nothing that will bend a man's will like the recognition of divine love which it is blessedness to come in contact with, and to obey. You may try to sway him by motives of advantage and self-interest, and to thunder into his ears the pealing words of duty and right and 'ought,' and there is no adequate response. You cannot soften a heart by the hammers of the law. You cannot force a man to do right by brandishing before him the whip that punishes doing wrong. You cannot sway the will by anything but the heart; and when you can touch the deepest spring it moves the whole mass.

You have seen some ponderous piece of machinery, which resists all attempts of a puny hand laid upon it to make it revolve. But down in one corner is a little hidden spring. Touch that and with majestic slowness and certainty the mighty mass turns. You know those rocking-stones down in the south of England; tons of weight poised upon a pin point, and so exquisitely balanced that a child's finger rightly applied may move the mass. So the whole man is made mobile only by the touch of love; and the grace that comes to us, and says, 'If ye love Me, keep My commandments'—is, as I believe, the sole motive which will continuously and adequately sway the rebellious, self-centred wills of men, to obedience resulting in nobility of life.

The other aspect of this same great word is, in like manner, that which we need. What men want is, first of all, the will to be noble and good; and, second, the power to carry out the will. It is God that worketh in us both the willing and the doing. I

venture to affirm that there is no power known, either
to thinkers, or philanthropists, or doctrinaires, or
strivers after excellence in the world—no power known
and available which will lift a life to such heights of
beauty and self-sacrificing nobility, as will the power
that comes to us by communication of the grace that
is in Jesus Christ.

I am perpetually trying to insist, dear brethren,
upon this one thought, that the communication of
actual new life is the central gift of the Gospel; and
this new life it is, this nature endowed with new
desires, hopes, aims, capacities, which alone will lift
the whole man into unwonted heights of beauty and
serenity. It is the grace of God, the gift of His
Divine Spirit who will dwell with all of us, if we will,
which alone can be trusted to make men good.

And now, if that be true, what follows? Surely
this, that for all you who have, in any measure, caught
a glimpse of what you ought to be, and have been
more or less vainly trying to realise your ideal, and
reach your goal, there is a better way than the way
of self-centred and self-derived and self-dependent
effort. There is the way of opening your hearts and
spirits to the entrance and access of that great power,
the grace of our Lord Jesus Christ, which will do in
us and for us all that we know we ought to do, and
yet feel hampered and hindered in performing.

Oh, dear friends! there are many of you, I believe,
who have more or less spasmodically and interruptedly,
but with a continual recurrence to the effort, sought
to plant your feet firmly in the paths of righteousness,
and have more or less failed. Listen to this Gospel,
and accept it, and put it to the proof. The love of
God which is in Christ Jesus, and the life which that

love brings in its hands, for all of us who will trust it, will dwell in you if you will, and mould you into His own likeness, and the law of the spirit of life which was in Christ Jesus will make us free from the law of sin and death.

All noble living is a battle. Can you and I, with our ten thousand, meet him that cometh against us with his twenty, the temptations of the world and of its Prince? Send for the reinforcements, and Jesus Christ will come and teach your hands to war and your fingers to fight. All noble life is self-denial, coercion, restraint; and can my poor, feeble hands apply muscular force enough to the brake to keep the wheels clogged, and prevent them from whirling me downhill into ruin? Let Him come and put His great gentle hand on the top of yours, and that will enable you to scotch the wheels, and make self-denial possible. All noble life is a building up by slow degrees from the foundation. And can you and I complete the task with our own limited resources, and our own feeble strengths? Will not 'all that pass by begin to mock' us and say, 'This man began to build and was not able to finish'? That is the epitaph written over all moralities and over all lives which, catching some glimpse of the good and the true and the noble, have tried, apart from Christ, to reproduce them in themselves. Frightful gaps, and an unfinished, however fair structure end them all. Go to Him. 'His hand hath laid the foundation of the house, His hand shall also finish it.' He who is Himself the foundation-stone is also the headstone of the corner, which is brought forth with shouting of 'Grace! Grace unto it!'

I need not, I suppose, linger to remind you what

important and large lessons these thoughts carry, not only for men who are trying to work at the task of mending and making their own characters, but on the larger scale, for all who seek to benefit and elevate their fellows. Brethren, it is not for me to depreciate any workers who, in any department, and by any methods, seek, and partially effect, the elevation of humanity. But I should be untrue to my own deepest convictions, and unfaithful to the message which God's providence has given it to me as my life's task to proclaim, if I did not declare that nothing will truly *re-form* humanity, society, the nation, the city, except that which re-creates the individual: 'the grace of our Lord Jesus Christ' entering into their midst.

II. And so, secondly, and very briefly, notice the lesson we get here as to how we should think of our own attainments.

I have already pointed out that there are two beautiful touches in my text. The Apostle traces everything that he is, in his character and in his Christian standing and in his Apostolic work and success, to that grace that has come down upon him, and clothed his nakedness with so glorious a garment. And then, in addition to that, he modestly, and with a fine sense of dignity, refrains from parading his attainments or his achievements, and says, 'It is not for me to estimate what I am; it is for you to do it.' True, indeed, in the next verse he does set forth, in very lofty language, his claims to be in nothing behind the very chiefest of the Apostles, and 'to have laboured more abundantly than they all.' But still the spirit of that humble and yet dignified silence runs through the whole context. 'By the grace of God I am—what I am.'

Well, then, it is not necessary for a man to be ignorant, or to pretend that he is ignorant, of what he can do. We hear a great deal about the unconsciousness of genius. There is a partial truth in it; and possibly the highest examples of power and success, in any department of mental or intellectual effort, are unaware of their achievements and stature. But if a man can do a certain kind of service there is no harm whatever in his recognising the fact that he can do it. The only harm is in his thinking that because he can, he is a very fine fellow, and that the work itself is a great work; and so setting himself up above his brethren. There is a vast deal of hypocrisy in what is called unconsciousness of power. Most men who have been chosen and empowered to do a great work for God or for men, in any department, have been aware that they could do it. But the less we think about ourselves, in any way, the better. The more entire our recognition of the influx of grace on which we depend for keeping our reservoir full, the less likelihood there will be of touchy self-assertion, the less likelihood of the misuse of the powers that we have. If we are to do much for God, if we are to keep what we have already attained, if we are to make our own lives sweet and beautiful, if we are to be invested with any increase of capacity, or led to any higher heights of nobleness and Christlikeness, we must copy, and make a conscious effort to copy, these two things, which marked the Apostle's estimate of himself—a distinct recognition that we are only reservoirs and nothing more—'What hast thou that thou hast not received? Why then dost thou glory as if thou hadst not received it?'—and a humble waiving aside of the attempt to determine what it is that we are. For however clearly a man may know his own powers and achievements, it is hard for him to estimate the relations of these to his whole character.

So, dear brethren, although it is a very homely piece of advice, and may seem to be beneath the so-called dignity of the pulpit, let me venture just to remind you that self-conceit is no disease peculiar to the ten-talented people, but is quite as rife, if not a good deal rifer, among those with one talent. They are very humble when it comes to work, and are quite contented to wrap the one talent up in a napkin then; but when it comes to self-assertion, or what they expect to receive of recognition from others, they need to be reminded quite as much as their betters in endowment—'By the grace of God I am what I am.'

III. And so, lastly, one word about the responsibility for our co-operation with the grace, in order to the accomplishment of its results.

'The grace which was bestowed upon me was not in vain,' says Paul. 'Not I, but the grace of God which was with me, and so I laboured more abundantly than they all.' That is to say, God in His giving love; Christ with His ever out-flowing Spirit, move round our hearts, and desire to enter. But the grace, the love, the gifts of the love may all be put away by our unfaithfulness, by our non-receptivity, by our misuse, and by our negligence. Paul yielded himself to the grace that was brought to work upon him. Have you yielded yourselves?

Paul said, 'By the grace of God I am what I am.' He could not have said that, could he, if he had known that the most part of what he was was dead against

God's will and purpose? Has God anything to do
with making you what you are, or has it been the
devil that has had the greater share in it? This man,
because he knew that he had submitted himself to
the often painful, searching, crucifying, self-restrain-
ing and stimulating influences of the Gospel and Spirit
of Christ, could say, 'God's grace has made me what
I am, and I helped Him to make me.' And can you
say anything like that?

Take your life. In how many of its deeds has there
been present the consciousness of God and His love?
Take your character. How much of it has been shot
through and through, so to speak, by the fiery darts
of that cleansing, warming, consuming grace of God?
Are you daily being baptized in that Spirit, searched
by that Spirit, condemned by that grace? Is it the
grace of God, or nature and self and the world and
the flesh that have made you what you are?

Oh, brethren! let us cultivate the sense of our need
of this divine help, for it does not come where men
do not know how weak they are, and how much they
want it. The mountain tops are high,—yes! and
they are dry; there is no water there. The rivers
run in the green valleys deep down. 'God resisteth
the proud, and giveth grace to the humble.' Let us
see that we open our hearts to the reception of these
quickening and cleansing influences, for it is possible
for us to cover ourselves over with such an impene-
trable covering that that grace cannot pass through
it. Let us see to it that we keep ourselves in close
contact with the foundation of all this grace, even
Jesus Christ Himself, by desire, by faith, by love,
by communion, by meditation, by approximation, by
sympathy, by service. And let us see that we use the

grace that we possess. 'For to him that hath shall be given, and from him that hath not'—not possessing in any real sense because not utilising for its appointed purpose—'shall be taken away even that he hath.' Wherefore, brethren, I 'beseech you that ye receive not the grace of God in vain.'

THE UNITY OF APOSTOLIC TEACHING

'Whether it were I or they, so we preach, and so ye believed.'—1 Cor. xv. 11.

PARTY spirit and faction were the curses of Greek civic life, and they had crept into at least one of the Greek churches—that in the luxurious and powerful city of Corinth. We know that there was a very considerable body of antagonists to Paul, who ranked themselves under the banner of Apollos or of Cephas *i.e.* Peter. Therefore, Paul, keenly conscious that he was speaking to some unfriendly critics, hastens in the context to remove the possible objection which might be made, that the Gospel which he preached was peculiar to himself, and proceeds to assert that the whole substance of what he had to say to men, was held with unbroken unanimity by the other apostles. 'They' means all of *them*; and 'so' means the summary of the Gospel teaching in the preceding verses.

Now, Paul would not have ventured to make that assertion, in the face of men whom he knew to be eager to pick holes in anything that he said, unless he had been perfectly sure of his ground. There were broad differences between him and the others. But their partisans might squabble, as is often the case, and the men, whose partisans they were, be unanimous. There were differences of individual character, of temper, and of views about certain points of Christian truth. But there was an unbroken front of unanimity in regard to all that lies within the compass of that little word which covers so much ground—'*So* we preach.'

Now, I wish to turn to that outstanding fact—which does not always attract the attention which it deserves —of the absolute identity of the message which all the apostles and primitive teachers delivered, and to seek to enforce some of the considerations and lessons which seem to me naturally to flow from it.

I. First, then, I ask you to think of the fact itself— the unbroken unanimity of the whole body of Apostolic teachers.

As I have said, there were wide differences of characteristics between them, but there was a broad tract of teaching wherein they all agreed. Let me briefly gather up the points of unanimity, the contents of the one Gospel, which every man of them felt was his message to the world. I may take it all from the two clauses in the preceding context, 'how that Christ died for our sins according to the Scriptures, and that He was buried, and that He rose again the third day according to the Scriptures.' These are the things about which, as Paul declares, there was not the whisper of a dissentient voice. There is the vital centre which he declares every Christian teacher grasped as being the essential of his message, and in various tones and manners, but in substantial identity of content, declared to the world.

Now, what lies in it? The Person spoken of—the Christ, and all that that word involves of reference to the ancient and incomplete Revelation in the past, its shadows and types, its prophecies and ceremonies, its priesthood and its sacrifices; with all that it involves of reference to the ancient hopes on which a thousand generations had lived, and which either are baseless delusions, or are realised in Jesus—the Person whom all the Apostles proclaimed was One anointed from God as Prophet, Priest, and King; who had come into the world to fulfil all that the ancient system had shadowed by sacrifice, temple, and priest, and was the Monarch of Israel and of the world.

And not only were they absolutely unanimous in regard to the Person, but they were unbrokenly consentient in regard to the facts of His life, His death, and His Resurrection. But the proclamation of the external fact is no gospel. You must add the clause 'for our sins,' and then the record, which is a mere piece of history, with no more good news in it than the record of the death of any other martyr, hero, or saint, starts into being truly the good news for the world. The least part of a historical fact is the fact; the greatest part of it is the explanation of the fact, and the setting it in its place in regard to other facts, the exhibition of the principles which it expresses, and of the conclusions to which it leads. So the bare historical declaration of a death and a resurrection is transmuted into a gospel, by that which is the most important part of the Gospel, the explanation of the meaning of the fact—'He died for our sins.'

If redemption from sin through the death of a Person is the fundamental conception of the Gospel for the world, then it is clear that, for such a purpose, a divine nature in the Person is wanted. Your notion of what Christ came to do will determine your notion of who He is. If you only recognise that His work is to teach, or to show in exercise a fair human character, then you may rest content with the lower notion of His nature which sees in Him but the foremost of the sons of men. But if we grasp 'died for our sins,' then for such a task the incarnation of the Eternal Son of God is the absolute pre-requisite.

Still further, our text brings out the contents of this gospel as being the declaration of the Resurrection. On that I need not here and now dwell at any length. But these are the points, the Person, the two facts, death and resurrection, and the great meaning of the death—viz. the expiation for the world's sins: these are the things on which the whole of the primitive teachers of the Apostolic Church had one voice and one message.

Now, I do not suppose that I need spend any time in showing to you how the extant records bear out, absolutely, this contention of the Apostle's. I need only remind you how the opposition that was waged against him—and it was a very vigorous and a very bitter opposition—from a section of the Church, had no bearing at all upon the question of what he taught, but only upon the question of to whom it was to be taught. The only objection that the so-called Judaising party in the early Church had against Paul and his preaching, was not the Gospel that he declared, but his assertion that the Gentile nations might enter into the Church through faith in Jesus Christ, without passing through the gate of circumcision. Depend upon it, if there had been any, even the most microscopic, divergence on his part from the general, broad stream of Christian teaching, the sleepless, keen-eyed, unscrupulous enemies that dogged him all his days would have pounced upon it eagerly, and would never have ceased talking about it. But not one of them ever said a word of the sort, but allowed his teaching to pass, because it was the teaching of every one of the apostles.

If I had time, or if it were necessary, it would be easy to point you to the records that we have left of the Apostolic teaching, in order to confirm this unbroken unanimity. I do not need to spend time on that. Proof-texts are not worth so much as the fact that these doctrines are interwoven into the whole structure of the New Testament as a whole—just as they are into Paul's letters. But I may gather one or two sayings, in which the substance of each writer's teaching has been concentrated by himself. For instance, Peter speaks about being 'redeemed by the precious blood of Christ as of a Lamb without blemish and without spot,' and declares that 'He Himself bare our sins in His own body on the tree.' John comes in with his doxology: 'Unto Him that loved us, and loosed us from our sins in His own blood'; and it is his pen that records how in the heavens there echoed 'glory and honour and thanks and blessing, for ever and ever, to the Lamb that was slain, and has redeemed us unto God by His blood.' The writer of the Epistle to the Hebrews, steeped as he is in ceremonial and sacrificial ideas, and having for his one purpose to work out the thought that Jesus Christ is all that the ancient ritual, sacerdotal and sacrificial system shadows and foretells, sums up his teaching in the statement that Christ having come, a high priest of good things to come, 'through His own blood, entered in, once for all, into the holy place, having obtained eternal redemption for us.'

There were limits to the unanimity, as I have already said. Paul and Peter had a great quarrel about circumcision and related subjects. The Apostolic writings are wondrously diverse from one another. Peter is far less constructive and profound than Paul. Paul and Peter are both untouched with the mystic wisdom of the Apostle John. But, in regard to the facts that I have signalised, the divinity, the person of Jesus Christ, His death and Resurrection, and the significance to be attached to that death, they are absolutely one. The instruments in the orchestra are various, the tender flute, the ringing trumpet, and many another, but the note they strike is the same. 'Whether it were I or they, so we preach.'

II. Now, let me ask you to consider the only explanation of this unanimity.

Time was when the people, who did not believe in Christ's divinity and sacrificial death, tortured themselves to try and make out meanings for these epistles, which should not include the obnoxious doctrines. That is nearly antiquated. I suppose that there is nobody now, or next to nobody, who does not admit that, right or wrong, Paul, Peter, John—all of them—teach these two things, that Christ is the Eternal Son of the Father, and that His death is the Sacrifice for the world's sin. But they say that that is not the primitive, simple teaching of the Man of Nazareth; and that the unanimity is a unanimity of misapprehension of, and addition to, His words and to the drift of His teaching.

Now, just think what a huge—I was going to say—inconceivability that supposition is. For there is no point, say from the time at which the Apostle who wrote the words of my text, which was somewhere about the year 56 or 57 A.D.,—there is no point between that period, working backwards through the history of the Church to the Crucifixion, where you can insert such a tremendous revolution of teaching as this. There is no trace of such a change. Peter's earliest speeches, as recorded in Acts, are in some important respects less developed doctrinally than are the epistles, but Christ's Messiahship, death, and Resurrection, with which is connected the remission of sins, are as clearly and emphatically proclaimed as at any later time. So these points of the Apostolic testimony were preached from the first, and, if in preaching them, the witnesses perverted the simple teaching of the Carpenter of Nazareth, and ascribed to Him a character which He had not claimed, and to His death a power of which He had not dreamed, they did so at the very time when the impressions of His personality and teaching were most recent and strong. It seems to me, apart altogether from other considerations, that such a right-about-face movement on the part of the early teachers of Christianity, is an absolute impossibility, regard being had to the facts of the case, even if you make much allowance for possible errors in the record.

But I would make another remark. If misapprehension came in, if these men, in their unanimous declaration of Christ's death as the Sacrifice for sin, were not fairly representing the conclusions inevitable from the facts of Christ's life and death, and from His own words, is it not an odd thing that the same misapprehension affected them all? When people misconceive a teacher's doctrine, they generally differ in the nature of their misconceptions, and split into sections and parties. But here you have to account for the fact that every man of them, with all their diversity of idiosyncrasy and character, tumbled into the same pit

of error, and that there was not one of them left sane
enough to protest. Does that seem to be a likely
thing?

And what about the worth of the teacher's teaching,
that did not guard its receivers from such absolute
misapprehension as that? If the whole Church unani-
mously mistook everything that Jesus Christ had said
to them, and unwarrantably made out of Him what
they did, on this hypothesis, I do not think that there
is much left to honour or admire in a teacher, whose
teaching was so ambiguous, as that it led all that
received it into such an error as that into which, by
the supposition, they fell.

No, brethren; they were one, because their Gospel
was the only possible statement of the principles that
underlay, and the conclusions that flowed from, the
plain facts of the life and the teaching of Jesus Christ.
I am not going to spend time in quoting His own
words. I can only refer to one or two of them very
succinctly. 'Destroy this Temple, and in three days I
will raise it up.' 'As Moses lifted up the serpent in the
wilderness, even so must the Son of Man be lifted up.'
'My flesh is the bread which I will give for the life of
the world.' 'The Son of Man came not to be ministered
unto, but to minister, and to give His life a ransom for
many.' 'This is My body broken for you; take, eat, in
remembrance of Me.' 'This is My blood, shed for many
for the remission of sins; this do ye, as often as ye
drink it, in remembrance of Me.' What possible explanation, doing justice to these words, is there, except
'Jesus Christ died for our sins according to the Scriptures'? And how could men who had heard them with
their own ears, and with their own eyes had seen
Him risen from the dead and ascending into heaven, do

otherwise than eagerly, enthusiastically, at the cost of all, and with unhesitating voice of unbroken unanimity, ' so preach ' ?

I quite admit that in Christ's teaching in the gospels you will not find the articulate drawing out into doctrinal statement of the principles that underlay, and the conclusions that flow from, the historical fact of Christ's propitiatory death. I do not wonder at that, nor do I admit that it is any argument against the truth of the divine revelation which is made in these doctrinal statements, to allege that we find nothing corresponding to them in Jesus Christ's own words. The silence is not as absolute as is alleged, as the quotations which I have made, and which might have been multiplied, do distinctly enough show. Even if it were more absolute than it is, the silence is by no means unintelligible. Christ had to offer the Sacrifice before the Sacrifice could be preached. He Himself warned His disciples against accepting His own words prior to the Cross, as the conclusive and ultimate revelation. 'I have many things to say unto you, but you cannot carry them now.' There was need that the Cross should be a fact before it was evolved into a doctrine. And so I venture to say that the unanimity of the preaching is only explicable on the ground of that preaching in both its parts—its assertion of Jesus' Messiahship and of His propitiatory death— being the repetition on the housetop of the lessons which they had heard in the ear from Him.

III. Note, briefly, the lesson from this unanimity.

Let us distinctly apprehend where is the living heart of the Gospel—that it is the message of redemption by the incarnation and sacrifice of the Son of God. There follows from that incarnation and sacrifice all the great teaching about the work of the Divine Spirit in men, dwelling in them for evermore. But the beginning of all is, 'Christ died for our sins according to the Scriptures.' And, brethren, that message meets, as nothing else meets, the deepest needs of every human soul. It is able, as nothing else is able, to open out into a whole encyclopædia and universe of wisdom and truth and power. If we strike it out of our conception of Christianity, or if we obscure it as being the very palpitating centre of the whole, then feebleness will creep over the Christianity that is *minus* a Cross, or does not see in it the Sacrifice for the world's sin. You may cast overboard the sails to lighten the ship. If you do, she lies a log on the waters. And if, for the sake of meeting new phases of thought, Christian churches tamper with this central truth, they have flung away their means of progress and of power.

Let me say again, and in a word only, that the considerations that I have been trying to submit to you in this sermon, show us the limits within which the modern cry of 'Back to the Christ of the Gospels,' is right, and where it may be wrong. I believe that in former days, and to some extent in the present day, we evangelical teachers have too much sometimes talked rather about the doctrines than about the Person who is the doctrines. And if the cry of 'Back to the Christ' means, 'Do not talk so much about the Atonement and Propitiation; talk about the Christ who atones,' then, with all my heart, I say, 'Amen!' But put the Person in the foreground, the living-loving, the dying-loving, the risen-loving Christ, put Him in the foreground. But if it is implied, as I am afraid it is often implied, that the Christ of the Gospels is one and the Christ of the epistles is another, and that to go

back to the Christ of the gospels means to drop
'died for our sins according to the Scriptures,' and to
retain only the non-miraculous, moral and religious
teachings that are recorded in the three first gospels,
then I say that it is fatal for the Church, and it is false
to the facts, for the Christ of the epistles is the Christ
of the gospels : the difference only being that in the
one you have the facts, and in the other you have their
meaning and their power.

So, lastly, let this text teach us what we ourselves
have to do with this unanimous testimony. 'So
we preach, and so ye believed.' Brother! Do you
believe *so*? That is to say, is your conception of
the Gospel the mighty redemptive agency which is
wrought by the Incarnate Son of God, who was
crucified for our offences, and rose that we might
live, and is glorified that we, too, may share His
glory? Is that your Gospel? But do not be content
with an intellectual grasp of the thing. 'So ye
believed' means a great deal more than 'I believe
that Christ died for our sins.' It means 'I believe
in the Christ who did die for my sins.' You must
cast yourself as a sinful man on Him; and, so casting,
you will find that it is no vain story which is commended to us by all these august voices from the past,
but you will have in your own experience the verifica-
tion of the fact that He died for our sins, in your own
consciousness of sins forgiven, and new love bestowed;
and so may turn round to Paul, the leader of the
chorus, and to all the apostolic band, and say to them,
'Now I believe, not because of thy saying, but because
I have seen Him, and myself heard Him.'

the

i

THE CERTAINTY AND JOY OF THE
RESURRECTION

'But now is Christ risen from the dead . . . the first fruits of them that slept.'
1 COR. XV. 20.

THE Apostle has been contemplating the long train of
dismal consequences which he sees would arise if we
only had a dead Christ. He thinks that he, the Apostle,
would have nothing to preach, and we, nothing to
believe. He thinks that all hope of deliverance from
sin would fade away. He thinks that the one fact
which gives assurance of immortality having vanished,
the dead who had nurtured the assurance have
perished. And he thinks that if things were so, then
Christian men, who had believed a false gospel, and
nourished an empty faith, and died clinging to a baseless hope, were far more to be pitied than men who
had had less splendid dreams and less utter illusions.

Then, with a swift revulsion of feeling, he turns
away from that dreary picture, and with a change of
key, which the dullest ear can appreciate, from the
wailing minors of the preceding verses, he breaks
into this burst of triumph. 'Now'—things being as
they are, for it is the logical 'now,' and not the
temporal one—things being as they are, 'Christ is
risen from the dead, and that as the first fruits of them
that slept.'

Part of the ceremonial of the Passover was the presentation in the Temple of a barley sheaf, the first of
the harvest, waved before the Lord in dedication to
Him, and in sign of thankful confidence that all the
fields would be reaped and their blessing gathered.

There may be some allusion to that ceremony, which coincided in time with the Resurrection of our Lord, in the words here, which regard that one solitary Resurrection as the early ripe and early reaped sheaf, the pledge and the prophecy of the whole ingathering.

Now there seem to me, in these words, to ring out mainly two things—an expression of absolute certainty in the fact, and an expression of unbounded triumph in the certainty of the fact.

And if we look at these two things, I think we shall get the main thoughts that the Apostle would impress upon our minds.

I. The certainty of Christ's Resurrection.

'Now *is* Christ risen,' says he, defying, as it were, doubt and negation, and basing himself upon the firm assurance which he possesses of that historical fact. 'Ah!' you say, 'seeing is believing; and he had evidence such as we can never have.' Well! let us see. Is it possible for us, nineteen centuries nearly after that day, to catch some echo of this assured confidence, and in the face of modern doubts and disbeliefs, to reiterate with as unfaltering assurance as that with which they came from his glowing lips, the great words of my text? Can we, logically and reasonably, as men who are guided by evidence and not by feeling, stand up before the world, and take for ours the ancient confession: 'I believe in Jesus Christ, His only Son, our Lord, who suffered under Pontius Pilate, was crucified, dead, and buried. The third day He rose again from the dead'? I think we can.

The way to prove a fact is by the evidence of witnesses. You cannot argue that it would be very convenient, if such and such a thing should be true; that great moral effects would follow if we believed it was true, and so on. The way to do is to put people who have seen it into the witness-box, and to make sure that their evidence is worth accepting.

And at the beginning of my remarks I wish to protest, in a sentence, against confusing the issues about this question of the Resurrection of Jesus Christ in that fashion which is popular nowadays, when we are told that miracle is impossible, and *therefore* there has been no Resurrection, or that death is the end of human existence, and that *therefore* there has been no Resurrection. That is not the way to go about ascertaining the truth as to asserted facts. Let us hear the evidence. The men who brush aside the testimony of the New Testament writers, in obedience to a theory, either about the impossibility of the supernatural, or about the fatal and final issues of human death, are victims of prejudice, in the strictest meaning of the word; and are no more logical than the well-known and proverbial reasoner who, when told that facts were against him, with sublime confidence in his own infallibility, is reported to have said, 'So much the worse for the facts.' Let us deal with evidence, and not with theory, when we are talking about alleged facts of history.

So then, let me remind you that, in this chapter from which my text is taken, we have a record of the Resurrection of Jesus Christ, older than, and altogether independent of, the records contained in the gospels, which are all subsequent in date to it; that this Epistle to the Corinthians is one of the four undisputed Epistles of the Apostle, which not the most advanced school of modern criticism has a word to say against; that, therefore, this chapter, written, at the latest, some seven and twenty years after the date of the Crucifixion, carries us up very close to that event; that it shows that the Resurrection was *universally* believed all over the Church, and therefore must have then been long believed; that it enables us to trace the same belief as universal, and in undisputed possession of the field among the churches, at the time of Paul's conversion, which cannot be put down at much more than five or six years after the Crucifixion, and that so we are standing in the presence of absolutely contemporaneous testimony. This is not a case in which a belief slowly and gradually grew up. Whether we accept the evidence or not, we are bound to admit that it is strictly contemporaneous testimony to the fact of Christ's Resurrection.

And the witnesses are reliable and competent, as well as contemporaneous. The old belief that their testimony was imposture is dead long ago; as, indeed, how could it live? It would be an anomaly, far greater than the Resurrection, to believe that these people, Mary, Peter, John, Paul, and all the rest of them, were conspirators in a lie, and that the fairest system of morality and the noblest consecration that the world has ever seen, grew up out of a fraud, like flowers upon a dunghill. That theory will not hold water; and even those who will not accept the testimony have long since confessed that it will not. But the Apostle, in my context, seems to think that that is the only tenable alternative to the other theory that the witnesses were veracious, and I am disposed to believe that he is right. He says, 'If Christ be not risen, then, are we' the utterly impossible thing of 'false witnesses to God,' devout perjurers, as the phrase might be paraphrased; men who are lying to please God. If Christ be not risen, they have sworn to a thing that they know to be untrue, in order to advance His cause and His kingdom. If that theory be not accepted, there is no other about these men and their message that will hold water for a minute, except the admission of its truth.

The fashionable modern one, that it was hallucination, is preposterous. Hallucinations that five hundred people at once shared! Hallucinations that lasted all through long talks, spread at intervals over more than a month! Hallucinations that included eating and drinking, speech and answer; the clasp of the hand and the feeling of the breath! Hallucinations that brought instruction! Hallucinations that culminated in the fancy that a gathered multitude of them saw Him going up into heaven! The hallucination is on the other side, I think. They have got the saddle on the wrong horse when they talk about the Apostolic witnesses being the victims of hallucination. It is the people who believe it possible that they should be who are so. The old argument against miracles used to say that it is more consonant with experience that testimony should be false, than that a miracle should be true. I venture to say it is a much greater strain on a man's credulity, to believe that *such* evidence is false than that *such* a miracle, so attested, is true. And I, for my part, venture to think that the reasonable men are the men who listen to these eye-witnesses when they say, ' We saw Him rise '; and echo back in answer the triumphant certitude, ' Christ is risen indeed! '

There is another consideration that I might put briefly. A very valuable way of establishing facts is to point to the existence of other facts, which indispensably require the previous ones for their explanation. Let me give you an illustration of what I mean.

I believe in the Resurrection of Jesus Christ, amongst other reasons, because I do not understand how it was possible for the Church to exist for a week after the Crucifixion, unless Jesus Christ rose again. Why was it that they did not all scatter? Why was it that the spirit of despondency and the tendency to separation, which were beginning to creep over them when they were saying: 'Ah! it is all up! We *trusted* that this *Lk 2 v:* had been He,' did not go on to their natural issue? How came it that these people, with their Master taken away from the midst of them, and the bond of union between them removed, and all their hopes crushed did not say: 'We have made a mistake, let us go back to Gennesareth and take to our fishing again, and try and forget our bright illusions'? That is what John the Baptist's followers did when he died. Why did not Christ's do the same? Because Christ rose again and re-knit them together. When the Shepherd was smitten, the flock would have been scattered, and never drawn together any more, unless there had been just such a thing as the Resurrection asserts there was, to reunite the dispersed and to encourage the depressed. And so I say, Christianity with a *dead* Christ, and a Church gathered round a grave from which the stone has *not* been rolled away, is more unbelievable than the miracle, for it is an absurdity.

Then there is another thing that I would say in a word. Let me put an illustration to explain what I mean. Suppose, after the execution of King Charles I., in some corner of the country a Pretender had sprung up and said, 'I am the King!' the way to end that would have been for the Puritan leaders to have taken people to St. George's Chapel, and said, 'Look! there is the coffin, there is the body, is that the

king, or is it not?' Jesus Christ was said to have
risen again, within a week of the time of His death.
The rulers of the nation had the grave, the watch, the
stone, the seal. They could have put an end to the pestilent nonsense in two minutes, if it had been nonsense, by
the simple process of saying, 'Go and look at the tomb,
and you will see Him there.' But this question has never
been answered, and never will be—What became of
that sacred corpse if Jesus Christ did not rise again from
the dead? The clumsy lie that the rulers told, that the
disciples had stolen away the body, was only their
acknowledgment that the grave was empty. If the
grave were empty, either His servants were impostors,
which we have seen it is incredible that they were, or
the Christ was risen again.

And so, dear brethren, for many other reasons
besides this handful that I have ventured to gather
and put before you, and in spite of the prejudices of
modern theories, I lift up here once more, with unfaltering certitude, the glad message which I beseech
you to accept: 'Christ is risen, the first fruits of them
that slept.'

II. So much, then, for the first point in this passage.
A word or two about the second—the triumph in the
certitude of that Resurrection.

As I remarked at a previous point of this discourse,
the Apostle has been speaking about the consequences
which would follow from the fact that Christ was not
raised. If we take all these consequences and reverse
them, we get the glad issues of His Resurrection, and
understand why it was that this great burst of triumph
comes from the Apostle's lips. And though I must
necessarily treat this part of my subject very inadequately, let me try to gather together the various

points on which, as I think, our Easter gladness ought to be built.

First, then, I say, the risen Christ gives us a complete Gospel. A dead Christ annihilates the Gospel. 'If Christ be not risen,' says the Apostle, 'our preaching,' by which he means not the act but the substance of his preaching, 'is vain.' Or, as the word might be more accurately rendered, 'empty.' There is nothing in it; no contents. It is a blown bladder; nothing in it but wind.

What was Paul's 'preaching'? It all turned upon these points—that Jesus Christ was the Son of God; that He was Incarnate in the flesh for us men; that He died on the Cross for our offences; that He was raised again, and had ascended into Heaven, ruling the world and breathing His presence into believing hearts; and that He would come again to be our Judge. These were the elements of what Paul called 'his Gospel.' He faces the supposition of a dead Christ, and he says, 'It is all gone! It is all vanished into thin air. I have nothing to preach if I have not a Cross to preach which is man's deliverance from sin, because on it the Son of God hath died, and I only know that Jesus Christ's sacrifice is accepted and sufficient, because I have it attested to me in His rising again from the dead.'

Dear brethren, on the fact of the Resurrection of Jesus Christ is suspended everything which makes the Gospel a gospel. Strike that out, and what have you left? Some beautiful bits of moral teaching, a lovely life, marred by tremendous mistakes about Himself and His own importance and His relation to men and to God; but you have got nothing left that is worth calling a gospel. You have the cross rising there,

gaunt, black, solitary; but, unless on the other side of
the river you have the Resurrection, no bridge will
ever be thrown across the black gulf, and the Cross
remains 'dead, being alone.' You must have a Resurrection to explain the Cross, and then the Life and the
Death tower up into the manifestation of God in the
flesh and the propitiation for our sins. Without it
we have nothing to preach which is worth calling a
gospel.

Again, a living Christ gives faith something to lay
hold of. The Apostle here in the context twice says,
according to the Authorised Version, that a dead Christ
makes our faith 'vain.' But he really uses two different words, the former of which is applied to
'preaching,' and means literally 'empty,' while the
latter means 'of none effect' or 'powerless.' So there
are two ideas suggested here which I can only touch
with the lightest hand.

The risen Christ puts some contents, so to speak, into
my faith; He gives me something for it to lay hold of.

Who can trust a *dead* Christ, or who can trust a
human Christ? That would be as much a blasphemy
as trusting any other man. It is only when we recognise Him as declared to be the Son of God, and that by
the Resurrection from the dead, that our faith has
anything round which it can twine, and to which it
can cleave. That living Saviour will stretch out His
hand to us if we look to Him, and if I put my poor,
trembling little hand up towards Him, He will bend to
me and clasp it. You cannot exercise faith unless you
have a risen Saviour, and unless you exercise faith in
Him your lives are marred and sad.

Again, if Christ be dead, our faith, if it could exist,
would be as devoid of effect as it would be empty of

substance. For such a faith would be like an infant
seeking nourishment at a dead mother's breast, or men
trying to kindle their torches at an extinguished lamp.
And chiefly would it fail to bring the first blessing
which the believing soul receives through and from a
risen Christ, namely, deliverance from sin. If He
whom we believed to be our sacrifice by His death and
our sanctification by His life has not risen, then, as
we have seen, all which makes His death other than a
martyr's vanishes, and with it vanish forgiveness
and purifying. Only when we recognise that in His
Cross explained by His Resurrection, we have redemption through His blood, even the forgiveness of sins,
and by the communication of the risen life from the
risen Lord possess that new nature which sets us free
from the dominion of our evil, is faith operative in
setting us free from our sins.

So, dear friends, the risen Christ gives us something
for faith to lay hold of, and will make it the hand by
which we grasp His strong hand, which lifts us 'out
of the horrible pit and the miry clay, and sets our
feet upon a rock.' But if He lie dead in the grave your
faith is vain, because it grasps nothing but a shadow;
and it is vain as being purposeless; you are yet in your
sins.

The last thought is that the risen Christ gives us the
certitude of our Resurrection. I do not for a moment
mean to say that, apart from the Resurrection of Jesus
Christ, the thought, be it a wish or a dread, of immortality, has not been found in men, but there is all the
difference in the world between forebodings, aspirations, wishes it were so, fears that it might be so, and
the calm certitude that it is so. Many men talked
about a western continent, but Columbus went there

and came back again, and that ended doubt. Many men before, and apart from Jesus, have cherished thoughts of an immortal life beyond the grave, but He has been there and returned. And that, and, as I believe, that only puts the doctrine of immortality upon an irrefragable foundation; and we can say, 'Now, I know that there is that land beyond.' They tell us that death ends everything. Modern materialism, in all its forms, asserts that it is the extinction of the personality. Jesus Christ died, and went through it, and came out of it the same, and I will trust Him. Brethren, the set of opinion amongst the educated and cultured classes in England, and all over Europe, at this moment, proves to anybody who has eyes to see, that for this generation, rejection of immortality will follow certainly on the rejection of Jesus Christ. And for England to-day, as for Greece when Paul sent his letter to Corinth, the one light of certitude in the great darkness is the fact that Jesus Christ hath died, and is risen again.

If you will let Him, He will make you partakers of His own immortal life. 'The first fruits of them that slept' is the pledge and the prophecy of all the waving abundance of golden grain that shall be gathered into the great husbandman's barns. The Apostle goes on to represent the resurrection of 'them that are Christ's' as a consequence of their union to Jesus. He has conquered for us all. He has entered the prison-house and come forth bearing its iron gates on His shoulders, and henceforth it is not possible that we should be holden of it. There are two resurrections—one, that of Christ's servants, one that of others. They are not the same in principle —and, alas, they are awfully different in issue. 'Some shall wake to everlasting life, and some to shame and everlasting contempt.'

Let me beseech you to make Jesus Christ the life of your dead souls, by humble, penitent trust in Him. And then, in due time, He will be the life of your transformed bodies, changing these into the likeness of the body of His glory, 'according to the working whereby He is able even to subdue all things unto Himself.'

THE DEATH OF DEATH

'But now is Christ risen from the dead, and become the first-fruits of them that slept. 21. For since by man came death, by man came also the resurrection of the dead. . . . 50. Now this I say, brethren, that flesh and blood cannot inherit the kingdom of God; neither doth corruption inherit incorruption. 51. Behold, I shew you a mystery; We shall not all sleep, but we shall all be changed, 52. In a moment, in the twinkling of an eye, at the last trump, (for the trumpet shall sound;) and the dead shall be raised incorruptible, and we shall be changed. 53. For this corruptible must put on incorruption, and this mortal must put on immortality. 54. So when this corruptible shall have put on incorruption, and this mortal shall have put on immortality, then shall be brought to pass the saying that is written, Death is swallowed up in victory. 55. O death, where is thy sting? O grave, where is thy victory? 56. The sting of death is sin; and the strength of sin is the law. 57. But thanks be to God, which giveth us the victory, through our Lord Jesus Christ. 58. Therefore, my beloved brethren, be ye stedfast, unmoveable, always abounding in the work of the Lord, forasmuch as ye know that your labour is not in vain in the Lord.'—1 COR. xv. 20, 21; 50-58.

THIS passage begins with the triumphant ringing out of the great fact which changes all the darkness of an earthly life without a heavenly hope into a blaze of light. All the dreariness for humanity, and all the vanity for Christian faith and preaching, vanish, like ghosts at cock-crow, when the Resurrection of Jesus rises sun-like on the world's night. It is a historical fact, established by the evidence proper for such,— namely, the credible testimony of eye-witnesses. They could attest His rising, but the knowledge of the world-wide significance of it comes, not from testimony, but

from revelation. Those who saw Him risen join to
declare: 'Now is Christ risen from the dead,' but it is
a higher Voice that goes on to say, 'and become the
first-fruits of them that slept.'

That one Man risen from the grave was like the
solitary sheaf of paschal first-fruits, prophesying of
many more, a gathered harvest that will fill the great
Husbandman's barns. The Resurrection of Jesus is not
only a prophecy, showing, as it and it alone does, that
death is not the end of man, but that life persists
through death and emerges from it, like a buried river
coming again flashing into the light of day, but it is the
source or cause of the Christian's resurrection. The
oneness of the race necessitated the diffusion through
all its members of sin and of its consequence—physical
death. If the fountain is poisoned, all the stream will
be tainted. If men are to be redeemed from the power
of the grave, there must be a new personal centre of
life; and union with Him, which can only be effected
by faith, is the condition of receiving life from Him,
which gradually conquers the death of sin now, and
will triumph over bodily death in the final resurrection. It is the resurrection of Christians that Paul is
dealing with. Others are to be raised, but on a different
principle, and to sadly different issues. Since Christ's
Resurrection assures us of the future waking, it changes
death into 'sleep,' and that sleep does not mean unconsciousness any more than natural sleep does, but only
rest from toil, and cessation of intercourse with the
external world.

In the part of the passage, verses 50 to 58, the Apostle
becomes, not the witness or the reasoner, as in the
earlier parts of the chapter, but the revealer of a
'mystery.' That word, so tragically misunderstood,

has here its uniform scriptural sense of truth, otherwise unknown, made known by revelation. But before
he unveils the mystery, Paul states with the utmost
force a difficulty which might seem to crush all hope,
—namely, that corporeity, as we know it, is clearly
incapable of living in such a world as that future one
must be. To use modern terms, organism and environment must be adapted to each other. A fish must have
the water, the creatures that flourish at the poles
would not survive at the equator. A man with his
gross earthly body, so thoroughly adapted to his
earthly abode, would be all out of harmony with his
surroundings in that higher world, and its rarified air
would be too thin and pure for his lungs. Can there
be any possibility of making him fit to live in a
spiritual world? Apart from revelation, the dreary
answer must be 'No.' But the 'mystery' answers with
'Yes.' The change from physical to spiritual is clearly
necessary, if there is to be a blessed life hereafter.

That necessary change is assured to all Christians,
whether they die or 'remain till the coming of the Lord.'
Paul varies in his anticipations as to whether he and
his contemporaries will belong to the one class or the
other; but he is quite sure that in either case the
indwelling Spirit of Jesus will effect on living and dead
the needful change. The grand description in verse 52,
like the parallel in 1 Thessalonians iv. 16, is modelled
on the account of the theophany on Sinai. The trumpet
was the signal of the Divine Presence. That last
manifestation will be sudden, and its startling breaking in on daily commonplace is intensified by the
reduplication: 'In a moment, in the twinkling of an
eye.' With sudden crash that awful blare of 'loud,
uplifted angel trumpet' will silence all other sounds,

and hush the world. The stages of what follows are distinctly marked. First, the rising of the dead changed in passing through death, so as to rise in incorruptible bodies, and then the change of the bodies of the living into like incorruption. The former will not be found naked, but will be clothed with their white garments; the latter will, as it were, put on the glorious robes above the 'muddy vesture of decay,' or, more truly, will see the miracle of these being transfigured till they shine 'so as no fuller on earth could white them.' The living will witness the resurrection of the dead; the risen dead will witness the transformation of the living. Then both hosts will be united, and, through all eternity, 'live together,' and that 'with Him.' Paul evidently expects that he and the Corinthians will be in the latter class, as appears by the 'we' in verse 52. He, as it were, points to his own body when he says, recurring to his former thought of the necessity of harmony between organism and environment, '*this* corruptible must put on incorruption.' Here 'corruption' is used in its physical application, though the ethical meaning may be in the background.

The Apostle closes his long argument and revelation with a burst, almost a shout, of triumph. Glowing words of old prophets rush into his mind, and he breathes a new, grander meaning into them. Isaiah had sung of a time when the veil over all nations *25: 6* should be destroyed 'in this mountain,' and when death should be swallowed up for ever; and Paul *: 8* grasps the words and says that the prophet's loftiest anticipations will be fulfilled when that monster, whose insatiable maw swallows down youth, beauty, strength, wisdom, will himself be swallowed up. Hosea had *13 : 14* prophesied of Israel's restoration under figure of a resurrection, and Paul grasps *his* words and fills them with a larger meaning. He modifies them, in a manner on which we need not enlarge, to express the great Christian thought that death has conquered man but that man in Christ will conquer the conqueror. With swift change of metaphor he represents death as a serpent, armed with a poisoned sting, and that suggests to him the thought, never far away in his view of man, that death's power to slay is derived from—or, so to say, concentrated in—sin; and that at once raises the other equally characteristic and familiar thought that law stimulates sin, since to know a thing to be forbidden creates in perverse humanity an itching to do it, and law reveals sin by setting up the ideal from which sin is the departure. But just as the tracks in Paul's mind were well worn, by which the thought of death brought in that of sin, and that of sin drew after it that of law, so with equal closeness of established association, that of law, condemnatory and slaying, brought up that of Christ, the all-sufficient refuge from that gloomy triad—Death, Sin, Law. Through union with Him each of us may possess His immortal risen life, in which Death, the engulfer, is himself engulfed; Death, the conqueror, is conquered utterly and for ever ; Death, the serpent, has his sting drawn, and is harmless. That participation in Christ's life is begun even here, and God 'giveth us the victory' now, even while we live outward lives that must end in death, and will give it perfectly in the resurrection, when 'they cannot die any more,' and death itself is dead.

The loftiest Christian hopes have close relation to the lowliest Christian duties, and Paul's triumphant song ends with plain, practical, prose exhortations to steadfastness, unmovable tenacity, and abundant fruitfulness, the motive and power of which will be found in the assurance that, since there is a life beyond, all labour here, however it may fail in the eyes of men, will not be in vain, but will tell on character and therefore on condition through eternity. If our peace does not rest where we would fain see it settle, it will not be wasted, but will return to us again, like the dove to the ark, and we shall 'self-enfold the large results of' labour that seemed to have been thrown away.

STRONG AND LOVING

'Watch ye, stand fast in the faith, quit you like men, be strong. 14. Let all your things be done with charity.'—1 Cor. xvi. 13, 14.

THERE is a singular contrast between the first four of these exhortations and the last. The former ring sharp and short like pistol-shots; the last is of gentler mould. The former sound like the word of command shouted from an officer along the ranks; and there is a military metaphor running all through them. The foe threatens to advance; let the guards keep their eyes open. He comes nearer; prepare for the charge, stand firm in your ranks. The battle is joined; 'quit you like men'—strike a man's stroke—'be strong.'

And then all the apparatus of warfare is put away out of sight, and the captain's word of command is softened into the Christian teacher's exhortation: 'Let all your deeds be done in charity.' For love is better than fighting, and is stronger than swords. And yet, although there is a contrast here, there is also a sequence and connection. No doubt these exhortations, which are Paul's last word to that Corinthian Church on whom he had lavished in turn the treasures of his

manifold eloquence, indignation, argumentation, and
tenderness, reflected the deficiencies of the people to
whom he was speaking.   They were schismatic and
factious to the very core, and so they needed the
exhortation to be left last in their ears, as it were, that
everything should be done in love.   They were ill-
grounded in regard to the very fundamental doctrines
of the faith, as all Paul's argumentation about the
resurrection proves, and so they needed to be bidden to
'stand fast in the faith.'   Their slothful carelessness
as to the discipline of the Christian life, and their
consequent feebleness of grasp of the Christian verities,
made them loose-braced and weak in all respects, and
incapacitated them for vigorous warfare.   Thus, we
see a picture in these injunctions of the sort of
community that Paul had to deal with in Corinth,
which yet he called a Church of saints, and for which
he loved and laboured.   Let me then run over and try
to bring out the importance and mutual connection of
what I may call this drill-book for the Christian
warfare, which is the Christian life.

'Watch ye.'   That means one of two things certainly,
probably both—Keep awake, and keep your eyes open. ⟩
Our Lord used the same metaphor, you remember, very
frequently, but with a special significance.   On His lips
it generally referred to the attitude of expectation of
His coming in judgment.   Paul uses sometimes the
figure with the same application, but here, distinctly,
it has another.   As I said, there is the military idea
underlying it.   What will become of an army if the
sentries go to sleep?   And what chance will a Christian
man have of doing his *devoir* against his enemy, unless
he keeps himself awake, and keeps himself alert?
Watchfulness, in the sense of always having eyes open

for the possible rush down upon us of temptation and
evil, is no small part of the discipline and the duty of
the Christian life.   One part of that watchfulness
consists in exercising a very rigid and a very constant
and comprehensive scrutiny of our motives.   For there
is no way by which evil creeps upon us so unobserved,
as when it slips in at the back door of a specious motive.
Many a man contents himself with the avoidance of
actual evil actions, and lets any kind of motives come
in and out of his mind unexamined.   It is all right to
look after our *doings*, but 'as a man *thinketh* in his
heart, so is he.'   The good or the evil of anything that
I do is determined wholly by the motive with which I
do it.   And we are a great deal too apt to palm off
deceptions on ourselves to make sure that our motives
are right, unless we give them a very careful and
minute scrutiny.   One side of this watchfulness, then,
is a habitual inspection of our motives and reasons for
action.   'What am I doing this for?' is a question that
would stop dead an enormous proportion of our activity,
as if you had turned the steam off from an engine.   If
you will use a very fine sieve through which to strain
your motives, you will go a long way to keeping your
actions right.   We should establish a rigid examination
for applicants for entrance, and make quite sure that
each that presents itself is not a wolf in sheep's clothing.
Make them all bring out their passports.   Let every
vessel that comes into your harbour remain isolated
from all communication with the shore, until the health
officer has been on board and given a clean bill. 'Watch
ye,' for yonder, away in the dark, in the shadow of the
trees, the black masses of the enemy are gathered, and
a midnight attack is but too likely to bring a bloody
awakening to a camp full of sleepers.

My text goes on to bring the enemy nearer and nearer and nearer. 'Watch ye'—and if, not unnoticed, they come down on you, 'stand fast in the faith.' There will be no keeping our ranks, or keeping our feet—or at least, it is not nearly so likely that there will be—unless there has been the preceding watchfulness. If the first command has not been obeyed, there is small chance of the second's being so. If there has not been any watchfulness, it is not at all likely that there will be much steadfastness. Just as with a man going along a crowded pavement, a little touch from a passer-by will throw him off his balance, whereas if he had known it was coming, and had adjusted his poise rightly, he would have stood against thrice as violent a shock, so, in order that we may stand fast, we must watch. A sudden assault will be a great deal less formidable when it is a foreseen assault.

'Stand fast *in the faith.*' I take it that this does not mean 'the thing that we believe,' which use of the word 'faith' is the ecclesiastical, but not the New Testament meaning. In Scripture, faith means not the body of truths that we believe, but the act of believing them. This further command tells us that, in addition to our watchfulness, and as the basis of our steadfastness, confidence in the revelation of God in Jesus Christ will enable us to keep our feet whatever comes against us, and to hold our ground, whoever may assault us.

But remember that it is not because I have faith that I stand fast, but because of that in which I have faith. My feet may be well shod—and it used to be said that a soldier's shoes were of as much importance in the battle as his musket—my feet may be well shod, but if they are not well planted upon firm ground I never shall be able to stand the collision of the foe. So then, it is not my grasp of the blessed truth, God in Christ my Friend and Helper, but it is that truth which I grasp at, that makes me strong. Or, to put it into other words, it is the foothold, and not the foot that holds it, that ensures our standing firm. Only there is no steadfastness communicated to us from the source of all stability, except by way of our faith, which brings Christ into us. 'Watch ye; stand fast in the faith.'

The next two words of command are very closely connected, though not quite identical. 'Quit you like men.' Play a man's part in the battle; strike with all the force of your muscles. But the Apostle adds, 'be strong.' You cannot play a man's part unless you are. 'Be strong'—the original would rather bear 'become strong.' What is the use of telling men to 'be strong'? It is a waste of words, in nine cases out of ten, to say to a weak man, 'Pluck up your courage, and show strength.' But the Apostle uses a very uncommon word here, at least uncommon in the New Testament, and another place where he uses it will throw light upon what he means: 'Strengthened with might by His Spirit in the inner man.' Then is it so vain a mockery to tell a poor, weak creature like me to become strong, when you can point me to the source of all strength, in that 'Spirit of power and of love and of a sound mind'? We have only to take our weakness there to have it stiffened into strength; as people put bits of wood into what are called 'petrifying wells,' which infiltrate into them mineral particles, that do not turn the wood into stone, but make the wood as strong as stone. So my manhood, with all its weakness, may have filtered into it divine strength, which will brace me for all needful duty, and make me 'more than conqueror through Him that loved us.' Then, it is not

mockery and cruelty, vanity and surplusage to preach
'Quit you like men; be strong, and be a man'; because
if we will observe the plain and not hard conditions,
strength will come to us according to our day, in
fulfilment of the great promises: 'My grace is sufficient
for thee; and My strength is made perfect in weakness.'

And now we have done with the fighting words of
command, and come to the gentler exhortation: 'Let
all your things be done in charity.'

That was a hard lesson for these Corinthians who
were splitting themselves into factions and sects, and
tearing each other's eyes out in their partisanship for
various Christian teachers. But the advice has a much
wider application than to the suppression of squabbles
in Christian communities. It is the sum of all commandments of the Christian life, if you will take love
in its widest sense, in the sense, that is, in which it is
always used in Paul's writings. We cut it into two
halves, and think of it as sometimes meaning love to
God, and sometimes love to man. The two are
inseparably inter-penetrated in the New Testament
writings; and so we have to interpret this supreme
commandment in the whole breadth and meaning of
that great word *Love*. And then it just comes to this,
that love is the victor in all the Christian warfare. If
we love God, at any given moment, consciously having
our affection engaged with Him, and our heart going
out to Him, do you think that any evil or temptation
would have power over us? Should we not see them
as they are, to be devils in disguise? In the proportion
in which I love God I conquer all sin. And at the
moment in which that great, sweet, all-satisfying light
floods into my soul, I see through the hollowness and
the shams, and detect the ugliness and the filth of the

R

things that otherwise would be temptations. If you desire to be conquerors in the Christian fight, remember that the true way of conquest is, as another Apostle says, 'Keep yourselves in the love of God.' 'Let all your things be done in charity.'

And, further, how beautifully the Apostle here puts the great truth that we are all apt to forget, that the strongest type of human character is the gentlest and most loving, and that the mighty man is not the man of intellectual or material force, such as the world idolises, but the man who is much because he loves much. If we would come to supreme beauty of Christian character, there must be inseparably manifested in our lives, and lived in our hearts, strength and love, might and gentleness. That is the perfect man, and that was the union which was set before us, in the highest form, in the 'Strong Son of God, Immortal Love,' whom we call our Saviour, and whom we are bound to follow. His soldiers conquer as the Captain of their salvation has conquered, when watchfulness and steadfastness and courage and strength are all baptized in love and perfected thereby.

ANATHEMA AND GRACE

'The salutation of me Paul with mine own hand. 22. If any man love not the Lord Jesus Christ, let him be Anathema Maran-atha. 23. The grace of our Lord Jesus Christ be with you. 24. My love be with you all in Christ Jesus.'—1 COR. xvi. 21-24.

TERROR and tenderness are strangely mingled in this parting salutation, which was added in the great characters shaped by Paul's own hand, to the letter written by an amanuensis. He has been obliged, throughout the whole epistle, to assume a tone of

remonstrance abundantly mingled with irony and
sarcasm and indignation. He has had to rebuke the
Corinthians for many faults, party spirit, lax morality,
toleration of foul sins, grave abuses in their worship
even at the Lord's Supper, gross errors in opinion in
the denial of the Resurrection. And in this last solemn
warning he traces all these vices to their fountain-
head—the defect of love to Jesus Christ—and warns of
their fatal issue. 'Let him be Anathema.'

But he will not leave these terrible words for his
last. The thunder is followed by gentle rain, and the
sun glistens on the drops; 'The grace of our Lord
Jesus Christ be with you all.' Nor for himself will he
let the last impression be one of rebuke or even of
warning. He desires to show that his heart yearns
over them all; so he gathers them all—the partisans;
the poor brother that has fallen into sin; the lax ones
who, in their misplaced tenderness, had left him in his
sin; the misguided reasoners who had struck the
Resurrection out of the articles of the Christian creed
—he gathers them all into his final salutation, and he
says, 'Take and share my love—though I have had to
rebuke—amongst the whole of you.'

Is not that beautiful? And does not the juxta-
position of such messages in this farewell go deeper
than the revelation of Paul's character? May we not
see, in these terrible and tender thoughts thus inextricably intertwined and braided together, a revelation
of the true nature both of the terror and the tenderness of the Gospel which Paul preached? It is from
that point of view that I wish to look at them now.

I. I take first that thought—the terror of the fate of
the unloving.

Now, I must ask you for a moment's attention in

regard to these two untranslated words, *Anathema Maran-atha*. The first thing to be noticed is that the latter of them stands independently of the former, and forms a sentence by itself, as I shall have to show you presently. Anathema' means an offering, or a thing devoted; and its use in the New Testament arises from its use in the Greek translation of the Old Testament, where it is employed for persons and things that, in a peculiar sense, were set apart and devoted to God. In the story of the conquest of Canaan, for instance, we read of Jericho and other places, persons, or things that were, as our version somewhat unfortunately renders it, 'accursed,' or as it ought rather to be rendered, 'devoted,' or 'put under a ban.' And this 'devotion' was of such a sort as that the things or persons devoted were doomed to destruction. All the dreadful things that were done in the Conquest were the consequences of the persons that endured them being thus 'consecrated,' in a very dreadful sense, or set apart for God. The underlying idea was that evil things brought into contact with Him were necessarily destroyed with a swift destruction. That being the meaning of the word, it is clear that its use in my text is distinctly metaphorical, and that it suggests to us that the unloving, like those cities full of uncleanness, when they are brought into contact with the infinite love of the coming Judge, shrivel up and are destroyed.

The other word 'Maran-atha,' as I said, is to be taken as a separate sentence. It belongs to the dialect, which was probably the vernacular of Palestine in the time of Paul, and to which belong, for the most part, the other untranslated words that are scattered up and down the Gospels, such as 'Aceldama,' 'Ephphatha,' and the like. It means 'our Lord comes.' Why Paul

chose to use that untranslated scrap of another tongue
in a letter to a Gentile Church we cannot tell.   Perhaps
it had come to be a kind of watchword amongst the
early Jewish Christians, which came naturally to his
lips.   But, at any rate, the use of it here is distinctly to
confirm the warning of the previous clause, by pointing to the time at which that warning shall be fulfilled.
'If any man love not the Lord Jesus Christ, let him be
devoted and destroyed.   Our Lord comes.'   The only
other thing to be noticed by way of introduction is
that this first clause is not an imprecation, nor any
wish on the part of the Apostle, but is a solemn prophetic warning (acquiesced in by every righteous heart)
of that which will certainly come.   The significance of
the whole may be gathered into one simple sentence—
The coming of the Lord of Love is the destruction of
the unloving.

'Our Lord comes.'   Paul's Christianity gathered
round two facts and moments—one in the past, Christ
has come; one in the future, Christ will come.   For
memory, the coming by the cradle and the Cross; for
hope, the coming on His throne in glory; and between
these two moments, like the solid piers of a suspension
bridge, the frail structure of the Present hangs swinging.   In this day men have lost their expectation of the
one, and to a large extent their faith in the other.   But
we shall not understand Scripture unless we seek to
make as prominent in our thoughts as on its pages
that second coming as the complement and necessary
issue of the first.   It stands stamped on every line.   It
colours all the New Testament views of life.   It is used
as a motive for every duty, and as a magnet to draw
men to Jesus Christ by salutary dread.   There is no
hint in my text about the time of the Lord's coming,

no disturbing of the solemnity of the thought by non-essential details of chronology, so we may dismiss these from our minds. The fact is the same, and has the same force as a motive for life, whether it is to be fulfilled in the next moment or thousands of years hence, provided only that you and I are to be there when He comes.

There have been many comings in the past, besides the comings in the flesh. The days of the Lord that have already appeared in the history of the world are not few. One characteristic is stamped upon them all, and that is the swift annihilation of what is opposed to Him. The Bible has a set of standing metaphors by which to illustrate this thought of the Coming of the Lord—a flood, a harvest when the ears are ripe for the sickle, the waking of God from slumber, and the like; all suggesting similar thoughts. *The* day of the Lord, *the* coming of the Lord, will include and surpass all the characteristics which these lesser and premonitory judgment days presented in miniature. I do not enlarge on this theme. I would not play the orator about it if I could; but I appeal to your consciences, which, in the case of most of us, not only testify of right and wrong, but of responsibility, and suggest a judge to whom we are responsible. And I urge on each, and on myself, this simple question: Have I allowed its due weight on my life and character to that watchword of the ancient church—*Maran-atha*, ' our Lord cometh'?

Now, the coming of the Lord of Love is the annihilation of the unloving. The destruction implied in Anathema does not mean the cessation of Being, but a death which is worse than death, because it is a death in life. Suppose a man with all his past annihilated,

with all its effort foiled and crushed, with all its possessions evaporated and disappeared, and with his
memory and his conscience stung into clear-sighted
activity, so that he looks back upon his former self
and into his present self, and feels that it is all waste
and chaos, would not that fulfil the word of my text—
'Let him be Anathema'? And suppose that such a
man, in addition to these thoughts, and as the root and
the source of them, had ever the quivering consciousness that he was and must be in the presence of an
unloved Judge; have you not there the naked bones of
a very dreadful thing, which does not need any tawdry
eloquence of man to make it more solemn and more
real? The unloving heart is always ill at ease in the
presence of Him whom it does not love. The unloving
heart does not love, because it does not trust, nor see
the love. Therefore, the unloving heart is a heart that
is only capable of apprehending the wrathful side of
Christ's character. It is a heart devoid of the fruits of
love which are likeness and righteousness, 'without
which no man shall see the Lord,' nor stand the flash
of the brightness of His coming. So there is no cruelty
nor arbitrariness in the decree that the heart that
loves not, when brought into contact with the infinite
Lord of Love, must find in the touch death and not life,
darkness and not light, terror and not hope. Notice
that Paul's negation *is* a negation and not an affirmation. He does not say 'he that hateth,' but 'he that
doth not love.' The absence of the active emotion of
love, which is the child of faith, the parent of righteousness, the condition of joy in His presence, is
sufficient to ensure that this fate shall fall upon a
man. I durst not enlarge. I leave the truth on your
hearts.

II. Secondly, notice the present grace of the coming
Lord. 'Our Lord cometh. The grace of our Lord
Jesus Christ be with you all.' These two things are
not contradictory, but we often deal with them as if
they were. And some men lay hold of the one side of
the antithesis, and some men lay hold of the other, and
rend them apart, and make antagonistic theories of
Christianity out of them. But the real doctrine puts
the two together and says there is no terror without
tenderness, and there is no tenderness without terror.
If we sacrifice the aspects of the divine nature, as
revealed to us in the gentle Christ, which kindle a
wholesome dread, we have, all unwittingly, robbed the
aspects of the divine nature, which warm in us a
gracious love, of their power to inflame and to illuminate. You cannot have love which is anything nobler
than facile good nature and unrighteous indifference,
unless you have along with it aspects of God's character and government which ought to make some men
afraid. And you cannot keep these latter aspects from
being exaggerated and darkened into a Moloch of
cruelty, unless you remember that, side by side with
them, or rather underlying them and determining
them, are aspects of the divine nature to which only
child-like confidence and calm beatific returns of love
do rightly respond. The terror of the Lord is a garb
which our sins force upon the love of the Lord, and
when the one is presented it brings with it the other.
Never should they be parted in our thoughts or in our
teaching.

Note what that present grace is. It is a tenderness
which gathers into its embrace all these imperfect,
immoral, lax, heretical people in Corinth, as well as
everywhere else—'The grace of our Lord Jesus Christ

be with *you all.*' There were men in that church that
said, 'I am of Paul, I of Apollos, I of Cephas, I of
Christ.' There were men in that church that had
defiled their souls and their flesh, and corrupted the
community, and blasphemed the name of Christ by
such foul, sensual sin as was 'not even named among
the Gentiles.' There were men in that church so dead
to all the sanctities even of the communion-table as
that, with the bread between their teeth and the wine-
cup in their hands, one was hungry and another
drunken. There were men in that church, whose
Christianity was so anomalous and singularly fragmentary that they did not believe in the resurrection
of the dead. And yet Paul flings the great rainbow, as
it were, of Christ's enclosing love over them all. And
surely the love which gathers in such people leaves
none outside its sweep; and the tenderness which
stoops from heaven to pity, to pardon, to cleanse such
is a tenderness to which the weakest, saddest, sinful-
lest, foulest of the sons of men may confidently resort.
Let nothing rob you of this assurance, that Christ, the
coming Lord, is present with us all, and with all our
weak and wicked brethren, in the full condescension
of His all-embracing, all-hoping, all-forgetting, and all-
restoring love. All that we need, in order to get its
full sunshine into our hearts, is that we trust Him
utterly, and, so trusting, love Him back again with
that love which is the fulfilling of the Law and the
crown of the Gospel.

III. And now, lastly, note the tenderness, caught
from the Master Himself, of the servant who rebukes.

This last message of love from the Apostle himself,
in verse 24, is quite anomalous. There is no other
instance in his letters where he introduces himself and

his own love at the end, after he has pronounced the solemn benediction commending to Christ's grace. But here, as if he had felt that he must leave an impression of himself on their minds, which corresponded to the impression of his Master that he desired to leave, he deviates from his ordinary habit, and makes his last word a personal word—'*My love* be with you all in Christ Jesus.' Rebuke is the sign of love. Sharp condemnation may be the language of love. Plain warning of possible evils is the simple duty of love. So Paul folds all whom he has been rebuking in the warm embrace of his proffered love, which was the very cause of his rebuke. The healing balm of this closing message was to be applied to the wounds which his keen edged words had made, and to show that they were wounds by a surgeon, not by a foe. In effect, this parting smile of love says, 'I am not become your enemy because I tell you the truth; I show my love to you by the plainness and roughness of my words.' Generalise that, free it from its personal reference, and it just comes to this: There never was a shallower sneer than the sneer which is cast at Christianity, as if it were harsh, 'ferocious,' or unloving, when it preaches the terror of the Lord. No! rather, because the Gospel *is* a Gospel, it must speak plainly about death and destruction to the unloving. The danger signal is not to be blamed for a collision, which it is hoisted to avert; and it is a strange sign of an unfeeling and unsympathetic, or of a harsh and gloomy system, that it should tell men where they are driving, in order that they may never reach the miserable goal. 'Knowing, therefore, the terror of the Lord, we persuade men.' And when people say to us preachers, 'Is that your Gospel, a Gospel that talks about everlasting

destruction from the presence of the Lord at the glory
of His coming—is that your Gospel?' We can only
answer, 'Yes, it is! Because, so to talk, may by God's
mercy, secure that some who hear shall never know
anything of the wrath, save the hearing of it with the
ear, and may, by the warning of it, be drawn to the
Rock of Ages for safety and shelter from the storm.'

Therefore, dear friends, the upshot of all that I have
been feebly trying to say is just this; let us lay hold
with all our hearts, and by simple faith, of the present
grace of the coming, loving Lord and Judge. You can
do it. It is your only hope to do it. *Have* you done it?
If so, then you may lift up your heads to the throne,
and be glad, as those who know that their Friend and
Deliverer will come at last, to help, to bless, to save.
If not, dear friend, take the warning, that not to love
is to be shrivelled like a leaf in the flame, at that
coming which is life to them that love, and destruction
to all besides. 'Herein is our love made perfect, that
we may have boldness before Him in the day of judgment.'

II. CORINTHIANS

GOD'S YEA; MAN'S AMEN

'For how many soever be the promises of God, in Him is the yea: wherefore also through Him is the Amen.'—2 COR. i. 20 (R.V.).

THIS is one of the many passages the force and beauty of which are, for the first time, brought within the reach of an English reader by the alterations in the Revised Version. These are partly dependent upon the reading of the text and partly upon the translation. As the words stand in the Authorised Version, 'yea' and 'amen' seem to be very nearly synonymous expressions, and to point substantially to the same thing— viz. that Jesus Christ is, as it were, the confirmation and seal of God's promises. But in the Revised Version the alterations, especially in the pronouns, indicate more distinctly that the Apostle means two different things by the 'yea' and the 'amen.' The one is God's voice, the other is man's. The one has to do with the certainty of the divine revelation, the other has to do with the certitude of our faith in the revelation. When God speaks in Christ, He confirms everything that He has said before, and when we listen to God speaking in Christ, our lips are, through Christ, opened to utter our assenting 'Amen' to His great promises. So, then, we have the double form of our Lord's work, covering the whole ground of His relations to man, set forth in these two clauses, in the one of which

God's confirmation of His past revelations by Jesus Christ is treated of, and in the other of which the full and confident assent which men may give to that revelation is set before us. I deal, then, with these two points—God's certainties in Christ, and man's certitudes through Christ.

Now these two things do not always go together. We may be very certain, as far as our persuasion is concerned, of a very doubtful fact, or we may be very doubtful, as far as our persuasion is concerned, of a very certain fact. We speak about truths or facts as being certain, and we ought to mean by that, not how we think about them, but what they are in the evidence on which they rest. A certain truth is a truth which has its evidence irrefragable; and the only fitting attitude for men, in the presence of a certain truth, is to have a certitude of the truth. And these two things are, our Apostle tells us, both given to us in and through Jesus Christ. Let me deal, then, with these two sides.

I. First, God's certainties in Christ.

Of course the original reference of the text is to the whole series of great promises given in the Old Testament. These, says Paul, are sealed and confirmed to men by the revelation and work of Jesus Christ, but it is obvious that the principle which is good in reference to them is good on a wider field. I venture to take that extension, and to ask you to think briefly about some of the things that are made for us indubitably certain in Jesus Christ.

And, first of all, there is the certainty about God's heart. Everywhere else we have only peradventures, hopes, fears, guesses more or less doubtful, and roundabout inferences as to His disposition and attitude towards us. As one of the old divines says somewhere, 'All other ways of knowing God are like the bended bow. Christ is the straight string.' The only means by which, indubitably, as a matter of demonstration, men can be sure that God in the heavens has a heart of love towards them is by Jesus Christ. For consider what will make us sure of that. Nothing but facts; words are of little use, arguments are of little use. A revelation, however precious, which simply says to us, 'God is Love' is not sufficient for our need. We want to see love in operation if we are to be sure of it, and the only demonstration of the love of God is to witness the love of God in actual working. And you get it—where? On the Cross of Jesus Christ. I do not believe that anything else irrefragably establishes the fact for the yearning hearts of us poor men who want love, and yet cannot grope our way in amidst the mysteries and the clouds in providence and nature, except this—'Herein is love, not that we loved God, but that He loved us, and sent His Son to be the propitiation for our sins.'

The question may arise in some minds, Is there any need for proving God's love? The question never arose except within the limits of Christianity. It is only men who have lived all their lives in an atmosphere saturated by Christian sentiment and conviction that ever come to the point of saying, 'We do not want historical revelation to prove to us the fact of a loving God.' They would never have fancied that they did not need the revelation unless, unconsciously to themselves, and indirectly, all their thoughts had been coloured and illuminated by the revelation that they profess they reject. God as Love is 'our dearest faith, our ghastliest doubt,' and the only way to make

absolutely certain of the fact that His heart is full of
mercy to us is to look upon Him as He stands revealed
to us, not merely in the words of Christ, for, precious
as they are, these are the smallest part of His revelation, but in the life and in the death which open for
us the heart of God. Remember what He said Himself, *not* ' He who hath listened to Me, doth understand
the Father,' but ' He that hath *seen* Me hath seen the
Father.' ' In Him is yea,' and the hopes and shadowy
fore-revelations of the loving heart of God are confirmed by the fact of His life and death. God *establishes*,
not 'commends' as our translation has it, ' His love
towards us in that whilst we were yet sinners Christ
died for us.'

Further, in Him we have the certainty of pardon.
Every deep heart-experience amongst men has felt the
necessity of having a clear certainty and knowledge
about forgiveness. Men do not feel it always. A man
can skate over the surface of the great deeps that lie
beneath the most frivolous life, and may suppose, in
his superficial way of looking at things, that there is
no need for any definite teaching about sin and the
mode of dealing with it. But once bring that man
face to face, in a quiet hour, with the facts of his life
and of a divine law, and all that superficial ignoring
of evil in himself and of the dread of punishment and
consequences, passes away. I am sure of this, that no
religion will ever go far and last long and work
mightily, and lay a sovereign hand upon human life,
which has not a most plain and decisive message to
preach in reference to pardon. And I am sure of this,
that one reason for the comparative feebleness of
much so-called Christian teaching in this generation
is just that the deepest needs of a man's conscience are

not met by it. In a religion on which the whole spirit of a man may rest itself, there must be a very plain message about what is to be done with sin. The only message which answers to the needs of an awakened conscience and an alarmed heart is the old-fashioned message that Jesus Christ the Righteous has died for us sinful men. All other religions have felt after a clear doctrine of forgiveness, and all have failed to find it. Here is the divine 'Yea!' And on it alone we can suspend the whole weight of our soul's salvation. The rope that is to haul us out of the horrible pit and the miry clay had much need to be tested before we commit ourselves to it. There are plenty of easy-going superficial theories about forgiveness predominant in the world to-day. Except the one that says, 'In whom we have redemption through His blood, even the forgiveness of sin,' they are all like the rope let down into the dark mine to lift the captives beneath, half of the strands of which have been cut on the sharp edge above, and when the weight hangs on to it, it will snap. There is nothing on which a man who has once learned the tragical meaning and awful reality and depth of the fact of his transgression can suspend his forgiveness, except this, that 'Christ has died, the just for the unjust, to bring us unto God.' 'In Him the promise is yea.'

And, again, we have in Christ divine certainties in regard to life. We have in Him the absolutely perfect pattern to which we are to conform our whole doings. And so, notwithstanding that there may, and will still be many uncertainties and much perplexity, we have the great broad lines of morals and of duty traced with a firm hand, and all that we need to know of obligation and of perfectness lies in this—Be like Jesus

Christ! So the solemn commandments of the ethical side of Divine Revelation, as well as the promises of it, get their 'yea' in Jesus Christ, and He stands the Law of our lives.

We have certainties for life, in the matter of protection, guidance, supply of all necessity, and the like, treasured and garnered in Jesus Christ. For He not only confirms, but fulfils, the promises which God has made. If we have that dear Lord for our very own, and He belongs to us as He does belong to them who love Him and trust Him, then in Him we have in actual possession these promises, how many soever they be, which are given by God's other words.

Christ is Protean, and becomes everything to each man that each man requires. He is, as it were, 'a box where sweets compacted lie.' 'In Him are hid all the treasures,' not only of wisdom and knowledge, but of divine gifts, and we have but to go to Him in order to have that which at each moment as it emerges, we most require. As in some of those sunny islands of the Southern Pacific, one tree supplies the people with all that they need for their simple wants, fruit for their food, leaves for their houses, staves, thread, needles, clothing, drink, everything—so Jesus Christ, this Tree of Life, is Himself the sum of all the promises, and, having Him, we have everything that we need.

And, lastly, in Christ we have the divine certainties as to the Future over which, apart from Him, lie cloud and darkness. As I said about the revelation of the heart of God, so I say about the revelation of a future life—a verbal revelation is not enough. We have enough of arguments; what we want is facts. We have enough of man's peradventures about a future life, enough of evidence more or less valid to show

s

that it is 'probable,' or 'not inconceivable,' or 'more likely than not,' and so on and so on. What we want is that somebody shall cross the gulf and come back again, and so we get in the Resurrection of Christ the one fact on which men may safely rest their convictions of immortality, and I do not think that there is a second anywhere. On it alone, as I believe, hinges the whole answer to the question—'If a man die, shall he live again?' This generation is brought, in my reading of it, right up to this alternative—Christ's Resurrection,—or we die like the brutes that perish. 'All the promises of God in Him are yea.'

II. And now a word as to the second portion of my text—viz. man's certitudes, which answer to God's certainties.

The latter are *in* Christ, the former are *through* Christ. Now it is clear that the only fitting attitude for professing Christians in reference to these certainties of God is the attitude of unhesitating affirmation and joyful assent. Certitude is the fitting response to certainty.

There should be some kind of correspondence between the firmness with which we grasp, the tenacity with which we hold, the assurance with which we believe, these great truths, and the rock-like firmness and immovableness of the evidence upon which they rest. It is a poor compliment to God to come to His most veracious affirmations, sealed with the broad seal of His Son's life and death, and to answer with a hesitating 'Amen,' that falters and almost sticks in our throat. Build rock upon rock. Be sure of the certain things. Grasp with a firm hand the firm stay. Immovably cling to the immovable foundation; and though you be but like the limpet on the rock hold fast by the Rock, as the limpet does; for it is an insult to the certainty of the revelation, when there is hesitation in the believer.

I need not dwell for more than a moment upon the lamentable contrast which is presented between this certitude, which is our only fitting attitude, and the hesitating assent and half belief in which so many professing Christians pass their lives. The reasons for that are partly moral, partly intellectual. This is not a day which is favourable to the unhesitating avowal of convictions in reference to an unseen world, and many of us are afraid of being called narrow, or dogmatisers, and think it looks like breadth, and liberality, and culture, and I know not what, to say 'Well! perhaps it is, but I am not quite sure; I think it is, but I will not commit myself.' All the promises of God, which in Him are yea, ought through Him to get from us an 'Amen.'

There is a great deal that will always be uncertain. The firmer our convictions, the fewer will be the things that they grasp; but, if they be few, they will be large, and enough for us. These truths certified in Christ concerning the heart of God, the message of pardon, the law for life, the gifts of guidance, defence, and sanctifying, the sure and certain hope of immortality —these things we ought to be sure about, whatever borderland of uncertainty may lie beyond them. The Christian verb is 'we *know*,' not 'we hope, we calculate, we infer, we think,' but 'we *know*.' And it becomes us to apprehend for ourselves the full blessedness and power of the certitude which Christ has given to us by the certainties which he has brought us.

I need not speak about the blessedness of such a calm assurance, about the need of it for power, for peace, for effort, for fixedness in the midst of a world and age of change. But I must, before I close, point you to the only path by which that certitude is attainable. '*Through* Him is the amen.' He is the Door. The truths which He confirms are so inextricably intertwined with Himself that you cannot get them and put away Him. Christ's relation to Christ's Gospel is not the relation of other teachers to their words. You may accept the words of a Plato, whatever you think of the Plato who spoke the words. But you cannot separate Christ and His teaching in that fashion, and you must have *Him* if you are to get *it*. So, faith in Him, the intellectual acceptance of Him, as the authoritative and infallible Revealer, the bowing down of heart and will to Him as our Commander and our Lord, the absolute trust in Him as the foundation of all our hope and the source of all our blessedness—that is the way to certitude, and there is no other road that we can take.

If thus we keep near Him, our faith will bring us the present experience and fulfilment of the promises, and we shall be sure of them, because we have them already. And whilst men are asking, 'Do we know anything about God? Is there a God at all? Is there such a thing as forgiveness? Can anybody find anywhere absolute rules for his life? Is there anything beyond the grave but mist and darkness?' we can say, 'One thing I know, Jesus Christ is my Saviour, and in Him I know God, and pardon, and duty, and sanctifying, and safety, and immortality; and whatever is dark, this, at least, is sun-clear.' Get high enough up and you will be above the fog; and while the men down in it are squabbling as to whether there is anything outside the mist, you, from your sunny station, will see the far-off coasts, and haply catch some whiff of perfume from their shore, and see some glinting of a glory upon the shining turrets of 'the city that hath foundations.' We have a present possession of all the promises of God; and whoever doubts their certitude, the man who knows himself a son of God by faith, and has experience of forgiveness and guidance and answered prayer and hopes whose 'sweetness yieldeth proof that they were born for immortality,' *knows* the things which others question and doubt.

So live near Jesus Christ, and, holding fast by His hand, you may lift up your joyful 'Amen' to every one of God's 'Yeas.' For in Him we know the Father, in Him we know that we have the forgiveness of sins, in Him we know that God is near to bless and succour and guide, and in Him 'we know that, though our earthly house were dissolved, we have a building of God.' Wherefore we are always confident; and when the Voice from Heaven says 'Yea!' our choral shout may go up 'Amen! Thou art the faithful and true witness.'

ANOINTED AND STABLISHED

'Now He which stablisheth us with you in Christ, and hath anointed us, is God.'—2 COR. i. 21.

THE connection in which these words occur is a remarkable illustration of the Apostle's habit of looking at the most trivial things in the light of the highest truths. He had been obliged, as the context informs us, to abandon an intended visit to Corinth. The miserable crew of antagonists, who yelped at his heels all his life, seized this change of purpose as the occasion for a double-barrelled charge.

They said he was either fickle and infirm of purpose, or insincere, and saying 'Yea' with one side of his mouth and 'Nay' with the other. He rebuts this accusation with apparently quite disproportionate vehemence and great solemnity. He points in the context to the faithfulness of God, to the firm Gospel which he had preached, to God's great 'Yea!' as his answer. He says in effect, 'How could I, with such a word burning in my heart, move in a region of equivocation and double-dealing; or how could I, whose whole being is saturated with so firm and stable a Gospel, be unreliable and fickle? The message must make the messenger like itself. Communion with a faithful God must make faith-keeping men; the certainties of God's "Yea," and the certitudes of our "Amen," must influence our characters.' And so to suppose that a man, influenced by Christianity, is a weak, double-dealing, unsteadfast man is a contradiction in terms. In the text he carries his argument a step further, and points, not only to the power of the Gospel to steady and confirm, but also to the fact that God Himself communicates to the believing soul Christian stability by the anointing which He bestows.

So, then, we have in these words the declaration that inflexible, immovable steadfastness is a mark of a Christian, and that this Christian steadfastness, without which there is no Christianity worth the naming, is a direct gift from God Himself by means of that great anointing which He confers upon men. To that thought, in one or two of its aspects, I ask your attention.

I. Notice the deep source of this Christian steadfastness.

The language of the original, carefully considered,

seems to me to bear this interpretation, that the 'anointing' of the second clause is the means of the 'establishing' of the first—that is to say, that God confers Christian steadfastness of character by the bestowment of the unction of His Divine Spirit.

Now notice how deep Paul digs in order to get a foundation for a common virtue. There are many ways by which men may cultivate the tenacity and steadfastness of purpose which ought to mark us all. Much discipline may be brought to bear in order to secure that; but the text says that the deepest ground upon which it can be rested is nothing less divine and solemn than this, the actual communication to men, to feeble, vacillating, fluctuating wills, and treacherous, wayward, wandering hearts, of the strength and fixedness which are given by God's own Spirit.

I suppose I need not remind you that from beginning to end of Scripture, 'anointing' is taken as the symbol of the communication of a true divine influence. The oil poured on the head of prophet, priest, and king was but the expression of the communication to the recipient of a divine influence which fitted him as well as designated him, for the office that he filled. And although it is aside from my present purpose, I may just, in a sentence, point to the felicity of the emblem. The flowing oil smoothes the surface upon which it is spread, supples the limbs, and is nutritive and illuminating; thus giving an appropriate emblem of the secret, silent, quickening, nourishing, enlightening influences of that Spirit which God gives to all His sons.

And inasmuch as here this oil of the Divine Spirit is stated as being the true ground and basis of

Christian steadfastness, it is obvious that the anointing intended cannot be that of mere designation to, and inspiration for, apostolic or other office, but must be the universal possession of all Christian men and women. 'Ye,' says another Apostle, speaking to the whole democracy of the Christian Church, and not to any little group of selected aristocrats therein—'ye have an unction from the Holy One,' and every man and woman who has a living grasp of the living Christ, receives from Him this great gift.

Then, notice further that this anointing by a Divine Spirit, which is a true source of life to those that possess it, is derived from, and parallel with, Christ's anointing. We use the word 'Christ' as a proper name, and forget what it means. The 'Christ' is *the Anointed One*. And do you think that it was a mere accident, or the result of a scanty vocabulary, which compelled the Apostle, in these two contiguous clauses, to use cognate words when he said:—'He that establisheth us with you in the *Anointed*, and hath *anointed* us, is God'? Did he not mean to say thereby, 'Each of you in a very true sense, if you are a Christian, is a *Christ*'? You, too, are anointed; you, too, are God's Messiahs. On you in a measure the same Spirit rests which dwelt without measure in Him. The chief of Christ's gifts to the Church is the gift of His own life. All His brethren are anointed with the oil that was poured upon His head, even as the oil upon Aaron's locks percolated to the very skirts of his garments. Being anointed with the anointing which was on Him, all His people may claim an identity of nature, may hope for an identity of destiny, and are bound to a prolongation of part of His function and a similarity of character. If He by that anointing was made

Prophet, Priest, and King for the world, all His children partake of these offices in subordinate but real fashion, and are prophets to make God known to men, priests to offer up spiritual sacrifices, and kings at least over themselves, and, if they will, over a world which obeys and serves those that serve and love God. Ye are anointed—'Messiahs' and 'Christs,' by derivation of the life of Jesus Christ.

And if these things be true, it is plain enough how this divine unction, which is granted to all Christians, lies at the root of steadfastness.

We talk a great deal about the gentleness of Christ; we cannot celebrate it too much, but we may forget that it is the gentleness of strength. We do not sufficiently mark the masculine features in that character, the tremendous tenacity of will, the inflexible fixedness of purpose, the irremovable constancy of obedience in the face of all temptations to the contrary. The figure that rises before us is that of the Christ yearning over weaklings far oftener than it is that of the Christ with knitted brow, and tightened lips, and far-off gazing eye, 'steadfastly setting His face to go to Jerusalem,' and followed as He pressed up the rocky road from Jericho, by that wondering group, astonished at the rigidity of purpose that was stamped on His features. That Christ gives us His Spirit to make us tenacious, constant, righteously obstinate, inflexible in the pursuit of all that is lovely and of good report, like Himself. That Divine Spirit will cure the fickleness of our natures; for our wills are never fixed till they are fixed in obedience, and never free until they elect to serve Him. That Divine Spirit will cure the wandering of our hearts and bind us to Himself. It will lift us above the selfish and cowardly dependence on externals and surroundings, men and things, in which we are all tempted to live. We are all too like aneroid barometers, that go up and down with every variation of a foot or two in our level, but if we have the Spirit of Christ dwelling in us, it will cut the bonds that bind us to the world, and give us possession of a deeper love than can be sustained by, or is derived from, these superficial sources. The true possession of the Divine Spirit, if I might use such a metaphor, sets a man on an insulating stool, and all the currents that move round about him are powerless to reach him. If we have that Divine Spirit within us, it will give us an experience of the preciousness and the truth, the certitude and the sweetness, of Christ's Gospel, which will make it impossible that we should ever 'cast away the confidence which has such 'recompense of reward.' No man will be surely bound to the truth and person of Christ with bonds that cannot be snapped, except he who in his heart has the knowledge of Him which is possession, and by the gift of the Divine Spirit is knit to Jesus Christ.

So, dear friends, whilst the world is full of wise words about steadfastness, and exalts determination of character and fixity of purpose, rightly, as the basis of much good, our Gospel comes to us poor, light, thistledown creatures, and lets us see how we can be steadfast and settled by being fastened to a steadfast and settled Christ. When storms are raging they lash light articles on deck to holdfasts. Let us lash ourselves to the abiding Christ, and we, too, shall abide.

II. In the next place, notice the aim or purpose of this Christian steadfastness.

'He stablisheth us with you in Christ,' or as the original has it even more significantly, *into* or *'unto* Christ.' Now that seems to me to imply two things—first, that our steadfastness, made possible by our possession of that Divine Spirit, is steadfastness in our relations to Jesus Christ. We are established in reference or in regard to Him. In other words, what Paul here means is, first, a fixed conviction of the truth that He is the Christ, the Son of God, the Saviour of the world, and my Saviour. That is the first step. Men who are steadfast without their intellect guiding and settling the steadfastness are not steadfast, but obstinate and pigheaded. We are meant to be guided by our understandings, and no fixity is anything better than the immobility of a stone, unless it be based upon a distinct and whole-brained intellectual acceptance of Jesus Christ as the All-in-all for us, for life and death, for inward and outward being.

Paul means, next, a steadfastness in regard to Christ in our trust and love   Surely if from Him there is for ever streaming out an unbroken flow of tenderness, there should be ever on our sides an equally unbroken opening of our hearts for the reception of His love, and an equally uninterrupted response to it in our grateful affection. There can be no more damning condemnation of the vacillations and fluctuations of Christian men's affections than the steadfastness of Christ's love to them. He loves ever; He is unalterable in the communication and effluence of His heart. Surely it is most fitting that we should be steadfast in our devotion and answering love to Him. And Paul means not only fixedness of intellectual convict' on and continuity of loving response, but also habitual obedience, which is always ready to do His will.

So we should answer His 'Yea!' with our 'Amen!' and having an unchanging Christ to rest upon, we should rest upon Him unchanging. The broken, fluctuating affections and trusts and obediences which mark so much of the average Christian life of this day are only too sad proofs of how scant our possession of that Spirit of steadfastness must be supposed to be. God's 'Yea' is answered by our faltering 'Amen'; God's truth is hesitatingly accepted; God's love is partially returned; God's work is slothfully and negligently done. 'Be ye steadfast, unmovable, always abounding in the work of the Lord.'

Another thought is suggested by these words—viz. that such steadfastness as we have been trying to describe has for its result a deeper penetration into Jesus Christ and a fuller possession of Him. The only way by which we can grow nearer and nearer to our Lord is by steadfastly keeping beside Him. You cannot get the spirit of a landscape unless you sit down and gaze, and let it soak into you. The cheap tripper never sees the lake. You cannot get to know a man until you summer and winter with him. No subject worth studying opens itself to the hasty glance. Was it not Sir Isaac Newton who used to say, 'I have no genius, but I keep a subject before me'? 'Abide in Me; as the branch cannot bear fruit except it abide in the vine, no more can ye except ye abide in Me.' Continuous, steadfast adhesion to Him is the condition of growing up into His likeness, and receiving more and more of His beauty into our waiting hearts. 'Wait on the Lord; wait, I say, on the Lord.'

III. Lastly, notice the very humble and commonplace sphere in which the Christian steadfastness manifests itself.

It was nothing of more importance than that Paul had said he was going to Corinth, and did not, on which he brings all this array of great principles to bear. From which I gather just this thought, that the highest gifts of God's grace and the greatest truths of God's Word are meant to regulate the tiniest things in our daily life. It is no degradation to the lightning to have to carry messages. It is no profanation of the sun to gather its rays into a burning glass to light a kitchen fire with. And it is no unworthy use of the Divine Spirit that God gives to His children, to say it will keep a man from hasty and precipitate decisions as to little things in life, and from chopping and changing about, with a levity of purpose and without a sufficient reason. If our religion is not going to influence the trifles, what is it going to influence? Our life is made up of trifles, and if these are not its field, where is its field? You may be quite sure that, if your religion does not influence the little things, it will never influence the great ones. If it has not power enough to guide the horses when they are at a slow, sober walk, what do you think it will do when they are at a gallop and plunging? 'He that is faithful in that which is least is faithful also in much.' So let us see to two things—first, that all our religion is worked into our life, for only so much of it as is so inwrought is our religion—and, second, that all our life is brought under the sway of motives derived from our religion; for only in proportion as it is, will it be pure and good.

And as regards this special virtue and prime quality of steadfastness and fixedness of purpose, you can do no good in the world without it. Unless a man can hold his own, and turn an obstinate negative to the temptations that lie thick about him, he will never come to any good at all, either in this life or in the next. The basis of all excellence is a wholesome disregard of externals, and the cultivation of a strong self-reliant and self-centred, because God-trusting and Christ-centred, will. And I tell you, especially you young men and women, if you want to do or be anything worth doing or being, you must try to get your natures hardened into being 'steadfast, unmovable.' There is only one infallible way of doing it, and that is to let the 'strong Son of God' live in you, and in Him to find your strength for resistance, your strength for obedience, your strength for submission. 'I have set the Lord always before me; because He is at my right hand, I shall not be moved.'

There are two types of men in the world. The one has his emblem in the chaff, rootless, with no hold, swept out of the threshing-floor by every gust of wind. That the picture of many whose principles lie at the mercy of the babble of tongues round about them, whose rectitude goes at a puff of temptation, like the smoke out of a chimney when the wind blows; who have no will for what is good, but live as it happens. The other type of man has his emblem in the tree, rooted deep, and therefore rising high, with its roots going as far underground as its branches spread in the blue, and therefore green of leaf and rich of fruit. 'We are made partakers of Christ if we hold fast the beginning of our confidence, steadfast until the end.'

SEAL AND EARNEST

'Who hath also sealed us, and given the earnest of the Spirit in our hearts.'
2 COR. i. 22.

THERE are three strong metaphors in this and the preceding verse—'anointing,' 'sealing,' and 'giving the earnest'—all of which find their reality in the same divine act. These three metaphors all refer to the same subject, and what that subject is is sufficiently explained in the last of them. The 'earnest' consists of 'the Spirit in our hearts,' and the same explanation might have been appended to both the preceding clauses, for the 'anointing' is the anointing of the Spirit, and the 'seal' is the seal of the Spirit. Further, these three metaphors all refer to one and the same act. They are not three things, but three aspects of one thing, just as a sunbeam might be regarded either as the source of warmth, or of light, or of chemical action. So the one gift of the one Spirit, 'anoints,' 'seals,' and is the 'earnest.' Further, these three metaphors all declare a universal prerogative of Christians. Every man that loves Jesus Christ has the Spirit in the measure of his faith, 'and if any man have not the Spirit of Christ he is none of His.'

I. Note the first metaphor in the text—the 'seal' of the Spirit.

A seal is impressed upon a recipient material made soft by warmth, in order to leave there a copy of itself. Now it is not fanciful, nor riding a metaphor to death, when I dwell upon these features of the emblem in order to suggest their analogies in Christian life. The Spirit of God comes into our spirits, and by gentle contact impresses upon the material, which was intractable until it was melted by the genial warmth of faith and love, the likeness of Himself, but yet so as that prominences correspond to the hollows, and what is in relief in the one is sunk in the other. Expand that general statement for a moment or two.

The effect of all the divine indwelling, which is the characteristic gift of Christ to every Christian soul, is to mould the recipient into the image of the divine inhabitant. There is in the human spirit—such are its dignity amidst its ruins, and its nobility shining through its degradation—a capacity of receiving that image of God which consists not only in voluntary and intelligent action and the consciousness of personal being, but in the love of the things that are fair, and in righteousness, and true holiness. His Spirit, entering into a heart, will make that heart wise with its own wisdom, strong with some infusion of its own strength, gracious with some drops of its own grace, gentle with some softening from its own gentleness, holy with some purity reflected from its own transcendent whiteness. The Spirit, which is life, moulds the heart into which it enters to a kindred, and, therefore, similar life.

There are, however, characteristics in this 'seal' of the Spirit which are not so much copies as correspondences. That is to say, just as what is convex in the seal is concave in the impression, and *vice versâ*, so, when that Divine Spirit comes into our spirits, its promises will excite faith, its gifts will breed desire; to every bestowment there will answer an opening receptivity. Recipient love will correspond to the love that longs to dispense, the sense of need to the divine fulness and sufficiency, emptiness to abundance, prayers to promises; the cry 'Abba! Father'! the yearning consciousness of sonship, to the word 'Thou art My

Son'; and the upward eye of aspiration and petition, and necessity, and waiting, to the downward glance of love bestowing itself. The open heart answers to the extended hand, and the seal which God's Spirit impresses upon the heart that is submitted to it, has the two-fold character of resemblance in moral nature and righteousness, and of correspondence as regards the mysteries of the converse between the recipient man and the giving God.

Then, mark that the material is made capable of receiving the stamp, because it is warmed and softened. That is to say, faith must prepare the heart for the sanctifying indwelling of that Divine Spirit. The hard wax may be struck with the seal, but it leaves no trace. God does not do with man as the coiner does with his blanks, put them cold into a press, and by violence from without stamp an image upon them, but He does as men do with a seal, warms the wax first, and then, with a gentle, firm touch, leaves the likeness there. So, brother! learn this lesson: if you wish to be good, lie under the contact of the Spirit of righteousness, and see that your heart is warm.

Still further, note that this aggregate of Christian character, in likeness and correspondence, is the true sign that we belong to God. The seal is the mark of ownership, is it not? Where the broad arrow has been impressed, everybody knows that that is royal property. And so this seal of God's Divine Spirit, in its effects upon my character, is the one token to myself and to other people that I belong to God, and that He belongs to me. Or, to put it into plain English, the best reason for any man's being regarded as a Christian is his possession of the likeness and correspondence to God which that Divine Spirit gives. Likeness and correspondence, I say, for the one class of results is the more open for the observation of the world, and the other class is of the more value for ourselves. I believe that Christian people ought to have, and are meant by that Divine Spirit dwelling in them to have, a consciousness that they are Christians and God's children, for their own peace and rest and joy. But you cannot use that in demonstration to other people; you may be as sure of it as you will, in your inmost hearts, but it is no sign to anybody else. And, on the other hand, there may be much of outward virtue and beauty of character which may lead other people to say about a man: '*That* is a good Christian man, at any rate,' and yet there may be in the heart an all but absolute absence of any joyful assurance that we are Christ's, and that He belongs to us. So the two facts must go together. Correspondence, the spirit of sonship which meets His taking us as sons, the faith which clasps the promise, the reception which welcomes bestowment, must be stamped upon the inward life. For the outward life there must be the manifest impress of righteousness upon my actions, if there is to be any real seal and token that I belong to Him. God writes His own name upon the men that are His. All their goodness, their gentleness, patience, hatred of evil, energy and strenuousness in service, submission in suffering, with whatsoever other radiance of human virtue may belong to them, are really 'His mark!'

There is no other worth talking about, and to you Christian men I come and say, Be very sure that your professions of inward communion and happy consciousness that you are Christ's are verified to yourself and to others by a plain outward life of righteousness like the Lord's. Have you got that seal stamped upon your lives, like the hall-mark that says, 'This is genuine silver, and no plated Brummagem stuff'? Have you got that seal of a visible righteousness and every-day purity to confirm your assertion that you belong to Christ? Is it woven into the whole length of your being, like the scarlet thread that is spun into every Admiralty cable as a sign that it is Crown property? God's seal, visible to me and to nobody else, is my consciousness that I am His; but that consciousness is vindicated and delivered from the possibility of illusion or hypocrisy, only when it is checked and fortified by the outward evidence of the holy life which the Spirit of God has wrought.

Further, this sealing, which is thus the token of God's ownership, is also the pledge of security. A seal is stamped in order that there may be no tampering with what it seals; that it may be kept safe from all assaults, thieves, and violence. And in the metaphor of our text there is included this thought, too, which is also of an intensely practical nature. For it just comes to this—our true guarantee that we shall come at last into the sweet security and safety of the perfect state is present likeness to the indwelling Spirit and present reception of divine grace. The seal is the pledge of security, just because it is the mark of ownership. When, by God's Spirit dwelling in us, we are led to love the things that are fair, and to long after more posses- sion of whatever things are of good report, that is like God's hoisting His flag upon a newly-annexed territory. And is He going to be so careless in the preservation of His property as that He will allow that which is thus acquired to slip away from Him? Does He account us as of so small value as to hold us with so slack a hand? But no man has a right to rest on the assurance of

God's saving him into the heavenly kingdom, unless He is saving him at this moment from the devil and his own evil heart. And, therefore, I say the Christian character, in its outward manifestations and in its sweet inward secrets of communion, is the guarantee that we shall not fall. Rest upon Him, and He will hold you up. We are 'kept by the power of God unto salvation,' and that power keeps us and that final salvation becomes ours, 'through faith.'

II. Now, secondly, turn to the other emblem, that 'earnest' which consists in like manner 'of the Spirit.'

The 'earnest,' of course, is a small portion of purchase-money, or wages, or contract-money, which is given at the making of a bargain, as an assurance that the whole amount will be paid in due time. And, says the Apostle, this seal is also an earnest. It not only makes certain God's ownership and guarantees the security of those on whom it is impressed, but it also points onwards to the future, and at once guarantees that, and to a large extent reveals the nature of it. So, then, we have here two thoughts on which I touch.

The Christian character and experience are the earnest of the inheritance, in the sense of being its guarantee, inasmuch as the experiences of the Christian life here are plainly immortal. The Resurrection of Jesus Christ from the dead is the objective and external proof of a future life. The facts of the Christian life, its aspirations, its communion, its clasp of God as its very own, are the subjective and inward proofs of a future life. As a matter of fact, if you will take the Old Testament, you will see that the highest summits in it, to which the hope of immortality soared, spring directly from the experience of deep and blessed communion with the living God. When the Psalmist said 'Thou wilt not leave my soul in *Sheol*; neither wilt Thou suffer Thy Holy One to see corruption,' he was speaking a conviction that had been floated into his mind on the crest of a great wave of religious enjoyment and communion. And, in like manner, when the other Psalmist said, 'Thou art the strength of my heart, and my portion for ever,' he was speaking of the glimpse that he had got of the land that was very far off, from the height which he had climbed on the Mount of fellowship with God. And for us, I suppose that the same experience holds good. Howsoever much we may say that we believe in a future life and in a heaven, we really grasp them as facts that will be true about ourselves, in the proportion in which we are living here in direct contact and communion with God. The conviction of immortality is the distinct and direct result of the present enjoyment of communion with Him, and it is a reasonable result. No man who has known what it is to turn himself to God with a glow of humble love, and to feel that he is not turning his face to vacuity, but to a Face that looks on him with love, can believe that anything can ever come to destroy that communion. What have faith, love, aspiration, resignation, fellowship with God, to do with death? They cannot be cut through with the stroke that destroys physical life, any more than you can divide a sunbeam with a sword. It unites again, and the impotent edge passes through and has effected nothing. Death can shear asunder many bonds, but that invisible bond that unites the soul to God is of adamant, against which his scythe is in vain. Death is the grim porter that opens the door of a dark hole and herds us into it as sheep are driven into a slaughter-house. But to those who have learned what it is to lay a trusting hand in God's hand, the

grim porter is turned into the gentle damsel, who keeps
the door, and opens it for light and warmth and safety
to the hunted prisoner that has escaped from the
dungeon of life. Death cannot touch communion, and
the consciousness of communion with God is the earnest
of the inheritance.

It is so for another reason also. All the results of
the Divine Spirit's sealing of the soul are manifestly incomplete, and as manifestly tend towards completeness.
The engine is clearly working now at half-speed. It is
obviously capable of much higher pressure than it is
going at now. Those powers in the Christian man can
plainly do a great deal more than they ever have done
here, and are meant to do a great deal more. Is this
imperfect Christianity of ours, our little faith so soon
shattered, our little love so quickly disproved, our
faltering resolutions, our lame performances, our
earthward cleavings—are these things all that Jesus
Christ's bitter agony was for, and all that a Divine Spirit
is able to make of us? Manifestly, here is but a
segment of the circle, in heaven is the perfect round;
and the imperfections, so far as life is concerned, in the
work of so obviously divine an Agent, cry aloud for a
region where tendency shall become result, and all that
it was possible for Him to make us we shall become.
The road evidently leads upwards, and round that sharp
corner where the black rocks come so near each other
and our eyesight cannot travel, we may be sure it goes
steadily up still to the top of the pass, until it reaches
'the shining table-lands whereof our God Himself is
Sun and Moon,' and brings us all to the city set on a hill.

And, further, that divine seal is the earnest, inasmuch
as itself is part of the whole. The truest and the
loftiest conception that we can form of heaven is as

being the perfecting of the religious experience of earth. The shilling or two, given to the servant in old-fashioned days, when he was hired, is of the same currency as the balance that he is to get when the year's work is done. The small payment to-day comes out of the same purse, and is coined out of the same specie, and is part of the same currency of the same kingdom, as what we get when we go yonder and count the endless riches to which we have fallen heirs at last. You have but to take the faith, the love, the obedience, the communion of the highest moments of the Christian life on earth, and free them from all their limitations, subtract from them all their imperfections, multiply them to their superlative possibility, and endow them with a continual power of growth, and stretch them out to absolute eternity, and you get heaven. The earnest is of a piece with the inheritance.

So, dear brethren, here is a gift offered for us all, a gift which our feebleness sorely needs, a gift for every timid nature, for every weak will, for every man, woman, and child beset with snares and fighting with heavy tasks, the offer of a reinforcement as real and as sure to bring victory as when, on that day when the fate of Europe was determined, after long hours of conflict, the Prussian bugles blew, and the English commander knew that (with the fresh troops that came on the field) victory was made certain. So you and I may have in our hearts the Spirit of God, the spirit of strength, the spirit of love and of a sound mind, the spirit of adoption, the spirit of wisdom and of revelation in the knowledge of Him, to enlighten our darkness, to bind our hearts to Him, to quicken and energise our souls, to make the weakest among us strong, and the strong as an angel of God. And the condition on which

we may get it is this simple one which the Apostle
lays down ; '*After that ye believed,* ye were sealed with
that Holy Spirit of promise, which is the earnest of our
inheritance.' The Christ, who is the Lord and Giver of
the Spirit, has shown us how its blessed influences may
be ours when, on the great day of the feast, He stood
and cried with a voice that echoes across the centuries,
and is meant for each of us, ' If any man thirsts, let
him come unto Me and drink. He that believeth in
Me, out of his belly shall flow rivers of living water.
This spake He of the Spirit which they that believe on
Him should receive.'

THE TRIUMPHAL PROCESSION

'Thanks be unto God, which always leadeth us in triumph in Christ and maketh
manifest through us the savour of His knowledge in every place.'—2 COR. ii. 14
(R. V.)

I SUPPOSE most of us have some knowledge of what a
Roman Triumph was, and can picture to ourselves the
long procession, the victorious general in his chariot
with its white horses, the laurelled soldiers, the sullen
captives, with suppressed hate flashing in their sunken
eyes, the wreathing clouds of incense that went up
into the blue sky, and the shouting multitude of
spectators. That is the picture in the Apostle's mind
here. The Revised Version correctly alters the translation into 'Thanks unto God which always *leadeth us
in* triumph in Christ.'

Paul thinks of himself and of his coadjutors in
Christian work as being conquered captives, made to
follow their Conqueror and to swell His triumph. He
is thankful to be so overcome. What was deepest

degradation is to him supreme honour. Curses in many a strange tongue would break from the lips of the prisoners who had to follow the general's victorious chariot. But from Paul's lips comes irrepressible praise; he joins in the shout of acclamation to the Conqueror.

And then he passes on to another of the parts of the ceremonial. As the wreathing incense appealed at once to two senses, and was visible in its curling clouds of smoke, and likewise fragrant to the nostrils, so says Paul, with a singular combination of expression, 'He maketh *manifest*,' that is visible, the *savour* of His knowledge. From a heart kindled by the flame of the divine love there will go up the odour of a holy life visible and fragrant, sweet and fair.

And thus all Christians, and not Christian workers only in the narrower sense of the word, who may be doing evangelistic work, have set before them in these great words the very ideal and secret of their lives.

There are three things here, on each of which I touch as belonging to the true notion of a Christian life—the conquered captive; that captive partaking in the triumph of his Conqueror; and the conquered captive led as a trophy and a witness to the Conqueror's power. These three things, I think, explain the Apostle's thoughts here. Let me deal with them now.

I. First then, let us look at that thought of all Christians being in the truest sense conquered captives, bound to the chariot wheels of One who has overcome them.

The image implies a prior state of hostility and alienation. Now, do not let us exaggerate, let us take Paul's own experience. He is speaking about himself here; he is not talking doctrine, he is giving us autobiography, and he says, 'I was an enemy, and I have been conquered.'

What sort of an enemy was he? Well! He says that before he became a Christian he lived a pure, virtuous, respectable life. He was a man 'as touching the righteousness which is in the law, blameless.' Observant of all relative duties, sober, temperate, chaste; no man could say a word against him; he knew nothing against himself. His conscience acquitted him of wrong: 'I thought I ought to do many things,' as I did them. And yet, looking back from his present point of view upon a life thus adorned with many virtues, pure from all manifest corruption, to a large extent regulated by conscientious and religious motives of a kind, he says, 'Notwithstanding all that, I was an enemy.' Why? Because the retrospect let him see that his life was barren of the deepest faith and the purest love. And so I come to some of my friends here now, and I say to you, 'Change the name, and the story is true about you,' respectable people, who are trying to live pure and righteous lives, doing all duties that present themselves to you with a very tolerable measure of completeness and abominating and trying to keep yourselves from the things that your consciences tell you are wrong, yet needing to be conquered, in the deepest recesses of your wills and your hearts, before you become the true subjects of the true King. I do not want to exaggerate, nor to say of the ordinary run of people who listen to us preachers, that they commit manifest sins, 'gross as a mountain, open, palpable.' Some of you do, no doubt, for, in every hundred people, there are always some whose lives are foul and whose memories are stained and horrible; but the run of you are not like that. And yet I ask you, has your will been bowed and broken, and your heart overcome and conquered by this mighty Prince, the Prince of Peace, the Prince of Life? Unless it has, for all your righteousness and respectability, for all your outward religion and real religiousness of a sort, you are still hostile and rebellious, in your inmost hearts. That is the basis of the representation of my text.

What else does it suggest? It suggests the wonderful struggle and victory of weaponless love. As was said about the first Christian emperor, so it may be said about the great Emperor in the heavens, '*In hoc signo vinces!*' By this sign thou shalt conquer. For His only weapon is the Cross of His Son, and He fights only by the manifestation of infinite love, sacrifice, suffering, and pity. He conquers as the sun conquers the thick-ribbed ice by raying down its heat upon it, and melting it into sweet water. So God in Christ fights against the mountains of man's cold, hard sinfulness and alienation, and by the warmth of His own radiation turns them all into rivers that flow in love and praise. He conquers simply by forbearance and pity and love.

And what more does this first part of my text say to us? It tells us, too, of the true submission of the conquered captive; how we are conquered when we perceive and receive His love; how there is nothing else needed to win us all for Him except only that we shall recognise His great love to us.

This picture of the triumph comes with a solemn appeal and commandment to every one of us professing Christians. Think of these men, dragged at the conqueror's chariot-wheels, abject, with their weapons broken, with their resistance quelled, chained, yoked, haled away from their own land, dependent for life or death on the caprice of the general who rode before them there. It is a picture of what you Christian men and women are bound to be if you believe that God in Christ has loved you as we have been saying that He does. For abject submission, unconditional surrender, the yielding up of our whole will to Him, the yielding of all our possessions as His vassals—these are the duties that are correspondent to the facts of the case.

If we are thus won by infinite love, and not our own, but bought with a price, no conquered king, dragged at an emperor's chariot-wheels, was ever half as absolutely and abjectly bound to be his slave, and to live or die by his breath, as you are bound to your Master. You are Christians in the measure in which you are the captives of His spear and of His bow; in the measure in which you hold your territories as vassal kings, in the measure in which you say, stretching out your willing hands for the fetters, 'Lord! here am I, do with me as Thou wilt.' 'I am not mine own; be Thou my will, my Emperor, my Commander, my all.' Loyola used to say, as the law of his order, that every man that became a member of the Society of Jesus was to be like as a staff in a man's hand, or like as a corpse. It was a blasphemous and wicked claim, but it is but a poor fragmentary statement of the truth about those of us who enter the real Society of Jesus, and put ourselves in His hands to be wielded as His staff and His rod, and submit ourselves to Him, not as a corpse, but yield yourselves to our Christ 'as those that are alive from the dead.'

II. Now we have here, as part of the ideal of the Christian life, the conquered captives partaking in the triumph of their general.

Two groups made up the triumphal procession—the one that of the soldiers who had fought for, the other that of the prisoners who had fought against, the leader. And some commentators are inclined to believe that the Apostle is here thinking of himself and his fellows as belonging to the conquering army, and not to the conquered enemy. That seems to me to be less probable and in accordance with the whole image than the explanation which I have adopted. But be that as it may, it suggests to us this thought, that in the deepest reality in that Christian life of which all this metaphor is but the expression, they who are conquered foes become conquering allies. Or, to put it into other words—to be triumphed over by Christ is to triumph with Christ. And the praise which breaks from the Apostle's lips suggests the same idea. He pours out his thanks for that which he recognises as being no degradation but an honour, and a participation in his Conqueror's triumph.

We may illustrate that thought, that to be triumphed over by Christ is to triumph with Christ, by such considerations as these. This submission of which I have been speaking, abject and unconditional, extending to life and death, this submission and captivity is but another name for liberty. The man who is absolutely dependent upon Jesus Christ is absolutely independent of everything and everybody besides, himself included. That is to say, to be His slave is to be everybody else's master, and when we bow ourselves to Him, and take upon us the chains of glad obedience, and life-deep as well as life-long consecration, then He breaks off all other chains from our hands, and will not suffer that any others should have a share with Him in the possession of His servant. If you are His servants you are free from all besides; if you give yourselves up to Jesus Christ, in the measure in which you give yourselves up to Him, you will be set at liberty from the worst of all slaveries, that is the slavery of your own will and your own weakness, and your own tastes and fancies. You will be set at liberty from dependence upon men, from thinking about their opinion. You will be set at liberty from your dependence upon externals, from feeling as if you could not live unless you had this, that, or the other person or thing. You will be emancipated from fears and hopes which torture the men who strike their roots no deeper than this visible film of time which floats upon the surface of the great, invisible abyss of Eternity. If you have Christ for your Master you will be the masters of the world, and of time and sense and men and all besides; and so, being triumphed over by Him, you will share in His triumph.

And again, we may illustrate the same principle in yet another way. Such absolute and entire submission of will and love as I have been speaking about is the highest honour of a man. It was a degradation to be dragged at the chariot-wheels of conquering general, emperor, or consul—it broke the heart of many a barbarian king, and led some of them to suicide rather than face the degradation. It is a degradation to submit ourselves, even as much as many of us do, to the domination of human authorities, or to depend upon men as much as many of us do for our completeness and our satisfaction. But it is the highest ennobling of humanity that it shall lay itself down at Christ's feet, and let Him put His foot upon its neck. It is the exaltation of human nature to submit to Christ. The true nobility are those that 'come over with the Conqueror.' When we yield ourselves to Him, and let Him be our King, then the patent of nobility is given to us, and we are lifted in the scale of being. All our powers and faculties are heightened in their exercise, and made more blessed in their employment, because we have bowed ourselves to His control. And so to be triumphed over by Christ is to triumph with Christ.

And the same thought may be yet further illustrated. That submission which I have been speaking about so unites us to our Lord that we share in all that belongs to Him and thus partake in His triumph. If in will and heart we have yielded ourselves to Him, he that is thus joined to the Lord is one spirit, and all 'mine is Thine, and all Thine is mine.' He is the Heir of all things, and all things of which He is the Heir are our possession. 'All things are yours, and ye are Christ's.' Thus His dominion is the dominion of all that love Him, and His heritage is the heritage of all those that have joined themselves to Him; and no sparkle of the glory that falls upon His head but is reflected on the heads of His servants. The 'many crowns' that He wears are the crowns with which He crowns His followers.

Thus, my brother, to be overcome by God is to overcome the world, to be triumphed over by Christ is to share in His triumph; and he over whom Incarnate love wins the victory, like the patriarch of old in his mystical struggle, conquers in the hour of surrender; and to him it is said: 'As a prince thou hast power with God and hast prevailed.'

III. Lastly, a further picture of the ideal of the Christian life is set before us here in the thought of these conquered captives being led as the trophies and the witnesses of His overcoming power.

That idea is suggested by both halves of our verse. Both the emblem of the Apostle as marching in the triumphal procession, and the emblem of the Apostle as yielding from his burning heart the fragrant visible odour of the ascending incense, convey the same idea, viz. that one great purpose which Jesus Christ has in conquering men for Himself, and binding them to His chariot wheels, is that from them may go forth the witness of His power and the knowledge of His name.

That opens very wide subjects for our consideration which I can only very briefly touch upon. Let me just for an instant dwell upon some of them. First, the fact that Jesus Christ, by His Cross and Passion, is able to conquer men's wills, and to bind men's hearts to Him, is the highest proof of His power. It is an entirely unique thing in the history of the world. There is nothing the least like it anywhere else. The passionate attachment which this dead Galilean peasant is able to evoke in the hearts of people all these centuries after His death, is an unheard of and an unparalleled thing. All other teachers 'serve their generations by the will of God,' and then their names become speedily less and less powerful, and thicker and thicker mists of oblivion wrap them round until they disappear. But time has no power over Christ's influence. The bond which binds you and me to Him nineteen centuries after His death is the very same in quality as, and in degree is often far deeper and stronger than, the bond which united to Him the men that had seen Him. It stands as an unique fact in the history of the world, that from Christ of Nazareth there rays out through all the ages the spiritual power which absolutely takes possession of men, dominates them and turns them into His organs and instruments.

This generation prides itself upon testing all things by an utilitarian test, and about every system says:— 'Well, let us see it working.' And I do not think that Christianity need shrink from the test. With all its imperfections, the long procession of holy men and women who, for nineteen centuries, have been marching through history, owning Christ as their Conqueror, and ascribing all their goodness to Him, is a witness to His power to sway and to satisfy men, the force of whose testimony it is hard to overthrow. And I would like to ask the simple question: Will any system of belief or of no belief, except the faith in Christ's atoning sacrifice, do the like for men? He leads through the world the train of His captives, the evidence of His conquests.

And then, further, let me remind you that out of this representation there comes a very stimulating and solemn suggestion of duty for us Christian people. We are bound to live, setting forth whose we are, and what He has done for us. Just as the triumphal procession took its path up the Appian Way and along the side of the Forum to the altar of the Capitol, wreathed about by curling clouds of fragrant incense, so we should march through the world encompassed by the sweet and fragrant odour of His name, witnessing for Him by word, witnessing for Him by character, speaking for Him and living like Him, showing in our life that He rules us, and professing by our words that He does; and so should manifest His power.

Still further, Paul's thanksgiving teaches us that we should be thankful for all opportunities of doing such work. Christian men and women often grudge their services and grudge their money, and feel as if the necessities for doing Christian work in the world were

U

rather a burden than an honour. This man's generous heart was so full of love to his Prince that it glowed with thankfulness at the thought that Christ had let him do such things for Him. And He lets you do them if you will.

So, dear friends, it comes to be a very solemn question for us. What part are we playing in that great triumphal procession? We are all of us marching at His chariot wheels, whether we know it or not. But there were two sets of people in the old triumph. There were those who were conquered by force and unconquered in heart, and out of their eyes gleamed unquenchable malice and hatred, though their weapons were broken and their arms fettered. And there were those who, having shared in the commander's fight, shared in his triumph and rejoiced in his rule. And when the procession reached the gate of the temple, some, at any rate, of the former class were put to death before the gates. I pray you to remember that if we are dragged after Him reluctantly, the word will come: 'These, mine enemies, which would not that I should reign over them, bring hither and slay them before Me.' Whereas, on the other hand, for those who have yielded heart and soul to Him in love and submission born of the reception of His great love, the blessed word will come: 'He that overcometh shall inherit all things.' Which of the two parts of the procession do you belong to, my friend? Make your choice where you shall march, and whether you will be His loyal allies and soldiers who share in His triumph, or His enemies, who, overcome by His power, are not melted by His love. The one live, the other perish.

TRANSFORMATION BY BEHOLDING

'We all, with open face beholding as in a glass the glory of the Lord, are changed into the same image.'—2 Cor. iii. 18.

THIS whole section of the Epistle in which our text occurs is a remarkable instance of the fervid richness of the Apostle's mind, which acquires force by motion, and, like a chariot-wheel, catches fire as it revolves. One of the most obvious peculiarities of his style is his habit of 'going off at a word.' Each thought is, as it were, barbed all round, and catches and draws into sight a multitude of others, but slightly related to the main purpose in hand. And this characteristic gives at first sight an appearance of confusion to his writings. But it is not confusion, it is richness. The luxuriant underwood which this fertile soil bears, as some tropical forest, does not choke the great trees, though it drapes them.

Paul's immediate purpose seems to be to illustrate the frank openness which ought to mark the ministry of Christianity. He does this by reference to the veil which Moses wore when he came forth from talking with God. There, he says in effect, we have a picture of the Old Dispensation—a partial revelation, gleaming through a veil, flashing through symbols, expressed here in a rite, there in a type, there again in an obscure prophecy, but never or scarcely ever fronting the world with an unveiled face and the light of God shining clear from it. Christianity is, and Christian teachers ought to be, the opposite of all this. It has, and they are to have, no esoteric doctrines, no hints where plain speech is possible, no reserve, no use of symbols and ceremonies to overlay truth, but an in-

telligible revelation in words and deeds, to men's
understandings. It and they are plentifully to declare
the thing as it is.

But he gets far beyond this point in his uses of his
illustration. It opens out into a series of contrasts
between the two revelations. The veiled Moses represents the clouded revelation of old. The vanishing
gleam on his face recalls the fading glories of that which
was abolished; and then, by a quick turn of association,
Paul thinks of the veiled readers in the synagogues,
copies, as it were, of the lawgiver with the shrouded
countenance; only too significant images of the souls
obscured by prejudice and obstinate unbelief, with
which Israel trifles over the uncomprehended letter of
the old law.

The contrast to all this lies in our text. Judaism had
the one lawgiver who beheld God, while the people
tarried below. Christianity leads us all, to the mount
of vision, and lets the lowliest pass through the fences,
and go up where the blazing glory is seen. Moses
veiled the face that shone with the irradiation of Deity.
We with unveiled face are to shine among men. He
had a momentary gleam, a transient brightness; we
have a perpetual light. Moses' face shone, but the
lustre was but skin deep. But the light that we have
is inward, and works transformation into its own
likeness.

So there is here set forth the very loftiest conception
of the Christian life as direct vision, universal, manifest to men, permanent, transforming.

I. Note then, first, that the Christian life is a life of
contemplating and reflecting Christ.

It is a question whether the single word rendered in
our version 'beholding as in a glass,' means that, or

'reflecting as a glass does.' The latter seems more in accordance with the requirements of the context, and with the truth of the matter in hand. Unless we bring in the notion of reflected lustre, we do not get any parallel with the case of Moses. Looking into a glass does not in the least correspond with the allusion, which gave occasion to the whole section, to the glory of God smiting him on the face, till the reflected lustre with which it glowed became dazzling, and needed to be hid. And again, if Paul is here describing Christian vision of God as only indirect, as in a mirror, then that would be a point of inferiority in us as compared with Moses, who saw Him face to face. But the whole tone of the context prepares us to expect a setting forth of the particulars in which the Christian attitude towards the manifested God is above the Jewish. So, on the whole, it seems better to suppose that Paul meant 'mirroring,' than 'seeing in a mirror.'

But, whatever be the exact force of the word, the thing intended includes both acts. There is no reflection of the light without a previous reception of the light. In bodily sight, the eye is a mirror, and there is no sight without an image of the thing perceived being formed in the perceiving eye. In spiritual sight, the soul which beholds is a mirror, and at once beholds and reflects. Thus, then, we may say that we have in our text the Christian life described as one of contemplation and manifestation of the light of God.

The great truth of a direct, unimpeded vision, as belonging to Christian men on earth, sounds strange to many of us. 'That cannot be,' you say; 'does not Paul himself teach that we see through a glass darkly? Do we not walk by faith and not by sight? "No man hath seen God at any time, nor can see Him"; and besides that absolute impossibility, have we not veils of flesh and sense, to say nothing of the covering of sin "spread over the face of all nations," which hide from us even so much of the eternal light as His servants above behold, who see His face and bear His name on their foreheads?'

But these apparent difficulties drop away when we take into account two things—first, the object of vision, and second, the real nature of the vision itself.

As to the former, who is the Lord whose glory we receive on our unveiled faces? He is Jesus Christ. Here, as in the overwhelming majority of instances where *Lord* occurs in the New Testament, it is the name of the manifested God our brother. The glory which we behold and give back is not the incomprehensible, incommunicable lustre of the absolute divine perfectness, but that glory which, as John says, we beheld in Him who tabernacled with us, full of grace and truth; the glory which was manifested in loving, pitying words and loveliness of perfect deeds; the glory of the will resigned to God, and of God dwelling in and working through the will; the glory of faultless and complete manhood, and therein of the express image of God.

And as for the vision itself, that seeing which is denied to be possible is the bodily perception and the full comprehension of the Infinite God; that seeing which is affirmed to be possible, and actually bestowed in Christ, is the beholding of Him with the soul by faith; the immediate direct consciousness of His presence the perception of Him in His truth by the mind, the feeling of Him in His love by the heart, the contact with His gracious energy in our recipient and opening spirits. Faith is made the antithesis of sight. It is so, in certain respects. But faith is also paralleled with and exalted above the mere bodily perception. He who believing grasps the living Lord has a contact with Him as immediate and as real as that of the eyeball with light, and knows Him with a certitude as reliable as that which sight gives. 'Seeing is believing,' says sense; 'Believing is seeing,' says the spirit which clings to the Lord, 'whom having not seen' it loves. A bridge of perishable flesh, which is not myself but my tool, connects me with the outward world. *It* never touches myself at all, and I know it only by trust in my senses. But nothing intervenes between my Lord and me, when I love and trust. Then Spirit is joined to spirit, and of His presence I have the witness in myself. He is the light, which proves its own existence by revealing itself, which strikes with quickening impulse on the eye of the spirit that beholds by faith. Believing we see, and, seeing, we have that light in our souls to be 'the master light of all our seeing.' We need not think that to know by the consciousness of our trusting souls is less than to know by the vision of our fallible eyes; and though flesh hides from us the spiritual world in which we float, yet the only veil which really dims God to us—the veil of sin, the one separating principle—is done away in Christ, for all who love Him; so as that he who has not seen and yet has believed, has but the perfecting of his present vision to expect, when flesh drops away and the apocalypse of the heaven comes. True, in one view, 'We see through a glass darkly'; but also true, 'We all, with unveiled face, behold and reflect the glory of the Lord.'

Then note still further Paul's emphasis on the universality of this prerogative—'We all.' This vision does not belong to any select handful; does not depend upon special powers or gifts, which in the nature of things can only belong to a few. The spiritual aristocracy of God's Church is not the distinction of the law-giver, the priest or the prophet. There is none of us so weak, so low, so ignorant, so compassed about with sin, but that upon our happy faces that light may rest, and into our darkened hearts that sunshine may steal.

In that Old Dispensation, the light that broke through clouds was but that of the rising morning. It touched the mountain tops of the loftiest spirits: a Moses, a David, an Elijah caught the early gleams; while all the valleys slept in the pale shadow, and the mist clung in white folds to the plains. But the noon has come, and, from its steadfast throne in the very zenith, the sun, which never sets, pours down its rays into the deep recesses of the narrowest gorge, and every little daisy and hidden flower catches its brightness, and there is nothing hid from the heat thereof. We have no privileged class or caste now; no fences to keep out the mob from the place of vision, while lawgiver and priest gaze upon God. Christ reveals Himself to all His servants in the measure of their desire after Him. Whatsoever special gifts may belong to a few in His Church, the greatest gift belongs to all. The servants and the handmaidens have the Spirit, the children prophesy, the youths see visions, the old men dream dreams. 'The mobs,' 'the masses,' 'the plebs,' or whatever other contemptuous name the heathen aristocratic spirit has for the bulk of men, makes good its standing within the Church, as possessor of Christ's chiefest gifts. Redeemed by Him, it can behold His face and be glorified into His likeness. Not as Judaism with its ignorant mass, and its enlightened and in-spired few—we *all* behold the glory of the Lord.

Again, this contemplation involves reflection, or giving forth the light which we behold.

They who behold Christ have Christ formed in them, as will appear in my subsequent remarks. But apart from such considerations, which belong rather to the next part of this sermon, I touch on this thought here for one purpose—to bring out this idea—that what we *see* we shall certainly *show*. That will be the inevitable result of all true possession of the glory of Christ. The necessary accompaniment of vision is reflecting the thing beheld. Why, if you look closely enough into a man's eye, you will see in it little pictures of what he beholds at the moment; and if our hearts are beholding Christ, Christ will be mirrored and mani-fested on our hearts. Our characters will show what we are looking at, and ought, in the case of Christian people, to bear His image so plainly, that men cannot but take knowledge of us that we have been with Jesus.

This ought to lead all of us who say that we have seen the Lord, to serious self-questioning. Do behold-ing and reflecting go together in our cases? Are our characters like those transparent clocks, where you can see not only the figures and hands, but the wheels and works? Remember that, consciously and uncon-sciously, by direct efforts and by insensible influences on our lives, the true secret of our being ought to come, and will come, forth to light. The convictions which we hold, the emotions that are dominant in our hearts, will mould and shape our lives. If we have any deep, living perception of Christ, bystanders looking into our faces will be able to tell what it is up yonder that is making them like the faces of the angels—even the vision of the opened heavens and of the exalted Lord. These two things are inseparable—the one describes the attitude and action of the Christian man towards Christ; the other the very same attitude and action in relation to men. And you may be quite sure that, if little light comes from a Christian character, little light comes into it; and if it be swathed in thick veils from men, there must be no less thick veils between it and God.

Nor is it only that our fellowship with Christ will, as a matter of course, show itself in our characters, and beauty born of that communion 'shall pass into our face,' but we are also called on, as Paul puts it here, to make direct conscious efforts for the communication of the light which we behold. As the context has it, God hath shined in our hearts, that we might give the light of the knowledge of the glory of God in the face of Christ Jesus. Away with all veils! No reserve, no fear of the consequences of plain speaking, no diplomatic prudence regulating our frank utterance, no secret doctrines for the initiated! We are to 're-nounce the hidden things of dishonesty.' Our power and our duty lie in the full exhibition of the truth. We are only clear from the blood of men when we, for our parts, make sure that if any light be hid, it is hid not by reason of obscurity or silence on our parts, but only by reason of the blind eyes, before which the full-orbed radiance gleams in vain. All this is as true for every one possessing that universal prerogative of seeing the glory of Christ, as it is for an Apostle. The business of all such is to make known the name of Jesus, and if from idleness, or carelessness, or selfishness, they shirk that plain duty, they are counteracting

God's very purpose in shining on their hearts, and going far to quench the light which they darken.

Take this, then, Christian men and women, as a plain practical lesson from this text. You are bound to manifest what you believe, and to make the secret of your lives, in so far as possible, an open secret. Not that you are to drag into light before men the sacred depths of your own soul's experience. Let these lie hid. The world will be none the better for your confessions, but it needs your Lord. Show Him forth, not your own emotions about Him. What does the Apostle say close by my text? 'We preach not ourselves, but Christ Jesus the Lord.' Self-respect and reverence for the sanctities of our deepest emotions forbid our proclaiming these from the house-tops. Let these be curtained, if you will, from all eyes but God's, but let no folds hang before the picture of your Saviour that is drawn on your heart. See to it that you have the unveiled face turned towards Christ to be irradiated by His brightness, and the unveiled face turned towards men, from which shall shine every beam of the light which you have caught from your Lord. 'Arise! shine, for thy light is come, and the glory of the Lord is risen upon thee!'

II. Notice, secondly, that this life of contemplation is therefore a life of gradual transformation.

The brightness on the face of Moses was only skin-deep. It faded away, and left no trace. It effaced none of the marks of sorrow and care, and changed none of the lines of that strong, stern face. But, says Paul, the glory which we behold sinks inward, and changes us as we look, into its own image. Thus the superficial lustre, that had neither permanence nor transforming power, becomes an illustration of the powerlessness of law to change the moral character into the likeness of the fair ideal which it sets forth. And, in opposition to its weakness, the Apostle proclaims the great principle of Christian progress, that the beholding of Christ leads to the assimilation to Him.

The metaphor of a mirror does not wholly serve us here. When the sunbeams fall upon it, it flashes in the light, just because they do not enter its cold surface. It is a mirror, because it does not drink them up, but flings them back. The contrary is the case with these sentient mirrors of our spirits. In them the light must first sink in before it can ray out. They must first be filled with the glory, before the glory can stream forth. They are not so much like a reflecting surface as like a bar of iron, which needs to be heated right down to its obstinate black core, before its outer skin glows with the whiteness of a heat that is too hot to sparkle. The sunshine must fall on us, not as it does on some lonely hill-side, lighting up the grey stones with a passing gleam that changes nothing, and fades away, leaving the solitude to its sadness; but as it does on some cloud cradled near its setting, which it drenches and saturates with fire till its cold heart burns, and all its wreaths of vapour are brightness palpable, glorified by the light which lives amidst its mists. So must we have the glory sink into us before it can be reflected from us. In deep inward beholding we must have Christ in our hearts, that He may shine forth from our lives.

And this contemplation will be gradual transformation. There is the great principle of Christian morals. 'We all beholding . . . are changed.' The power to which is committed the perfecting of our characters lies in looking upon Jesus. It is not the mere beholding, but the gaze of love and trust that moulds us by silent sympathy into the likeness of His wondrous beauty, who is fairer than the children of men. It was a deep, true thought which the old painters had, when they drew John as likest to his Lord. Love makes us like. We learn *that* even in our earthly relationships, where habitual familiarity with parents and dear ones stamps some tone of voice or look, or little peculiarity of gesture, on a whole house. And when the infinite reverence and aspiration which the Christian soul cherishes to its Lord are superadded, the transforming power of loving contemplation of Him becomes mighty beyond all analogies in human friendship, though one in principle with these. What a marvellous thing that a block of rude sandstone, laid down before a perfect marble, should become a copy of its serene loveliness just by lying there! Lay your hearts down before Christ. Contemplate Him. Love Him. Think about Him. Let that pure face shine upon heart and spirit, and as the sun photographs itself on the sensitive plate exposed to its light, and you get a likeness of the sun by simply laying the thing in the sun, so He will ' be formed in you.' Iron near a magnet becomes magnetic. Spirits that dwell with Christ become Christ-like. The Roman Catholic legends put this truth in a coarse way, when they tell of saints who have gazed on some ghastly crucifix till they have received, in their tortured flesh, the copy of the wounds of Jesus, and have thus borne in their body the marks of the Lord. The story is hideous and gross, the idea beneath is ever true. Set your faces towards the Cross with loving, reverent gaze, and you will ' be conformed unto His death,' that in due time you may ' be also in the likeness of His Resurrection.'

Dear friends, surely this message—'Behold and be like'—ought to be very joyful and enlightening to many of us, who are wearied with painful struggles after isolated pieces of goodness, that elude our grasp. You have been trying, and trying, and trying half your lifetime to cure faults and make yourselves better and stronger. Try this other plan. Let love draw you, instead of duty driving you. Let fellowship with Christ elevate you, instead of seeking to struggle up the steeps on hands and knees. Live in sight of your Lord, and catch His Spirit. The man who travels with his face northwards has it grey and cold. Let him turn to the warm south, where the midday sun dwells, and his face will glow with the brightness that he sees. 'Looking unto Jesus' is the sovereign cure for all our ills and sins. It is the one condition of running with patience 'the race that is set before us.' Efforts after self-improvement which do not rest on it will not go deep enough, nor end in victory. But from that gaze will flow into our lives a power which will at once reveal the true goal, and brace every sinew for the struggle to reach it. Therefore, let us cease from self, and fix our eyes on our Saviour till His image imprints itself on our whole nature.

Such transformation, it must be remembered, comes gradually. The language of the text regards it as a lifelong process. 'We *are* changed'; that is a continuous operation. 'From glory to glory'; that is a course which has well-marked transitions and degrees. Be not impatient if it be slow. It will take a lifetime. Do not fancy that it is finished with you. Life is not long enough for it. Do not be complacent over the partial transformation which you have felt. There is but a fragment of the great image yet reproduced in your soul, a faint outline dimly traced, with many a feature wrongly drawn, with many a line still needed, before it can be called even approximately complete. See to it that you neither turn away your gaze, nor relax your efforts till all that you have beheld in Him is repeated in you.

Likeness to Christ is the aim of all religion. To it conversion is introductory; doctrines, devout emotion, worship and ceremonies, churches and organisations are valuable as auxiliary. Let that wondrous issue of God's mercy be the purpose of our lives, and the end as well as the test of all the things which we call our Christianity. Prize and use them as helps towards it, and remember that they are helps only in proportion as they show us that Saviour, the image of whom is our perfection, the beholding of whom is our trans- formation.

III. Notice, lastly, that the life of contemplation finally becomes a life of complete assimilation.

'Changed into the same image, from glory to glory.' The lustrous light which falls upon Christian hearts from the face of their Lord is permanent, and it is progressive. The likeness extends, becomes deeper, truer, every way perfecter, comprehends more and more of the faculties of the man; soaks into him, if I may say so, until he is saturated with the glory; and in all the extent of his being, and in all the depth possible to each part of that whole extent, is like his Lord. That is the hope for heaven, towards which we may indefinitely approximate here, and at which we shall absolutely arrive there. There we expect changes which are impossible here, while compassed with this body of sinful flesh. We look for the merciful exercise of His mighty working to 'change the body of our lowliness, that it may be fashioned like unto the body of His glory'; and that physical change in the resurrection of the just rightly bulks very large in good men's expectations. But we are somewhat apt to think of the perfect likeness of Christ too much in connection with that transformation that begins only after death, and to forget that the main transformation must begin here. The glorious, corporeal life like our Lord's, which is promised for heaven, is great and wonderful, but it is only the issue and last result of the far greater change in the spiritual nature, which by faith and love begins here. It is good to be clothed with the immortal vesture of the resurrection, and in that to be like Christ. It is better to be like Him in our hearts. His true image is that we should feel as He does, should think as He does, should will as He does; that we should have the same sympathies, the same loves, the same attitude towards God, and the same attitude towards men. It is that His heart and ours should beat in full accord, as with one pulse, and possessing one life. Wherever there is the beginning of that oneness and likeness of spirit, all the rest will come in due time. As the spirit, so the body. The whole nature must be transformed and made like Christ's, and the process will not stop till that end be accomplished in all who love Him. But the beginning here is the main thing which draws all the rest after it as of course. 'If the Spirit of Him that raised up Jesus from the dead dwell in you, He that raised up Christ from the dead shall also quicken your mortal bodies, by His Spirit that dwelleth in you.'

And, while this complete assimilation in body and spirit to our Lord is the end of the process which begins here by love and faith, my text, carefully considered, adds a further very remarkable idea. 'We are all changed,' says Paul, 'into the *same* image.' Same as what? Possibly the same as we behold; but more probably the phrase, especially 'image' in the singular, is employed to convey the thought of the blessed likeness of all who become perfectly like Him. As if he had said, 'Various as we are in disposition and character, unlike in the histories of our lives, and all the influences that these have had upon us, differing in everything but the common relation to Jesus Christ, we are all growing like the same image, and we shall come to be perfectly like it, and yet each retain his own distinct individuality.' 'We being many are one, for we are all partakers of one.'

Perhaps, too, we may connect with this another idea which occurs more than once in Paul's Epistles. In that to the Ephesians, for instance, he says that the Christian ministry is to continue, till a certain point of progress has been reached, which he describes as our *all* coming to '*a* perfect *man*.' The whole of us together make a perfect man—the whole make one image. That is to say, perhaps the Apostle's idea is, that it takes the aggregated perfectness of the whole Catholic Church, one throughout all ages, and containing a multitude that no man can number, to set worthily forth anything like a complete image of the fulness of Christ. No one man, even raised to the highest pitch of perfection, and though his nature be widened out to perfect development, can be the full image of that infinite sum of all beauty; but the whole of us taken together, with all the diversities of natural character retained and consecrated, being collectively His body which He vitalises, may, on the whole, be a not wholly inadequate representation of our perfect Lord. Just as we

set round a central light sparkling prisms, each of
which catches the glow at its own angle, and flashes it
back of its own colour, while the sovereign completeness of the perfect white radiance comes from the
blending of all their separate rays, so they who stand
round about the starry throne receive each the light in
his own measure and manner, and give forth each a
true and perfect, and altogether a complete, image of
Him who enlightens them all, and is above them all.

And whilst thus all bear the same image, there is no
monotony; and while there is endless diversity, there
is no discord. Like the serene choirs of angels in the
old monk's pictures, each one with the same tongue of
fire on the brow, with the same robe flowing in the
same folds to the feet, with the same golden hair, yet
each a separate self, with his own gladness, and a
different instrument for praise in his hand, and his own
part in that 'undisturbed song of pure content,' we
shall all be changed into the same image, and yet each
heart shall grow great with its own blessedness, and
each spirit bright with its own proper lustre of individual and characteristic perfection.

The law of the transformation is the same for earth
and for heaven. Here we see Him in part, and beholding grow like. There we shall see Him as He is, and
the likeness will be complete. That Transfiguration of
our Lord (which is described by the same word as
occurs in this text) may become for us the symbol and
the prophecy of what we look for. As with Him, so
with us; the indwelling glory shall come to the surface,
and the countenance shall shine as the light, and the
garments shall be 'white as no fuller on earth can
white them.' Nor shall that be a fading splendour, nor
shall we fear as we enter into the cloud, nor, looking

on Him, shall flesh bend beneath the burden, and the
eyes become drowsy, but we shall be as the Lawgiver
and the Prophet who stood by Him in the lambent
lustre, and shone with a brightness above that which
had once been veiled on Sinai. We shall never vanish
from His side, but dwell with Him in the abiding
temple which He has built, and there, looking upon
Him for ever, our happy souls shall change as they
gaze, and behold Him more perfectly as they change,
for 'we know that when He shall appear we shall be
like Him, for we shall see Him as He is.'

LOOKING AT THE UNSEEN

'While we look not at the things which are seen, but at the things which are
not seen.'—2 Cor. iv. 18.

MEN may be said to be divided into two classes,
materialists and idealists, in the widest sense of those
two words. The mass care for, and are occupied by,
and regard as really solid good, those goods which can
be touched and enjoyed by sense. The minority—
students, thinkers, men of ideas, moralists, and the
like—believe in, and care for, impalpable spiritual
riches. Everybody admits that the latter class is
distinctly the higher. Now it is from no disregard to
the importance and reality of that broad distinction
that I insist, to begin with, that it is not the antithesis
which is in the Apostle's mind here. His notion of
'the things that are seen' and 'the things that are not
seen' is a much grander and wider one than that. By
'the things that are seen' he means the whole of this
visible world, with all its circumstances and relations,

and by 'the things that are not seen' he means the realities beyond the stars.

He means the same thing that we mean when we talk in a much less true and impressive contrast about the present and the future. To him the 'things that are not seen' are present instead of being, as we weakly and foolishly christen them, 'the future state.' And it makes all the difference whether we think of that august realm as lying far away ahead of us, or whether we·feel that it is, as it is, in very deed, all round about us, and pressing in upon us, only that 'the veil'—that is to say, our 'flesh'—has come between us and it. Do not habitually think of these two sets of objects according to that misleading distinction 'present' and 'future,' but think of them rather as 'the things that are seen,' and 'the things that are not seen.'

I. Now, first, I wish to say a word or two about what such a look will do for us.

Paul's notion is, as you will see if you look at the context, that if we want to understand the visible, or to get the highest good out of the things that are seen, we must bring into the field of vision 'the things that are not seen.' The case with which he is dealing is that of a man in trouble. He talks about light affliction which is but for a moment, working out a far more exceeding and eternal weight of glory, 'while we look at the things which are not seen.' But the principle on which that statement is made, of course, has its widest application to all sorts and conditions of human life.

And the thought that emerges from it directly is that only when we take the 'things that are not seen' into account, and make them the standard and the scale by which we judge all things, do we understand 'the things that are seen.' That triumphant paradox of the Apostle's about the heavy burdens that pressed upon him and his brethren, lifelong as these burdens were, which yet he calls 'light' and 'but for a moment' is possible only when we open the shutter of the dungeon which we fancied was the whole universe, and look out on to the fair land that stretches beyond. A man who has seen the Himalayas will not be much overwhelmed by the height of Helvellyn. They who look out into the eternities have the true measuring rod and standard by which to estimate the duration and intensity of the things that are present. We are all tempted to do as villagers in some little hamlet do —think that their small local affairs are the world's affairs, and mighty, until they have been up to London and seen the scale of things there. If you and I would let the steady light of Eternity, and the sustaining pressure of the 'exceeding weight of glory' pour into our minds, we should carry with us a standard which would bring down the greatness, dwindle the duration, lighten the pressure, of the most crushing sorrow, and would set in its true dimensions everything that is here. It is for want of that that we go on as we do, calculating wrongly what are the great things and what are the small things. When, like some of those prisoners in the Inquisition, the heavy iron weights are laid upon our half-crushed hearts, we are tempted to shriek, 'Oh, these will be my death!' instead of taking in that great vision which, as it makes all earthly riches dross, so it makes all crushing burdens and blows of sorrow light as a feather.

But, on the other hand, do not let us forget that this

same standard which thus dwindles, also magnifies the
small, and in a very solemn sense, makes eternal the
else fleeting things of this life. For there is nothing
that makes this present existence of ours so utterly
contemptible, insignificant, and transitory, as to block
out of our sight its connection with Eternity. And
there is nothing which so lifts the commonplace into
the solemn, and invests with everlasting and tremendous importance everything that a man does here, as to
feel that it all tells on his condition away beyond
there. The shafting is on this side of the wall, but the
work that it does is through the wall there, in the
other chamber; and you do not understand the cranks
and the wheels here unless you know that they go
through the partition and are doing something there
beyond. If you shut out Eternity from our life in
time, then it is an inexplicable riddle; and I, for my
part, would venture to say that in that case, the men
who answer the question, 'Is life worth living?' with
a distinct negative, are wise. It is a tale told by an
idiot, 'full of sound and fury, signifying nothing,'
unless the light of 'the things not seen' flashes and
flares in upon it.

Further, this look of which my text speaks is the
condition on which Time prepares for Eternity.

The Apostle is speaking about the effect of affliction
in making ready for us an eternal weight of glory,
and he says that is done while, or on condition that
during the suffering, we are looking steadfastly towards the 'things that are not seen.' But no outward
circumstances or events can prepare a weight of glory
for us hereafter, unless they prepare us for the glory.
Affliction works for us that blessed result, in the
measure in which it fits us for that result. And so you

will find that, only a verse or two after my text, Paul, using the same very significant and emphatic verb, writes inverting the order of things, and says 'He that hath wrought *us for* the self-same thing is God.' So that working the thing for us, and working us for the thing, are one and the same process. Or, to put it into plain English, our various duties and circumstances here will prepare the glory of Eternity for us if they prepare us for the glory of Eternity. But only in the measure in which these outward things do thus shape and mould our characters do they work out for us 'an exceeding weight of glory.'

It is often thought that a man has been so miserable here that God is sure to give him future blessedness to recompense him. Well! 'that depends.' If he has used his miserableness as he will use it when he lets the light of 'the things not seen' in upon it, then, certainly, it will work out for him the blessed results. But if he does not, then, as certainly, it will not. Whilst there are many ways by which character is hammered and moulded and shaped into that which is fit to be clothed upon with the glory that is yonder, one of the foremost of these is the passing through things temporal with a continual regard to the things that are eternal. If you want to understand to-day you must bring Eternity into the account, and if you want to use to-day you must use it with the light of the eternal world full upon it. The sum of it all is, brethren, that the things seen cannot be estimated in their true character, unless they are regarded in immediate connection with the things that are unseen; and that the things seen will only prepare an eternal weight of glory for us when they prepare us for an eternal weight of glory.

II. And so, I note that this look at the things not seen is only possible through Jesus Christ.

He is the only window which opens out and gives the vision of that far-off land. I, for my part, believe that, if I might use such a metaphor, He is the Columbus of the New World. Men believed, and argued, and doubted about the existence of it across the seas there, until a man went, and came back again, and then went to found a new city yonder. And men hoped for immortality, and believed after a fashion—some of them—in a future life, and dreaded that it might be true, and discussed and debated whether it was, but doubt clouded all minds, until One, our Brother, went away into the darkness, and came back again, in most respects as He had gone, and then departed once more to make ready a city in which all who love Him should finally dwell, and to which you and I may be sure that we shall emigrate. It is only in Jesus Christ that the look which my text enjoins is possible.

For not only has He given a certitude so that we need now not to say 'We think, we hope, we fear, we are pretty well sure, that there must be a life beyond,' but we can say 'We know.' Not only has He done this, but also in Him and His life of glory at God's right hand in heaven, is summed up all that we really can know about that future. We look into the darkness in vain; we look at Him, and, our knowledge, though limited, is blessed. All other adumbrations of a life beyond must necessarily be cast into the metaphorical forms or the negative symbols in which the New Testament abounds. We may speak of golden pavements, and thrones, and harps, and the like. We may say: 'No night there, no sighing, nor weeping, no

burdened hearts, no toil, no pain, for the former
things are passed away.' But a future life which is all
described in metaphors, and a future life of which we
know only that it is the negation of the disagreeables
and limitations of the present, is but a poor affair.
Here is the positive truth, 'To him that overcometh
will I grant to sit with Me on My throne.' 'We shall
be like Him, for we shall see Him as He is.' And beyond that nearness to Christ, blessed communion with
Christ, likeness to Christ, royalty derived from Christ,
I think we neither know nor need to know anything
about that life.

Not only is He our sole medium of knowledge and
Himself the revelation of our heaven, but it is only by
Him that man's thoughts and desires are drawn to,
and find themselves at home in, that tremendous
thought of immortality. I know not how it may be
with you, but I am not ashamed to confess that to me
the idea of eternal continuance of my conscious being
is an awful thought, rather depressing and bewildering
than delighting and attractive. I, for my part, do not
believe that men generally do grapple to their hearts,
with any gratitude or joy, that solemn belief of
immortal life unless they feel that it is life with, and
in, and like, Jesus Christ. 'To depart' is dreary, and it
is only when we can say 'and to be with Christ' that it
becomes distinctly 'far better.' He is, if I may so say,
at once telescope and star. By Him we see Him; we
see, seeing Him, that the things that are unseen all
cluster round Himself and become blessed.

III. And now, lastly, this look should be habitual
with all Christian people.

Paul takes it for granted that every Christian man
is, as the habitual direction of his thoughts, looking

towards those 'things that are not seen.' The original shows that even more distinctly than our translation, but our translation shows it plainly enough. He does not say 'works for us an exceeding weight of glory *for*,' but *'while'* we look, as if it were a matter of course. He took it for granted as to these Corinthians. I wonder if he would be warranted in taking it for granted about us?

Note what sort of a look it is which produces these blessed effects. The word which the Apostle employs here is a more pointed one than the ordinary one for 'seeing.' It is translated in other places in the New Testament, '*Mark*' them which walk so as ye have us for an ensample, and the like. And it implies a con-centrated, protracted effort and interested gaze. A man, standing on the deck of a ship, casts a languid eye for a moment out on to the horizon, and sees nothing. A keen-eyed sailor by his side shades his eyes with his hand, and shuts out cross-lights, and looks, and peers, and keeps his eyes steady, and he sees the filmy outline of the mountain land. If you look for a minute, not much caring whether you see anything or not, and then turn away, and get your eye dazzled with all those vulgar, crude, high colours round about you here on earth, it is very little that you will see of 'the things that are not seen.' Concentrated attention, and a steadfast look, are wanted to make the invisible visible. You have to alter the focus of your eye if you are to see the thing that is afar off.

There has to be a positive shutting out of all other things, as is emphatically taught in the text by putting first the not looking at 'the things that are seen.' Here they are pressing in upon our eyeballs, all round us, insisting on being looked at, and unless

we resolutely avert our eyes, we shall not see anything else. They monopolise us unless we resist the
intrusive appeals that they make to us. We are like
men down in some fertile valley, surrounded by rich
vegetation, but seeing nothing beyond the green sides
of the glen. We have to go up to the hill-top if
we are to look out over the flashing ocean, and behold
afar off the towers of the mother city across the
restless waves. Brethren, unless you shut out the
world you will never see the things that are not
seen.

Now, as I have said, the Apostle regards this conscious
effort at bringing ourselves into touch, in mind and
heart and faith, with 'the things that are not seen,' as
being a habitual characteristic of Christian men. I
am very much afraid that the present generation of
Christian people do not, in anything like the degree in
which they should, recreate and strengthen themselves
with the contemplation which he here recommends.
It seems to me, for instance, that we do not hear
nearly as much in pulpits about the life beyond the
grave as we used to do when I was a boy. And,
though I confess I speak from limited knowledge, it
seems to me that these great motives which lie in the
thought of Eternity and our place there, are by no
means as prominent in the minds of the Christian
people of this generation as they used to be. Partly,
I suppose, that arises from the wholesome emphasis
which has been given of late years to the present day,
and this-side-the grave effects of Christianity, upon
character and life. Partly it arises, I think, from the
half-consciousness of being surrounded by an atmosphere of scepticism and unbelief as to a future life,
and from the most unwise, inexpedient, and cowardly

yielding to the temptation to say very little about the distinctive features of Christianity, and to dwell rather upon those which are sure to be recognised by even unbelieving people. And it comes, too, from the lack of faith, which, again, it tends mightily to increase.

Oh, dear brethren! our consciences tell us what different people we should be if habitually there shone before us that great, solemn issue to which we are all tending. Variations in the atmosphere there will always be, and sometimes the distant outlines will be clearer and sharper than at others, and the colours will shine out more distinctly. But surely it should not be that our vision of the Eternal should be like the vision that dwellers amongst the mountains have of the summits. They say that some of the great peaks of the world are swathed in mist all day long, and that only for a few moments in the morning, or for a brief space in the evening, does the solemn summit gleam rosy in the light. And that, I am afraid, is very much like the degree in which most of us look at 'the things that are not seen,' and so we are feeble, and we do not understand 'the things that are not seen'; and we do not get the good out of them.

Dear brethren, let us turn away our eyes from the gauds that we can see, and open the eyes of our spirits on the things that are, the things where Christ is, sitting at the right hand of God. Surely, surely, it is madness that when two sets of objects are before us, the one lasting for a moment, and then dying down into black nothingness, and the other shining on for ever; and when our 'look' settles whether we shall share the fate of the one or of the other, we should choose to gaze with all our eyes and hearts at the

perishable and turn away from the permanent. Surely,
if it is true that the things which are seen are temporal, common-sense, and a reasonable regard for our
own well-being, bid us look at the eternal 'things
which are not seen,' since only so can the light and the
momentary afflictions, joys, sorrows, or circumstances,
work out for us, and work us for 'a far more exceeding
and eternal weight of glory.'

TENT AND BUILDING

'For we know that if our earthly house of this tabernacle be dissolved, we have
a building of God, an house not made with hands, eternal in the heavens.'—
2 COR. v. 1.

KNOWLEDGE and ignorance, doubt and certitude, are
remarkably blended in these words. The Apostle
knows what many men are not certain of; the Apostle
doubts as to what all men now are certain of. '*If* our
earthly house of this tabernacle be dissolved'—there is
surely no if about that. But we must remember that
the first Christians, and the Apostles with them, did
not know whether they might not survive till the
coming of Christ; and so not die, but 'be changed.'
And this possibility, as appears from the context, is
clearly before the Apostle's mind. Such a limitation of
his knowledge is in entire accordance with our Lord's
own words, 'It is not for you to know the times and
the seasons,' and does not in the smallest degree dero-
gate from his authority as an inspired teacher. But
his certitude is as remarkable as his hesitation. He
knows—and he modestly and calmly affirms the confidence, as possessed by all believers—that, in the
event of death coming to him or them, he and they

have a mansion waiting for their entrance; a body of glory like to that which Jesus already wears.

I. So my text mainly sets before us very strikingly the Christian certitude as to the final future.

I need not dwell, I suppose, upon that familiar metaphor by which the relation of man to his bodily environment is described as that of a man to his dwelling-place. Only I would desire, in a word, to emphasise this as being the first of the elements of the blessed certitude in which Christian people may expatiate— the clear, broad distinction between me and my physical frame. There is no more connection, says Paul, between us and the organisation in which we at present dwell than there is between a man and the house that he inhabits. 'The foolish senses crown' Death and call him lord; but the Christian's certitude firmly draws the line, and declares that the man, the whole personality, is undisturbed by anything that befalls his residence; and that he may pass unimpaired from one house to another, being in both the self-same person. And that is something to keep firm hold of in these days when we are being told that life and consciousness are but a function of organisation, and that if the one be annihilated the other cannot persist. No; though all illustrations and metaphors must necessarily fail, the two which lie side by side here in my text and its context are far truer than that pseudo-science— which is not science at all, but only inference from science—which denies that the man is one thing and his house altogether another.

Then again, note, as part of the elements of this Christian certitude, the blessed thought that a body is part of the perfection of manhood. No mere dim, ghostly future, where consciousness somehow persists, without environment or tools to act upon an outer world, completes the idea of God in reference to man. But the old trinity is the eternal trinity for humanity, body, soul, and spirit. Corporeity, with all that it means of definiteness, with all that it means of relation to an external universe, is the perfection of manhood. To dwell naked, as the Apostle says in the context, is a thing from which man shudderingly recoils; and it is not to be his final fate. Let us take this as no small gain in reference to our conceptions of a future—the emphatic drawing into light of that thought that for his perfection man requires body, soul, and spirit.

And now, if we turn for a moment to the characteristics of the two conditions with which my text deals, we get some familiar enough but yet great and strengthening thoughts. The 'earthly house of this tabernacle is dissolved,' or, more correctly, retaining the metaphor of the house, is to be pulled down—and in its place there comes a building of God, a 'house not made with hands, eternal in the heavens.'

Now the contrast that is drawn here, whilst it would run out into a great many other particulars, about which we know nothing, and therefore had better say nothing, revolves in the Apostle's mind mainly round these two 'earthly' as contrasted with 'in the heavens'; and 'tabernacle,' or tent, as contrasted, first of all with a 'building,' and then with the predicate 'eternal.'

That is to say, the first outstanding difference which arises before the Apostle as blessed and glorious, is the contrast between the fragile dwelling-place, with its thin canvas, its bending poles, its certain removal some day, and the permanence of that which is not a 'tent,' but a 'building' which is 'eternal.' Involved in that is the thought that all the limitations and weaknesses which are necessarily associated with the perishableness of the present abode are at an end for ever. No more fatigue, no more working beyond the measure of power, no more need for recuperation and repose; no more dread of sickness and weakness; no more possibility of decay. 'It is sown in corruption; it is raised in incorruption'—neither 'can they die any more.' Whether that be by reason of any inherent immortality, or by reason of the uninterrupted flow into the creature of the immortal life of Christ, to whom he is joined, is a question that need not trouble us now. Enough for us that the contrast between the Bedouin tent—which is folded up and carried away, and nothing left but the black circle where the cheerful hearth once glinted amidst the sands of the desert—and the stately mansion reared for eternity, is the contrast between the organ of the spirit in which we now dwell and that which shall be ours.

And the other contrast is no less glorious and wonderful. 'The *earthly* house of this tent' does not merely define the composition, but also the whole relations and capacities of that to which it refers. The 'tent' is 'earthly' not merely because, to use a kindred metaphor, it is a 'building of clay,' but because, by all its capacities, it belongs to, corresponds with, and is fitted only for, this lower order of things, the seen and the perishable. And, on the other hand, the 'mansion' is in 'the heavens,' even whilst the future tenant is a nomad in his tent. That is so, because the power which can create that future abode is 'in the heavens.' It is so called in order to express the security in which it is kept for those who shall one day enter upon it. And it is so, further, to express the order of things with which it brings its dwellers into contact. 'Flesh and blood cannot inherit the Kingdom of God; neither doth corruption inherit incorruption.' That future home of the spirit will be congruous with the region in which it dwells; fitted for the heavens in which it is now preserved. And thus the two contrasts—adapted to the perishable, and itself perishable, belonging to the eternal and itself incorruptible—are the two which loom largest before the Apostle's mind.

Let no man say that such ideas of a possible future bodily frame are altogether inconsistent with all that we know of the limitations and characteristics of what we call matter. 'There is one flesh of beasts and another of birds,' says Paul; 'there is one glory of the sun and another of the moon.' And his old-fashioned argument is perfectly sound to-day.

Do you know so fully all the possibilities of creation as that you are warranted in asserting that such a thing as a body which is the fit organ of the spirit, and is incorruptible like the heavens in which it dwells, is an impossibility? Surely the forms of matter are sufficiently varied to make us chary in asserting that other forms are impossible, to which there may belong, as characteristics, even these glorious ones of my text. The old story of the king in the tropics, who laughed to scorn some one who told him that water could be turned into a solid, may well be quoted in this connection. Let us be less confident that we know all that is to be known in regard to the sweep of God's creative power; and let us thankfully accept the teaching by which we, too, in all our ignorance, may be able to say, 'We know that . . . we have a building of God . . . eternal in the heavens.'

Now there is only one more remark that I wish to

Y

make about this part of my subject; and it is this, that
the teaching of my text and its context casts great
light—and I think by many people much-needed light
—on what the resurrection of the dead means. That
doctrine has been weighted with a great many incredi-
bilities and I venture to say absurdities, by well-
meaning misconceptions and exaggerations. We have
heard grand platitudes about 'the scattered dust being
gathered from the four winds of heaven,' and so on,
but the teaching of my text is that the contrast between the present physical frame and the future bodily
environment is utter and complete; and that resurrection does not mean the assuming again of the body
that is left behind and done with, but the reinvestiture
of the man with another body. And so the Scriptural
phrase is, not 'the resurrection of the body,' but 'the
resurrection of the dead.' It is a house 'in the heavens.'
It comes 'from heaven.'

We leave the tent. Life and thought

> . . . have gone away, side by side,
> Leaving doors and windows wide;
> Careless tenants they!

And they may well be careless, because in the heavens
they have another mansion, incorruptible and glorious.

We leave the 'tent'; we enter the 'building.' There
is nothing here of some germ of immortality being
somehow extricated from the ruins, and fostered into
glorious growth. Or, to take another metaphor of the
context, we strip off the garment and are naked; and
then we are clothed with another garment and are not
found naked. The resurrection of the dead is the clothing of the spirit with the house which is from heaven.
And there is as much difference between the two
habitations as there is between the grim, solid archi-

tecture of northern peoples, amidst snow and ice,
needed to resist the blasts, and to keep the life within
in an ungenial climate, and the light, graceful dwell-
ings of those who walk in an atmosphere of perpetual
sunshine in the tropics, as there is between the close-
knit and narrow-windowed and narrow-doored abode
in which we now have to pass our days, and that large
house, with broad windows that take in a mightier
sweep and new senses that have relation with new
qualities in the world then around us.   Therefore let us,
whilst we grope in the dark here, and live in a narrow
hovel in a back street, look forward to the time when
we shall dwell on the sunny heights in the great
pavilion which God prepares for them that love Him.

II. And now note, again, how we come to this certitude.

My text is very significantly followed by a 'for,'
which gives the reason of the knowledge in a very
remarkable manner.   'We know, . . . for in this we
groan, earnestly desiring to be clothed upon with our
house, which is from heaven.'   Now that singular
collocation of ideas may be set forth thus—whatever
longing there is in a Christian, God-inspired soul, that
longing is a prophecy of its own fulfilment.   We know
that there is a house, because of the yearning, which is
deepest and strongest when we are nearest God, and
likest what He would have us to be—the yearning to
be 'clothed upon with our house which is from heaven.'
That is a truth that goes a long way; though to enlarge
on it is irrelevant to our present purpose.   It has its
limitations, as is obvious from the context, in which
are human elements which are not destined to be
gratified, mingled with the yearning, which is of God,
and which is destined to be satisfied.   But this at least

we may firmly hold by, that just because God will not put men to confusion intellectually, and does not let them entertain uncherished—still less Himself foster and excite—longings which He does not mean to gratify, a Christian yearning for immortality is, to the man who feels it, a declaration that immortality is sure for him. 'Delight thyself in the Lord, and He shall give thee the desires of thine heart.' Whatsoever, in touching Him, we do deeply long for may have blended with it human elements, which will be dispersed unsatisfied, but the substance of it is a prophecy of its own fulfilment. And as surely as the stork in the heavens, flying southward, will reach the sunny lands which draw it from the grim northern winter, so surely may a man say, 'I know that I have a house in heaven, because I long for it, and shrink from being found naked.'

Of course such longing, such aspiration and revulsion are no proofs of a fact except there be some fact which changes them from mere vague desires, and makes these solid certainties. And such a fact we have in that which is the only proof that the world has received, of the persistence of life through death and the continuance of personal identity unchanged by the grave, and that is the Resurrection of Jesus Christ from the dead. Our faith in immortality does not depend merely on our own subjective desires and longings, but these desires and longings are quickened, confirmed, and certified by this great fact that Jesus Christ has risen from the dead; and therefore we know that the yearnings in us are not in vain. So we come to this certitude, first, by reason of his experience; and, second, by reason of the longings which that experience fosters, if it does not kindle, within our hearts.

And let no man take exception to the Apostle's word here, 'we know,' or tell us that 'Knowledge is of the things we see.' That is true, and not true. It is true in regard to what arrogates to itself the name of science. And we are willing to admit the limitation if the men who insist upon it will, on their sides, admit that there are other sources of certitude than so-called 'facts,' by which they mean merely material facts. If it is meant to assert that we are less sure of the love of God, of immortality, than we are of the existence of this piece of wood, or that flame of gas; then I humbly venture to say that there is another region of facts than those which are appreciable by sense; that the evidence upon which we rest our certitude of immortal blessedness is quite as valid, quite as true, quite as able to bear the weight of a leaning heart as anything that can be produced, in the nature of evidence, for the things round us. It is not, 'We fancy, we believe, we hope, we are pretty nearly sure,' but it is ' We *know* ... that we have a building of God.'

III. Lastly, note what this certitude does.

The Apostle tells us by the 'for' which lies at the beginning of my text, and makes it a reason for something that has preceded, and what has preceded is this, 'We look not at the things which are seen, but at the things which are not seen.'

That is to say, such a joyous, calm certitude draws men's thoughts away from this shabby and transitory present, and fixes them on the solemn majesties of that eternal future. Yes! and nothing else will. Take away the idea of resurrection, and the remaining idea of immortality is a poor, shadowy, impotent thing. There is no force in it; there is no blessedness in it; there is nothing in it for a man to lay hold of. And,

as a matter of fact, there is no vivid faith in a future
life without belief in the resurrection and bodily existence of the perfected dead.

And we shall not let our thoughts willingly go out
thither unless our own personal wellbeing there is very
sure to us. When we know that for us individually
there is that house waiting for us to enter into it, when
the Lord comes, then we shall not be unwilling to turn
our hearts and our desires thither. We look at the
things which are not seen, for we know that we have
a house eternal.

And such a certitude will also make a man willing to
accept the else unwelcome necessity of leaving the
tent, and for a while doing without the mansion. It is
that which the Apostle is speaking of in subsequent
verses, on which I cannot enter now. He says—and
therein speaks a universal experience—that men recoil
from the idea of having to lay aside this earthly body
and be 'naked.' But we know that we have that
glorious mansion waiting for us, and that till the day
comes when we enter upon it we may be lapt in Christ
instead, and, in that so-called intermediate state, may
have Him to surround us, Him to be to us the medium
by which we come into connection with anything external, and so can contentedly go away from our home
in the body; and go to our home in Christ. 'Wherefore, we are always confident, and willing rather to be
absent from the body, and to be at home with the
Lord.'

Oh, brethren! do we think of our future thus? If we
do, then let us lay to heart the final words of our
teacher in this part of his letter: 'Wherefore we make
it our aim, whether at home or absent, to be well-
pleasing unto Him.'

THE PATIENT WORKMAN

'Now He that hath wrought us for the self-same thing is God.'—2 Cor. v. 5.

THESE words penetrate deep into the secrets of God. They assume to have read the riddle of life. To Paul everything which we experience, outwardly or inwardly, is from the divine working. Life is to him no mere blind whirl, or unintelligent play of accidental forces, nor is it the unguided result of our own or of others' wills, but is the slow operation of the great Workman. Paul assumes to know the meaning of this protracted process, that it all has one design which we may know and grasp and further. And he believes that the clear perception of the divine purpose, and the habit of looking at everything as contributing thereto, will be a magic charm against all sorrow, doubt, despondency, or fear, for he adds, 'Therefore we are always confident.' So let us try to follow the course of thought which issues in such a blessed gift as that of a continual, courageous outlook, and buoyant though grave lightheartedness, because we discern what He means 'Who worketh all things according to the counsel of His own will.'

I. The first thought here is, God's purpose in all His working. 'He that hath wrought us for the self-same thing is God.'

What is that 'self-same thing'? To understand it we must look back for a moment to the previous context. The Apostle has been speaking about the instinctive reluctance which even good men feel at the prospect of dying and 'putting off the earthly house of this tabernacle.' He distinguishes between three different conditions in which the human spirit may be —dwelling in the earthly body, stripped of that, and 'clothed with the house which is from Heaven,' and to this last and highest state he sees that for him and for his brethren there were two possible roads. They might reach it either through losing the present body, in the act of death, and passing through a period of what he calls nakedness; or they might attain it by being 'superinvested,' as it were, with the glorious body which was to come to saints with Christ when He came; and so slip on, as it were, the wedding garment over their old clothes, without having to denude themselves of these. And he says that deep in the Christian heart there lay reluctance to take the former road and the preference for the latter. His longing was that that which is mortal might be 'swallowed up of life,' as some sand-bank in the tide-way may be gradually covered and absorbed by the rejoicing waters. And then he says, 'Now He that hath wrought us for this very thing, is God.'

Of course it is impossible that he can mean by this 'very thing' the second of the roads by which it was possible to reach the ultimate issue, because he did not know whether his brethren and he were to die or to be changed. He speaks in the context about death as a possible contingency for himself and for them,—' If our earthly house of this tabernacle were dissolved,' and so on. Therefore we must suppose that 'the self-same thing' of which he is thinking as the divine purpose in all His dealings with us, is not the manner in which we may attain that ultimate condition, but the con-

dition itself which, by one road or another, God's
children shall attain. Or, in other words, the highest
aim of the divine love in all its dealings with us
Christian men, is not merely a blessed spiritual life, but
the completion of our humanity in a perfect spirit
dwelling in a glorified body. Corporeity—the dwelling
in a body by which the pure spirit moves amidst pure
universes—is the highest end of God's will concerning
us.

That glorified body is described in our context in
wonderful words, which it would take me far too long
to do more than just touch upon. Here we dwell in a
tent, there we shall dwell in a building. Here in a house
made with hands, a corporeal frame derived from
parents by material transmission and intervention;
there we shall dwell in a building of which God is the
maker. Here we dwell in a crumbling clay tenement,
which rains dissolve, which lightning strikes, and
winds overthrow, and which finally lies on the ground
a heap of tumbled ruin. There we dwell in a building,
God's direct work, eternal, and knowing no corruption
nor change. Here we dwell in a body congruous with,
and part of, the perishable earthly world in which it
abides, and with which it stands in relation; there we
dwell in a house partaking of the nature of the heavens
in which it moves, a body that is the fit organ of a
perfect spirit.

And so, says Paul, the end of what God means with
us is not stated in all its wonderfulness, when we speak
of spirits imbued with His wisdom and surcharged
with His light and perfectness, but when we add to that
the thought of a fitting organ in which these spirits
dwell, whereby they can come into contact with an
external universe, incorruptible, and so reach the

summit of their destined completeness. 'The house
not made with hands,' eternal, the building of God in
the Heavens, is the end that God has in view for all
His children.

II. So, then, secondly, note the slow process of the
Divine Workman.

The Apostle employs here a very emphatic compound
term for 'hath wrought.' It conveys not only the idea
of operation, but the idea of continuous and somewhat
toilsome and effortful work, as if against the resistance
of something that did not yield itself naturally to the
impulse that He would bestow. Like some sculptor
with a hard bit of marble, or some metallurgist who has
to work the rough ore till it becomes tractable, so the
loving, patient, Divine Artificer is here represented as
labouring long and earnestly with a somewhat obstinate
material which can and does resist His loving touch,
and yet going on with imperturbable and patient hope,
by manifold touches, here a little and there a little, all
through life preparing a man for His purpose. The
great Artificer toils at His task, 'rising early' and
working long, and not discouraged when He comes
upon a black vein in the white marble, nor when the
hard stone turns the edge of His chisels.

Now I would have you notice that there lies in this
conception a very important thought, viz. God cannot
make you fit for heaven all at a jump, or by a simple
act of will. That is not His way of working. He can
make a world so, He cannot make a saint so. He can
speak and it is done when it is only a universe that has
to be brought into being; or He can say, 'Let there
be light,' and light springs at His word. But He cannot
say, and He does not say, Let there be holiness, and it
comes. Not so can God make man meet for the

'inheritance of the saints in light.' And it takes Him all His energies, for all a lifetime, to prepare His child for what He wants to make of him.

There is another thought here, which I can only touch, and that is that God cannot give a man that glorified body of which I have been speaking, unless the man's spirit is Christlike. He cannot raise a bad man at the resurrection with the body of His glory. By the necessities of the case it is confined to the purified, because it corresponds to their inward spiritual being. It is only a perfect spirit that can dwell in a perfect body. You could not put a bad man, Godless and Christless, into the body which will be fit for them whom Christ has changed first of all in heart and spirit into His own likeness. He would be like those hermit crabs that you see on the beach who run into any kind of a shell, whether it fits them or not, in order to get a house.

There are two principles at work in the resurrection of the dead. The glorified body is not the physical outcome of the material body here, but is the issue and manifestation, in visible form, of the perfect and Christlike spirit. Some shall rise to glory and immortality, some to shame and everlasting contempt. If we are to stand at the last with the body of our humiliation changed into a body of glory, we must begin by being changed in the spirit of our mind. As the mind is, so will the body be one day. But, passing from such thoughts as these, and remembering that the Apostle here is speaking only about Christian people, and the divine operations upon them, we may still extend the meaning of this significant word 'wrought' somewhat further, and ask you just to consider, and that very briefly, the three-fold processes which, in the divine working, terminate in, and contemplate, this great issue.

God has wrought us for it in the very act of making us what we are. Human nature is an insoluble enigma, if this world is its only field. Amidst all the waste, the mysterious waste, of creation, there is no more profligate expenditure of powers than that which is involved in giving a man such faculties and capacities, if this be the only field on which they are to be exercised. If you think of what most of us do in this world, and of what it is in us to be, and to do, it is almost ludicrous to consider the disproportion. All other creatures fit their circumstances; nothing in them is bigger than their environment. They find in life a field for every power. You and I do not. 'The foxes have holes, and the birds of the air have roosting-places.' They all correspond to their circumstances, but we have an infinitude of faculty lying half dormant in each of us, which finds no work at all in this present world. And so, looking at men as they are with eternity in their hearts, with natures that go reaching out towards infinity, the question comes up: 'Wherefore hast Thou made all men in vain? What is the use of us, and why should we be what we are, if there is nothing for us except this poor present?' God, or whoever made us, has made a mistake; and strangely enough, if we were not made, but evolved, evolution has worked out faculties which have no correspondence with the things around them.

Life and man are an insoluble enigma except on one hypothesis, and that is that this is a nursery-ground, and that the plants will be pricked out some day, and planted where they are meant to grow. The hearts that feel after absolute and perfect love, the spirits that can conceive the idea of an infinite goodness, the dumb desires, the blank misgivings that wander homeless amidst the narrowness of this poor earth, all these things proclaim that there is a region where they will find their nutriment and expatiate, and when we look at a man we can only say, He that hath wrought him for an infinite world, and an endless communion with a perfect good, is God.

Still further, another field of the divine operation to this end is in what we roughly call 'providences.' What is the meaning of all this discipline through which we are passed, if there is nothing to be disciplined for? What is the good of an apprenticeship if there is no journeyman's life to come after it, where the powers that have been slowly acquired shall be nobly exercised upon broader fields? Why should men be taken, as it were, and, like the rough iron from the ground,

> 'Be heated hot with hopes and fears,
> And plunged in baths of hissing tears,
> And battered with the shocks of doom,'

if, after all the process, the polished shaft is to be broken in two, and tossed away as rubbish? If death ends faculty, it is a pity that the faculty was so patiently developed. If God is educating us all in His school, and then means that, like some wastrel boys, we should lose all our education as soon as we leave its benches, there is little use in the rod, and little meaning in the training. Brethren! life is an insoluble riddle unless the purpose of it lie yonder, and unless all this patient training of our sorrows and our gladnesses, the warmth that expands and the cold that contracts the heart, the light that gladdens and the darkness that saddens the eye and the spirit, are equally meant for training us for the perfect life of a perfect soul moving a perfect body in a perfect universe. Here is a pillar in some ancient hall that has fallen into poor hands, and has had a low roof thrown across the centre of the chamber at half its height. In the lower half there is part of a pillar that means nothing; ugly, bare, evidently climbing, and passing through the aperture, and away above yonder is the carved capital and the great entablature that it carries. Who could understand the shaft unless he could look up through the aperture, and see the summit? And who can think of life as anything but a wretched fragment unless he knows that all which begins here runs upwards into the room above, and there finds its explanation and its completion?

But there is the third sphere of the divine operation. As in creation and in providence, so in all the work and mystery of our redemption, this is the goal that God has in view. It was not worth Christ's while to come and die, if nothing more was to come of it than the imperfect reception of His blessings and gifts which the noblest Christian life in this world presents. The meaning and purpose of the Cross, the meaning and purpose of all the patient dealings of His whispering Spirit, are that we shall be like our Divine Lord in spirit first, and in body afterwards.

And everything about the experiences of a true Christian spirit is charged with a prophecy of immortality. I have not time to dwell upon one point gathered from the context, that I intended to have insisted upon, viz. that the very desires which God's good Spirit works in a believing soul are themselves confirmations of their own fulfilment. But if you notice at your leisure the verses that precede my text,

you will find that the Apostle adduces the groanings of
'earnest desire to be clothed with our house which is
from Heaven,' as a proof that we *have* 'a building of
God, a house not made with hands.' That is to say,
every longing in a Christian heart when it is most filled
with that Spirit, and most in contact with God, and
which is the answer of that heart to a promise of
Christ—every such longing carries with it the assurance
of its own fulfilment. He that hath wrought it has
wrought it in order that the desire may fit us for its
answer, and that the open mouth may be ready for the
abundant filling which His grace designs. He works
upon us, therefore, by making us desire a gift, and then
He gives that which He desires. So let us cherish these
longings, not for the accident of escaping death, nor as
choosing the path by which we shall reach the blessed
issue, but longing for that great issue itself; and try
to keep more distinct and clear before all our minds
this thought, 'God means for me the participation in
Christ's glorified Manhood, and my attaining of that
Manhood is the end that He has in view in all that
He does with me.'

III. So I must say one word about the last thought
that is here, and that is the certainty and the confidence. 'Therefore we are always confident,' says the
Apostle.

'He that hath wrought us for the self-same thing is
God.' Then we may be sure that as far as He is concerned, the work will not be suspended nor vain. *This*
man does not begin to build and is unable to finish. This
workman has infinite resources, an unchanging purpose,
and infinite long-suffering. He will complete His task.

In the quarries of Egypt you will find gigantic stones,
half-dressed, and intended to have been transported to

some great temple. But there they lie, the work incomplete, and they never carried to their place. There are no half-polished stones in God's quarries. They are all finished where they lie, and then borne across the sea, like Hiram's from Lebanon, to the Temple on the hill. It is a certainty that God will finish His work; and since ' He that hath wrought us is God,' we may be sure that He will not stop till He has done.

But it is a certainty that you can thwart. It is an operation that you can counterwork. The potter in Jeremiah's parable was making a vessel upon his wheel, and the vessel was marred in his hand, and did not turn out what he wanted it. The meaning of the metaphor, which has often been twisted to express the very opposite, is that the potter's work may fail, that the artificer may be balked, that you can counterwork the divine dealing, and that all His purpose in your creation, in His providence and in His gift of His Son for your redemption, may come to nought as far as you are concerned. ' I beseech you that ye receive not the grace of God in vain.' 'In vain have I smitten your children,' wailed the Divine Love; 'they have received no correction.' In vain God lavishes upon some of us His mercies, in vain for some of us has Christ toiled and suffered and died. Oh, brother! do not let all God's work on you come to nought, but yield yourselves to it. Rejoice in the confidence that He is moulding your character, cheerfully welcome and accept the providences, painful as they may be, by which He prepares you for heaven. The chisel is sharp that strikes off the superfluous pieces of marble, and when the chisel cuts, not into marble, but into a heart, there is a pang. Bear it, bear it! and understand the meaning of the blow of the sculptor's mallet, and see in all life the divine hand working towards the accomplishment of His own loving purpose. Then if we turn to Him, amid the pains of His discipline and the joys of His gifts of grace, with recognition and acceptance of His meaning in them all, and cry to Him, 'Thy mercy, O Lord, endureth for ever, forsake not the work of Thine own hands,' we may be always confident, as knowing that 'the Lord will perfect that which concerneth us.'

THE OLD HOUSE AND THE NEW

'We are confident, I say, and willing rather to be absent from the body, and to be present with the Lord.'—2 COR. v. 8.

THERE lie in the words of my text simply these two things; the Christian view of what death is, and the Christian temper in which to anticipate it.

I. First, the Christian view of what death is.

Now it is to be observed that, properly speaking, the Apostle is not here referring to the state of the dead, but to the act of dying. The language would more literally and accurately be rendered 'willing to *go from* home, from the body, and to *go* home, to the Lord.' The moment of transition of course leads to a permanent state, but it is the moment of transition which is in view in the words. I need not remind you, I suppose, that the metaphor of the home is one which has already been dwelt upon in the early part of the chapter, where the contrast is drawn between the transitory house of 'this tent,' and the 'building of God,' the body of incorruption and glory which the saints at the Resurrection day shall receive. So, then,

z

the Christian view of the act of death is that it is simply a change of abode.

Very clearly and firmly does Paul draw the line between the man and his dwelling-place. Life is more than a result of organisation. Consciousness, thought, feeling, are more than functions of matter. No materialist philosopher has ever been, or ever will be, able to explain within the limits of his system the strange difference between the cause and the effect; how it comes to pass that at the one end of the chain there is an impression upon a nerve, and at the other there is pain; how at the one end there is the throb of an inch of matter in a man's skull, and at the other end there are thoughts that breathe and words that burn, and that live for ever. That brings us up to the edge of a gulf over which no materialist philosopher has ever been able to cast a bridge. The scalpel cannot cut deep enough to solve this mystery. Conscience as well as instinct cry out against the theory that the worker and the tools are inseparable. For such a theory reduces human actions to mechanical results, and shatters all responsibility. Man is more than his dwelling-place. You crush a shell on the beach with your heel, and you slay its tiny inhabitant. But you can pull down the tent, and pluck up its pegs, and roll up its canvas, and put it away in a dark corner, and the tenant is untouched. The foolish senses crown Death as last, and lord of all. But wisdom says, 'Life and thought have gone away side by side, leaving doors and windows wide,' and that is all that has happened.

Still further, my text suggests that to the Christian soul the departure from the one house is the entrance into the other. The home has been the body; the home is now to be Jesus Christ. And very beautiful and significant with meanings, which only experience will fully unfold, is the representation that the Lord Christ Himself assumes the place which the bodily environment has hitherto held.

That teaches us, at all events, that there is a new depth and closeness of union with Jesus waiting the Christian soul, when it lays aside the separating film of flesh. Here the bodily organisation, with its limitations, necessarily shuts us off from the closeness of intercourse which is possible for a naked soul. We know not how much separation may depend upon the immersing of the spirit in the fleshly tabernacle, but this we know, that, though here and now, by faith which dominates sense, souls can live in Christ even whilst they live in the body; yet there shall come a form of union so much more close, intimate, all-pervading, and all-encircling, as that the present union with Him by faith, precious as it is, shall be, as the Apostle calls it in our context, 'absence from the Lord.' 'We have to be discharged,' says an old thinker, 'of a great deal of what we call body, and then we shall be more truly ourselves,' and more truly united to Him who, if we are Christian people at all, is the self of ourselves and the life of our lives. No man knows how close he can nestle to the bosom of Christ when the film of flesh is rent away. Just as when in some crowded street of a great city some grimy building is pulled down, a sudden daylight fills the vacant space, and all the site that had been shut out from the sky for many years is drenched in sunshine, so when 'the earthly house of this tabernacle' is ruinated and falls, the light will flood the place where it stood, and to be 'absent from the body' shall be to be 'present with the Lord.'

May we go a step further and suggest that, perhaps,

in the bold metaphor of my text, there is an answer to the questions which so often rack loving and parted hearts? 'Do the dead know aught of what affects us here? and can they do aught but gaze on Him, and love, and rest?' If it be that there is any such analogy as seems to be dimly shadowed in my text, between the relation of the body on earth to the spirit that inhabits it, and that of Jesus Christ to him who dwells in Him, and is clothed by Him, then it may be that, as the flesh, so the Christ transmits to the spirit that has Him for its home impressions from the outside world, and affords a means of action upon that world. Christ may be, if I might so say, the sensorium of the disembodied spirit; and Christ may be the hand of the man who hath no other instrument by which to express himself. But all that is fancy perhaps, speculation certainly; and yet there seems to be a shadow of a foundation for at least entertaining the possibility of such a thought as that Jesus is the means of knowing and the means of acting to those who rest from their labours in Him, and dwell in peace in His arms. But be that as it may, the reality of a close communion and encircling by the felt presence of Jesus Christ, which, in its blessed closeness, will make the closest communion here seem to be obscure, is certainly declared in the words before us.

Then this transition is regarded in my text as being the work of a moment. It is not a long journey of which the beginning is 'to go *from* home, from the body,' and the end is 'to *go* home, to the Lord.' But it is one and the same motion which, looked at from the one side, is departure, and looked at from the other is arrival. The old saying has it, 'there is but a step between me and death.' The truth is, there is but a step between me and *life*. The mighty angel in the

Apocalypse, that stood with one foot on the firm land and the other on the boundless ocean, is but the type of the spirit in the brief moment of transition, when the consciousness of two worlds blends, and it is clothed upon with the house which is from heaven, in the very act of stripping off the earthly house of this tabernacle.

Nor need I remind you, I suppose, in more than a sentence, that this transition obviously leads into a state of conscious communion with Jesus Christ. The dreary figment of an unconscious interval for the dis-embodied spirit has no foundation, either in what we know of spirit, or in what is revealed to us in Scripture. For the one thing that seems to make it probable—the use of that metaphor of 'sleeping in Jesus'—is quite sufficiently accounted for by the notions of repose, and cessation of outward activity, and withdrawal of capacity of being influenced by the so-called realities of this lower world, without dragging in the unfounded notion of unconsciousness. My text is incompatible with it, for it is absurd to say of an unconscious spirit, clear of a bodily environment, that it is anywhere; and there is no intelligible sense in which the condition of such a spirit can be called being 'with the Lord.'

So, then, I think a momentary transition, with unin-terrupted consciousness, which leads to a far deeper and more wonderful and blessed sense of unity with Jesus Christ than is possible here on earth, is the true shape in which the act of death presents itself to the Christian thinker.

And remember, dear brethren, that is all we know. Nothing else is certain—nothing but this, 'with the Lord,' and the resulting certainty that therefore it is well with them. It is enough for our faith, for our comfort, for our patient waiting. They live in Christ, 'and there we find them worthier to be loved,' and certainly lapped in a deeper rest. 'Blessed are the dead that die in the Lord.'

II. In the next place, note the Christian temper in which to anticipate the transition.

'We are always courageous, and willing rather to leave our home in the body, and to go home to the Lord.' Now I must briefly remind you of how the Apostle comes to this state of feeling. He has been speaking about the natural shrinking, which belongs to all humanity, from the act of dissolution, considered as being the stripping off of the garment of the flesh. And he has declared, on behalf of himself and the early Christian Church, his own and their personal desire that they might escape from that trial by the path which seemed possible to the early Christians—viz. that of surviving until the return of Jesus Christ from Heaven, when they would be 'clothed upon with the house which is from Heaven,' without the necessity of stripping off that with which at present they are invested. Then he says—and this is a very remarkable thought—that just because this instinctive shrinking from death and yearning for the glorified body is so strong in the Christian heart, that is a sign that there is such a glorified body waiting for us. He says, 'we know that if our house . . . were dissolved, we have a building of God.' And his reason for knowing it is this, 'for in this we groan.' That is a bold position to say that a yearning in the Christian consciousness prophesies its own fulfilment. Our desires are the prophecies of His gifts. Then, on this certainty — which he deduces from the fact of the longing for it—on this certainty of the glorious, ultimate body of the Resurrec-

tion he bases his willingness expressed in the text, to
go through the unwelcome process of leaving the old
house, although he shrinks from it.

So, then, Christian faith does not destroy the natural
reluctance to put aside the old companion of our lives.
The old house, though it be smoky, dimly lighted, and,
by our own careless keeping, sluttish and grimy in
many a corner, yet is the only house we have ever
known, and to be absent from it is untried and strange.
There is nothing wrong in saying 'we would not be
unclothed but clothed upon.' Nature speaks there.
We may reverently entertain the same feelings which
our Pattern acknowledged, when He said, 'I have a
baptism to be baptized with, and how am I straitened
until it be accomplished.' And there would be nothing
sinful in repeating His prayer with His conditions, 'If
it be possible, let this cup pass from Me.'

But then the text suggests to us the large Christian
possessions and hope which counterwork this reluctance, in the measure in which we live lives of faith.
There is the assurance of that ultimate home in which
all the transiency of the present material organisation
is exchanged for the enduring permanence which knows
no corruption. The 'tent' is swept away to make room
for the 'building.' The earthly house is dissolved in
order that there may be reared round the homeless
tenant the house eternal, 'not made with hands,' God's
own work, which is waiting in the heavens; because
the power that shall frame it is there. Not only that
great hope of the 'body of His glory,' with which at
the last all true souls shall be invested, but further-
more, 'the earnest of the spirit,' and the blessed
experiences therefrom, resulting even here, ought to
make the unwelcome necessity less unwelcome. If the

firstfruits be righteousness and peace and joy of the
Holy Ghost, what shall the harvest be? If the 'earnest,'
the shilling given in advance, be so precious, what will
the whole wealth of the inheritance which it heralds
be when it is received?

For such reasons the transitory passage becomes less
painful and unwelcome. Who is there that would
hesitate to dip his foot into the ice-cold brook if he
knew that it would not reach above his ankles, and that
a step would land him in blessedness unimagined till
experienced?

Therefore the Christian temper is that of quiet
willingness and constant courage. There is nothing
hysterical here, nothing morbid, nothing overstrained,
nothing artificial. The Apostle says: 'I would rather
not. I should like if I could escape it. It is an unwelcome necessity; but when I see what I do see beyond,
I am ready. Since so it must be, I will go, not reluctantly, nor dragged away from life, nor clinging desper-
ately to it as it slips from my hands, nor dreading
anything that may happen beyond; but always courageous, and prepared to go whithersoever the path
may take me, since I am sure that it ends in His bosom.'
He is willing to go from the home of the body, because
to do that is to go home to Christ.

There are other references of our Apostle's, substantially of the same tone as that of my text, but with very
beautiful and encouraging differences. When he was
nearer his end, when it seemed to him as if the heads-
man's block was not very far off, his *willingness* had
intensified into 'having a *desire* to depart and to be
with Christ, which is far better.' And when the end
was all but reached, and he knew that death was
waiting just round the next turn in the road, he said,

with the confidence that in the midst of the struggle would have been vainglory, but at the end of it was a foretaste of the calm of Heaven, 'I have finished my course, I have kept the faith; henceforth there is laid up for me a crown of righteousness.' That is our model, dear brethren,—'always courageous,' afraid of nothing in life, in death, or beyond, and therefore willing to go from home from the body and to go home to the Lord.

Think of this man thus fronting the inevitable, with no excitement and with no delusions. Remember what Paul believed about death, about sin, about his own sin, about judgment, about hell. And then think of how to him death had made its darkness beautiful with the light of Christ's face, and all the terror was gone out of it. Do you think so about death? Do you shrink from it? Why? Why do you not take Paul's cure for the shrinking? If you can say, 'To me to live is Christ,' you will have no difficulty in saying, 'and to die is gain.' That is the only way by which you can come to such a temper, and then you will be willing to move from the cottage to the palace, and to wait in peace till you are shifted again into 'the building of God, the house not made with hands, eternal in the heavens.'

PLEASING CHRIST

'We labour that whether present or absent we may be accepted of Him.'
2 COR. v. 9.

WE do not usually care very much for, or very much trust, a man's own statement of the motives of his life, especially if in the statement he takes credit for lofty and noble ones. And it would be rather a dangerous experiment for the ordinary run of so-called Christian people to stand up and say what Paul says here, that the supreme design and aim towards which all their lives are directed is to please Jesus Christ. In his case the tree was known by its fruits. Certainly there never was a life of more noble self-abnegation, of more continuous heroism, of loftier aspiration and lowlier service than the life of which we see the very pulse in these words.

But Paul is not only professing his own faith, he is speaking in the name of all his brethren. 'We,' ought to include every man and woman who calls himself or herself a Christian. It is this setting of the will of Jesus Christ high up above all other commandments, and proposing to one's self as the aim that swallows up all other aims, that I may please Him— it is this, and not creeds, forms, opinions, professions, or even a faith that simply trusts in Him for salvation, that makes a true Christian. You are a Christian in the precise measure in which Christ's will is uppermost and exclusive in your life, and for all your professions and your orthodoxy and your worship and your faith, not one hair's-breadth further. Here is the signature and the common characteristic of all real Christians, 'We labour that whether present or absent we may be well-pleasing to Him.'

So then in looking together at these words now, I take three points, the supreme aim of the Christian life; the concentration of effort which that aim demands; and the insignificance to which it reduces all external things.

I. First, then, let me deal with that supreme aim of the Christian life.

The word which is, correctly enough, rendered

'accepted,' may more literally, and perhaps with a closer correspondence to the Apostle's meaning, be translated 'well-pleasing,' and the aim is this, not merely that we may be accepted, but that we may bring a smile into His face, and some joy and complacent delight in us into His heart, when He looks upon our doings. That pleasure of Jesus Christ in them that 'fear Him, and in them that hope in His mercy' and do His will is a present emotion that fills His heart in looking upon His followers, and it will be especially declared in the solemn, final judgment. We must keep in view both of these periods, if we would rightly understand the sweep of the aim which ought to be uppermost in all Christian people. Here and now in our present acts, we should so live as to occasion a present sentiment of complacent delight in us, in the heart of the Christ who sees us here and now and always. We should so live as that at that far-off future day when we shall 'all be manifested before the Judgment-seat of Christ,' the Judge may bend from His tribunal, and welcome us into His presence with a word of congratulation and an outstretched hand of loving reception. Set that two-fold aim before you, Christian men and women, else you will fail to experience the full stimulus of this thought.

Now such an aim as this implies a very wonderful conception of Jesus Christ's present relations to us. It is a truth that we may minister to His joy. It is a truth that just as really as you mothers are glad when you hear from a far-off land that your boy is doing well, and getting on, so Jesus Christ's heart fills with gladness when He sees you and me walking in the paths in which He would have us go. We often think about our dear dead that they cannot know of us and

our doings here, because the sorrow that would sometimes come from the contemplation of our evil, or of
our misfortunes, would trouble them in their serene
rest.   We know not how that may be, but this at least
we do know, that the Man Jesus Christ, who, like those
dear ones, 'was dead, and is alive for evermore,' in His
human nature has knowledge of all His children's
failures, as well as successes, and is affected with some
shadow of regret, or with some reality of delight,
according as they follow or stray from the paths in
which He would have them walk. If it be so with Him
it may be so with them; and though it be not so with
them it must be so with Him. So this strange, sweet,
tender, and powerful thought is a piece of plain prose,
that Christ is glad when you and I are good.

Does it need any word to emphasise the force of that
motive to a Christian heart that loves the Master?
Surely this is the great and blessed peculiarity of all
the morality of Christianity that it has all a personal
bearing and aspect, and that just as the sum of all our
duty is gathered up in the one command, 'Imitate
Christ,' so the motive for all our duty lies in 'If you
love Me, keep My commandments,' and the reward
which ought to stimulate more than anything besides
is the one thought, not, of what I shall get because I am
good, but of what I shall give Him by my obedience, a
joy in the heart that was stabbed through and through
by sorrow for my sake.   That we may please Him
'who pleased not Himself,' is surely the grandest
motive on which the pursuit of holiness, and the
imitation of Jesus Christ can ever be made to rest.
Oh! how different, and how much more blessed such
a motive and aim is than all the lower reasons for
which men are sometimes exhorted and encouraged to

be good! What a difference it is when we say, 'Do
that thing because it is right,' and when we say, 'Do
that thing because you will be happier if you do,' or
when we say, 'Do it because He would like you to do
it.' The one is all cold and abstract. To stand before
a man and simply say: 'Now go and do your duty,' is
a poor way of setting his feet upon a rock and establishing his goings. Duty is not a word that stirs men's
hearts, however it may awe their consciences. It rises
up before us like some goddess statuesque and serene,
with purity, indeed, in her deep and solemn eyes, but
with nothing appealing to our affections in her stern
lineaments. But when the thought of 'You ought'
melts into 'For my sake,' and through the dissolving
face of the cold marble goddess there shine the beloved lineaments of Him who 'wears the Godhead's
most benignant grace,' the smile upon His face becomes
a motive that touches all hearts. Transmute obligation
into gratitude, and in front of duty and appeals to self
put Christ, and all the harshness and difficulty and
burden and self-sacrifice of obedience becomes easy
and a joy.

Then let me remind you that this one supreme aim
of pleasing Jesus Christ can be carried on through all
life in every varying form, great or small. A blessed
unity is given to our whole being when the little things
and the big things, the easy things and the hard things,
deeds which are conspicuous and deeds which no eye
sees, are all brought under the influence of the one
motive and made co-operant to the one end. Drive
that one steadfast aim through your lives like a bar of
iron, and it will give the lives strength and consistency
—not rigidity, because they may still be flexible. Nothing will be too small to be consecrated by that

motive; nothing too great to own its power. You can please Him everywhere and always. The only thing that is inconsistent with pleasing Him is the thing which, alas! we do at all times and should do at no time, and that is to sin against Him. If we bear with us this as a conscious motive in every part of our day's work it will give us a quick discernment as to what is evil, which I believe nothing else will so surely give. If you desire life to be noble, uniform, dignified, great in its minutest acts and solemn in its very trifles, and if you would have some continual test and standard by which you can detect all spurious, apparent virtues, and discover lurking and masked temptations, carry this one aim clear and high above all else, and make it the purpose of the whole life, to be well-pleasing unto Him.

II. Now, in the next place, notice the concentrated effort which this aim requires.

The word rendered in my text 'labour' is a peculiar one, very seldom employed in Scripture. It means, in its most literal signification, to be fond of honour, or to be actuated by a love of honour; and hence it comes, by a very natural transition, to mean to strive to gain something for the sake of the honour connected with it. That is to say, it not only expresses the notion of diligent, strenuous effort, but it reveals the reason for that diligence and strenuousness in what I may call (for the word might almost be so rendered) the *ambition* of being honoured by pleasing Christ. So that the 'labour' of my text covers the whole ground, not only of the act but of its motive. The concentration of effort which such an aim requires may be enforced by one or two simple exhortations.

First, let me say that we ought, as Christian people, to

cultivate this noble ambition of pleasing Jesus Christ. Men have all got the love of approbation deep in them. God put it there for a good purpose, not that we might shape our lives so as to get others to pat us on the back, and say, 'Well done!' but that, in addition to the other solemn and sovereign motives for following the paths of righteousness, we might have this highest ambition to impel us on the road. And it is the duty of all Christians to see to it that they discipline themselves so as, in their own feelings, to put high above all the approbation or censure of their fellows the approbation or censure of Jesus Christ. That will take some cultivation. It is a great deal easier to shape our courses so as to get one another's praise. I remember a quaint saying in a German book. 'An old schoolmaster tried to please this one and that one, and it failed. "Well, then," said he, "I will try to please Christ." And that succeeded.'

And let me remind you that a second part of the concentration of effort which this aim requires is to strive with the utmost energy in the accomplishment of it. Paul did not believe that anybody could please Jesus Christ without a fight for it. His notion of acceptable service was service which a man suppressed much to render, and overcame much to bring. And I urge upon you this, dear brethren, that with all the mob of faces round about us which shut out Christ's face, and with all the temptations to follow other aims, and with the weaknesses of our own characters, it never was, is not, nor ever will be, an easy thing, or a thing to be done without a struggle and a dead lift, to live so as to be well-pleasing to Him.

Look at Paul's metaphors with which he sets forth the Christian life—a warfare, a race, a struggle, a building up of some great temple structure, and the like—all suggesting at the least the idea of patient, persistent, continuous toil, and most of them suggesting also the idea of struggle with antagonistic forces and difficulties, either within or without. So we must set our shoulders to the wheel, put our backs into our work. Do not think that you are going to be carried into the condition of conformity with Jesus Christ in a dream, or that the road to heaven is a primrose path, to be trodden in silver slippers. ' I will not offer unto the Lord that which doth cost me nothing,' and if you do, it will be worth exactly what it costs. There must be concentration of effort if we are to be well-pleasing to Him.

But then do not forget, on the other hand, that deeper than all effort, and the very spring and life of it, there must be the opening of our hearts for the entrance of His life and spirit, by the presence of which only are we well-pleasing to Christ. That which pleases Him in you and me is our likeness to Him. According to the old Puritan illustration, the refiner sat by the furnace until he could see in the molten metal his own face mirrored, and then he knew it was pure. So what pleases Christ in us is the reflection of Himself. And how can we get that likeness to Himself except by receiving into our hearts the Spirit that was in Christ Jesus, and will dwell in us, and will produce in us in our measure the same image that it formed in Him? ' Work *out* your own salvation,' because 'it is God that worketh *in* you.' Labour, concentrate effort, and above all open the heart to the entrance of that transforming power.

III. Lastly, let me suggest the utter insignificance to which this aim reduces all externals.

'We labour,' says Paul, 'that whether present or absent, we may be accepted.' What differences of condition are covered by that parenthetical phrase—'present or absent!' He talks about it as if it was a very small matter, does he not? And what is included in it? Whether a man shall be in the body or out of it; that is to say, whether he be alive or dead. Here is an aim then, so great, so lofty, so all-comprehensive that it reduces the difference between living in the world and being out of it, to a trifle. And if we stand so high up that these two varieties of condition dwindle into insignificance and seem to have melted into one, do you think that there is anything else that will be very big? If the difference between life and death is dwindled and dwarfed, what else do you suppose will remain? Nothing, I should think.

So if we only, by God's help, which will be given to us if we want it, keep this clear before us as the motive of all our life, then all the possible alternatives of human condition and circumstance will sink into insignificance, and from that lofty summit will 'show scarce so gross as beetles' in the air beneath our lofty station.

Whether we be rich or poor, solitary or beset by friends, happy or sad, hopeful or despairing, young or old, wearied or buoyant, learned or foolish, it matters not. The one aim lifts itself before us, and they in whose eyes shine the light of that great issue are careless of the road along which they pass. Do you enlist yourselves in the company that fires at the long range, and all those that take aim at the shorter ones will seem to be very pitifully limiting their powers.

Then remember that this same aim, and this same result may be equally pursued and attained whether

2 A

here or yonder. It is something to have a course of life which runs straight along, unbent aside, and not cut short off, by the change from earth to Heaven. And this felicity he only has who, amidst things temporal and insignificant, sees and seeks the eternal smile on the face of his unchanging Saviour. On earth, in death, through eternity, such a life will be homogeneous and of a piece; and when all other aims are hull down below the horizon, forgotten and out of sight, then still this will be the purpose, and yonder it will be the accomplished purpose, of each, to please the Lord Jesus Christ.

My dear friend, remember that in its full meaning this aim regards the future, and points onward to that great judgment-seat where you and I will certainly each of us give account of himself. Do you think that you will please Christ then? Do you think that when that day dawns, a smile of welcome will come into His eyes, and a glow of gladness at the meeting into yours? Or have you cause to fear that you will 'call on the rocks and the hills to cover you from the face of Him that sitteth on the Throne?'

We are all close by one another; our voices are very audible to each other. Do you learn, Christian people, that the first,—or at least a prime—condition of all Christian and Christ-pleasing life, is a wholesome disregard of what anybody says but Himself. The old Lacedæmonians used to stir themselves to heroism by the thought: 'What will they say of us in Sparta?' The governor of some outlying English colony minds very little what the people that he is set to rule think about him. He reports to Downing Street, and it is the opinion of the Home Government that influences him. You report to headquarters. Never mind what

anybody else thinks of you.   Your business is to please
Christ, and the less you trouble yourselves about pleasing men the more you will succeed in doing it.   Be
deaf to the tittle tattle of your fellow soldiers in the
ranks.   It is your Commander's smile that will be your
highest reward.

> ' Fame is no plant that grows on mortal soil,
> But lives and spreads aloft by those pure eyes,
> And perfect witness of all-judging Jove ;
> As he pronounces lastly on each deed,
> Of so much fame in heaven expect thy meed.'

THE LOVE THAT CONSTRAINS

'The love of Christ constraineth us.'—2 Cor. v. 14.

IT is a dangerous thing to be unlike other people.   It
is still more dangerous to be better than other people.
The world has a little heap of depreciatory terms
which it flings, age after age, at all men who have a
higher standard and nobler aims than their fellows.
A favourite term is 'mad.'   So, long ago they said, 'The
prophet is a fool; the spiritual man is mad,' and, in
His turn, Jesus was said to be 'beside Himself,' and
Festus shouted from the judgment-seat to Paul that
he was mad.   A great many people had said the same
thing about him before, as the context shows.   For the
verse before my text is: 'Whether we be beside ourselves, it is to God: or whether we be sober, it is for your
cause.'   Now the former clause can only refer to other
people's estimate of the Apostle.   No doubt there were
many things about him that gave colour to it.   He said
that a dead Man had appeared to him and spoken with
him.   He said that he had been carried up into the third
heaven.   He had a very strange creed in the judgment

of the times. He had abandoned a brilliant career for a very poor one. He was obviously utterly indifferent to the ordinary aims of men. He had a consuming enthusiasm. And so the world explained him satisfactorily to itself by the short and easy method of saying, 'Insane.' And Paul explained himself by the great word of my text, 'The love of Christ constraineth us.' Wherever there is a life adequately under the influence of Christ's love the results will be such as an unsympathising world may call madness, but which are the perfection of sober-mindedness. Would there were more such madmen! I wish to try to make one or two of them now, by getting some of you to take for your motto, 'The love of Christ constraineth us.'

I. Now the first thing to notice is this constraining love.

I need not spend time in showing that when Paul says here 'The love of Christ,' he means Christ's love to him, not his to Christ. That is in accordance with his continual usage of the expression; and it is in accordance with facts. For it is not my love to Jesus, but His love to me, that brings the real moulding power into my life, and my love to Him is only the condition on which the true power acts upon me. To get the fulcrum and the lever which will heave a life up to the heights you have to get out of yourselves.

Now Paul never saw Jesus Christ in this earthly life. Timothy, who is associated with him in this letter, and perhaps is one of the 'us,' never saw Him either. The Corinthian believers whom he is addressing had, of course, never seen Him. And yet the Apostle has not the slightest hesitation in taking that great benediction of Christ's love and spreading it over them all. That love is independent of time and of space; it includes humanity, and is co-extensive with it. Unturned away by unworthiness, unrepelled by non-responsiveness, undisgusted by any sin, unwearied by any, however numerous, foiling of its attempts, the love of Christ, like the great heavens that bend above us, wraps us all in its sweetness, and showers upon us all its light and its dew.

And yet, brethren, I would have you remember that whilst we thus try to paint, in poor, poor words, the universality of that love, we have to remember that it does not partake of the weakness that infects all human affections, which are only strong when they are narrow, and as the river expands it becomes shallow, and loses the force in its flow which it had when it was gathered between straiter banks, so as that a universal charity is almost akin to a universal indifference. But this love that grasps us all, this river that 'proceedeth from the Throne of God and of the Lamb,' flows in its widest reaches as deep and as impetuous in its career as if it were held within the narrowest of gorges. For Christ's universal love is universal only because it is individualising and particular. We love our nation by generalising and losing sight of the individuals. Christ loves the world because He loves every man and woman in it, and His grace enwraps all because His grace hovers over each.

> 'The sun whose beams most glorious are
> Despiseth no beholder,'

but the rays come straight to each eyeball. Be sure of this: that He who, when the multitude thronged Him and pressed Him, felt the tremulous, timid, scarcely perceptible touch of one woman's wasted finger on the hem of His garment, holds each of us in the grasp of

His love, which is universal, because it applies to each. You and I have each the whole radiance of it pouring down on our heads, and none intercepts the beams from any other. So, brethren, let us each feel not only the love that grasps the world, but the love that empties itself on me.

But there is one more remark that I wish to make in reference to this constraining love of Jesus Christ, and that is, that in order to see and feel it we must take the point of view that this Apostle takes in my text. For hearken how he goes on. 'The love of Christ constraineth us, because we thus judge, that if one died for all, then all died, and that He died for all,' etc. That is to say, the death of Christ for all, which is equivalent to the death of Christ for each, is the great solvent by which the love of God melts men's hearts, and is the great proof that Jesus Christ loves me, and thee, and all of us. If you strike out that conception you have struck out from your Christianity the vindication of the belief that Christ loves the world. What possible meaning is there in the expression, 'He died for all?' How can the fact of His death on a 'green hill' outside the gates of a little city in Syria have world-wide issues, unless in that death He bore, and bore away, the sins of the whole world? I know that there have been many—and there are many to-day—who not accepting what seems to me to be the very vital heart of Christianity—viz. the death of Christ for the world's sin, do yet cherish—as I think illogically—yet do cherish a regard for Him, which puts some of us who call ourselves 'orthodox,' and are tepid, to the blush. Thank God! men are often better than their creeds, as well as worse than them. But that fact does not affect what I am saying now, and what I beg you to take for

what you find it to be worth, that unless we believe
that Jesus Christ died for all, I do not know what claim
He has on the love of the world. We shall admire
Him, we shall bow before Him, as the very realised
ideal of humanity, though how this one Man has
managed to escape the taint of the all-pervading evil
remains, upon that hypothesis, very obscure. But love
Him? No! Why should I? But if I feel that His
death had world-wide issues, and that He went down
into the darkness in order that He might bring the
world into the light, then—and I am sure, on the wide
scale and in the long-run only then—will men turn to
Him and say, 'Thou hast died for me, help me to live
for Thee.' Brethren, I beseech you, take care of
emptying the death of Christ of its deepest meaning,
lest you should thereby rob His character of its chiefest
charm, and His name of its mightiest soul-melting
power. The love that constraineth is the love that
died, and died for all, because it died for each.

II. Now let me ask you to consider the echo of this
constraining love.

I said a moment or two ago that Christ's love to us is
the constraining power, and that ours to Him is but
the condition on which that power works. But between
the two there comes something which brings that
constraining love to bear upon our hearts. And so
notice what my text goes on to adduce as needful for
Christ's love to have its effect—namely, 'because we
thus judge,' etc. Then my estimate, my apprehension
of the love of Christ must come in between its manifestation and its power to grip, to restrain, to impel
me. If I may use such a figure, He stands, as it were,
bugle in hand, and blows the sweet strains that are
meant to set the echoes flying. But the rock must

receive the impact of the vibrations ere it can throw back the thinned echo of the music. Love must be believed and known ere it can be responded to.

Now the only answer and echo that hearts desire is the love of the beloved heart. We all know that in our earthly life. Love is as much a hunger to be loved as the outgoing of my own affection. The two things are inseparable, and there is nothing that repays love but love. Jesus Christ wishes each of us to love Him. If it is true that He loves me, then, intertwisted with the outgoing of His heart towards me is the yearning that my heart may go out towards Him. Dear brethren, this is no pulpit rhetoric, it is a plain, simple fact, inseparable from the belief in Christ's love—that He wishes you and every soul of man to love Him, and that, whatever else you bring, lip reverence, orthodox belief, apparent surrender, in the assay shop of His great mint all these are rejected, and the only metal that passes the fire is the pure gold of an answering love. Brethren! is that what you bring to Jesus Christ?

Love seeks for love, and our love can only be an echo of His. He takes the beginning in everything. If I am to love Him back again, I must have faith in His love to me. And if that be so, then the true way by which you, imperfect Christian people, can deepen and strengthen your love to Jesus Christ is not so much by efforts to work up a certain warmth of sentiment and glow of affection, as by gazing, with believing eyes of the heart, upon that which kindles your love to Him. If you want ice to melt, put it out into the sunshine. If you want the mirror to gleam, do not spend all your time in polishing it. Carry it where it can catch the ray, and it will flash it back in glory. 'We love Him because He first loved us.' Our love is an echo; be sure that you listen for the parent note, and link yourselves by faith with that great love which has come down from Heaven for us all.

But how can I speak about echoes and responses when I know that there are scores of men and women whom a preacher's words reach who would be ashamed of themselves, and rightly, if they exhibited the same callousness of heart and selfishness of ingratitude to some human, partial benefactor as they are not ashamed to have exhibited all their lives to Jesus Christ. Echo? Yes! your heartstrings are set vibrating fast enough whenever, in the adjoining apartment, an instrument is touched which is tuned to the same key as your heart. Pleasures, earthly aims, worldly gifts, the sweetnesses of human life, all these things set them thrilling, and you can hear the music, but your hearts are not tuned to answer to the note that is struck in 'He loved me and gave Himself for me.' The bugle is blown, and there is silence, and no echo, faint and far, comes whispering back. Brethren, we use no one else, in whose love we have any belief, a thousandth part so ill as we use Jesus Christ.

III. Now, lastly, let me say a word about the constraining influence of this echoed love.

Its first effect, if it has any real power in our hearts and lives, will be to change their centre, to decentralise. Look what the Apostle goes on to say: 'We thus judge that He . . . died for all, that they which live should not live henceforth unto themselves.' That is the great transformation. Secure that, and all nobleness will follow, and 'whatsoever things are lovely and of good report' will come, like doves to their windows, flocking into the soul that has ceased to find its centre in its poor rebellious self. All love derives its power to elevate, refine, beautify, ennoble, conquer, from the fact that, in lower degree, all love makes the beloved the centre, and not the self. Hence the mother's self-sacrifice, hence the sweet reciprocity of wedded life, hence everything in humanity that is noble and good. Love is the antagonist of selfishness, and the highest type of love should be, and in the measure in which we are under the influence of Christ's love will be, the self-surrendering life of a Christian man. I know that in saying so I am condemning myself and my brethren. All the same, it is true. The one power that rescues a man from the tyranny of living for self, which is the mother of all sin and ignobleness, is when a man can say 'Christ is my aim,' 'Christ is my object.' 'The life that I live in the flesh I live by the faith of the Son of God, who loved me and gave Himself for me.' There is no secret of self-annihilation, which is self-transfigura-tion, and, I was going to say, deification, like that of loving Christ with all my heart because He has loved me so.

Again, let me remind you that, on its lower reaches and levels, we find that all true affection has in it a strange power of assimilating its objects to one another. Just as a man and woman who have lived together for half a century in wedded life come to have the same notions, the same prejudices, the same tastes, and sometimes you can see their very faces being moulded into likeness, so, if I love Jesus Christ, I shall by degrees grow liker and liker to Him, and be 'changed into the same image, from glory to glory.'

Again, the love constrains, and not only constrains but impels, because it becomes a joy to divine and to do the will of the beloved Christ. 'My yoke is easy.'

Is it? It is very hard to be a Christian. His requirements are a great deal sterner than others. His yoke
is easy, not because it is a lighter yoke, but because it
is padded with love. And that makes all service a
sacrament, and the surrender of my own will, which is
the essence of obedience, a joy.

So, dear friends, we come here in sight of the unique
and blessed characteristic of all Christian morality,
and of all its practical exhortations, and the Gospel
stands alone as the mightiest moulding power in the
world, just because its word is 'love, and do as thou
wilt.' For in the measure of thy love will thy will
coincide with the will of Christ. There is nothing else
that has anything like that power. We do not want
to be told what is right. We know it a great deal
better than we practise it. A revelation from heaven
that simply told me my duty would be surplusage.
'If there had been a law that could have given life,
righteousness had been by the law.' We want a life,
not a law, and the love of Christ brings the life to us.

And so, dear friends, that life, restrained and impelled
by the love to which it is being assimilated, is a life of
liberty and a life of blessedness. In the measure in
which the love of Christ constrains any man, it makes
for him difficulties easy, the impossible possible, the
crooked things straight, and the rough places plain.
The duty becomes a delight, and self ceases to disturb.
If the love of God is shed abroad in a heart, and in the
measure in which it is, that heart will be at rest, and a
great peace will brood over it. Then the will bows in
glad submission, and all the powers arise to joyous
service. We are lords of the world and ourselves
when we are Christ's servants for love's sake; and
earth and its good are never so good as when the

power of His echoed love rules our lives. Do you know and believe that Christ loves you? Do you know and believe that you had a place in His heart when He hung on the Cross for the salvation of the world? Have you answered that love with yours, kindled by your faith in, and experience of, His? Is His love the overmastering impulse which urges you to all good, the mighty constraint that keeps you back from all evil, the magnet that draws, the anchor that steadies, the fortress that defends, the light that illumines, the treasure that enriches? Is it the law that commands, and the power that enables? Then you are blessed, though people will perhaps say that you are mad, whilst here; and you will be blessed for ever and ever.

THE ENTREATIES OF GOD

'Now then we are ambassadors for Christ, as though God did beseech . . . by us: we pray . . . in Christ's stead, be ye reconciled to God.'—2 COR. v. 20.

THESE are wonderful and bold words, not so much because of what they claim for the servants as because of what they reveal of the Lord. That thought, 'as though God did beseech,' seems to me to be the one deserving of our attention now, far rather than any inferences which may be drawn from the words as to the relation of preachers of the Gospel to man and to God. I wish, therefore, to try to set forth the wonderfulness of this mystery of a beseeching God, and to put by the side of it the other wonder and mystery of men refusing the divine beseechings.

Before doing so, however, I remark that the supplement which stands in our Authorised Version in this text is a misleading and unfortunate one. 'As though God did beseech *you*' and 'we pray *you*' unduly narrow the scope of the Apostolic message, and confuse the whole course of the Apostolic reasoning here. For he has been speaking of a world which is reconciled to God, and he finds a consequence of that reconciliation of the world in the fact that he and his fellow-preachers are entrusted with the word of reconciliation. The scope of their message, then, can be no narrower than the scope of the reconciliation; and inasmuch as that is world-wide the beseeching must be co-extensive therewith, and must cover the whole ground of humanity. It is a universal message that is set forth here. The Corinthians, to whom Paul was speaking, are, by his hypothesis, already reconciled to God, and the message which he has in trust for them is given in the subsequent words: 'We then, as workers together with God, beseech you also that ye receive not the grace of God in vain.' But the message, the pleading of the divine heart, 'be ye reconciled to God,' is a pleading that reaches over the whole range of a reconciled world. I take then, just these two thoughts, God beseeching man, and man refusing God.

I. God beseeching man.

Now notice how, in my text, there alternates, as if substantially the same idea, the thoughts that Christ and that God pray men to be reconciled. 'We are ambassadors on *Christ's* behalf, as though *God* did beseech you by us, we pray on *Christ's* behalf.' So you see, first, Christ the Pleader, then God beseeching, then Christ again entreating and praying. Could any man have so spoken, passing instinctively from the one thought to the other, unless he had believed that whatsoever things the Father doeth, these also doeth the Son

likewise; and that Jesus Christ is the Representative
of the whole Deity for mankind, so as that when He
pleads God pleads, and God pleads through Him. I do
not dwell upon this, but I simply wish to mark it in
passing as one of the innumerable strong and irrefragable testimonies to the familiarity and firmness
with which that thought of the divinity of Jesus Christ,
and the full revelation of the Father by Him, was
grasped by the Apostle, and was believed by the people
to whom he spoke. God pleads, therefore Christ
pleads, Christ pleads, therefore God pleads; and these
Two are One in their beseechings, and the voice of the
Father echoes to us in the tenderness of the Son.

So, then, let us think of that pleading. To sue for
love, to beg that an enemy will put away his enmity is
the part of the inferior rather than of the superior; is
the part of the offender rather than of the offended;
is the part of the vanquished rather than of the victor;
is the part surely not of the king but of the rebel.
And yet here, in the sublime transcending of all human
precedent and pattern which characterises the divine
dealing, we have the place of the suppliant and of
the supplicated inverted, and Love upon the Throne
bends down to ask of the rebel that lies powerless and
sullen at His feet, and yet is not conquered until his
heart be won, though his limbs be manacled, that he
would put away all the bitterness out of his heart, and
come back to' the love and the grace which are ready
to pour over him. 'He that might the vengeance best
have taken, finds out the remedy.' He against whom we
have transgressed prays us to be reconciled; and the
Infinite Love lowers Himself in that lowering which is,
in another aspect, the climax of His exaltation, to pray
the rebels to accept His amnesty.

Oh, dear brethren! this is no mere piece of rhetoric. What facts in the divine heart does it represent? What facts in the divine conduct does it represent? It represents these facts in the divine heart, that there is in it an infinite longing for the creature's love, an infinite desire for unity between Him and us.

There are wonderful significance and beauty in the language of my text which are lost in the Authorised Version; but are preserved in the Revised. 'We are ambassadors' not only '*for* Christ,' but '*on Christ's behalf.*' And the same proposition is repeated in the subsequent clause. 'We pray you,' not merely 'in Christ's stead,' though that is much, but '*on His account,*' which is more—as if it lay very near His heart that we should put away our enmity; and as if in some transcendent and wonderful manner the all-perfect, self-sufficing God was made glad, and the Master, who is His image for us, 'saw of the travail of His soul, and,' in regard to one man, 'was satisfied,' when the man lets the warmth of God's love in Christ thaw away the coldness out of his heart, and kindle there an answering flame. An old divine says, 'We cannot do God a greater pleasure or more oblige His very heart, than to trust in Him as a God of love.' He is ready to stoop to any humiliation to effect that purpose. So intense is the divine desire to win the world to His love, that He will stoop to sue for it rather than lose it. Such is at least part of the fact in the divine heart, which is shadowed forth for us by that wonderful thought of the beseeching God.

And what facts in the divine conduct does this great word represent? A God that beseeches. Well, think of the tears of imploring love which fell from Christ's eyes as He looked across the valley from Olivet, and saw the Temple glittering in the early sunshine. Think of 'O Jerusalem! Jerusalem! ... how often would I have gathered thy children together ... and ye would not.' And are we not to see in the Christ who wept in the earnestness of His desire, and in the pain of its disappointment, the very revelation of the Father's heart and the very action of the Father's arm? 'Come unto me, all ye that labour, and are heavy laden, and I will give you rest.' That is Christ beseeching and God beseeching in Him. Need I quote other words, gentle, winning, loving? Do we not feel, when looking upon Christ, as if the secret of His whole life was the stretching out imploring and welcoming hands to men, and praying them to grasp His hands, and be saved? But, oh, brethren! the fact that towers above all others, which explains the whole procedure of divinity, and is the keystone of the whole arch of revelation; the fact which reveals in one triple beam of light, God, man, and sin in the clearest illumination, is the Cross of Jesus Christ. And if that be not the very sublime of entreaty; and if any voice can be conceived, human or divine, that shall reach men's hearts with a more piercing note of pathetic invitation than sounds from that Cross, I know not where it is. Christ that dies, in His dying breath calls to us, and ' the blood of sprinkling speaketh better things than that of Abel'; inasmuch as its voice is, 'Come unto Me, and be ye saved, all the ends of the earth.'

Not only in the divine facts of the life and death of Jesus Christ, but in all the appeals of that great revelation which lies before us in Scripture; and may I say, in the poor, broken utterances of men whose harsh, thin voices try to set themselves, in some measure, to the sweetness and the fulness of His beseeching tones—

does God call upon you to draw close to Him, and put away your enmity. And not only by His Word written or ministered from human lips, but also by the patient providences of His love He calls and prays you to come. A mother will sometimes, in foolish fondness, coax her sullen child by injudicious kindness, or, in wise patience, will seek to draw the little heart away from the faults that she desires not to notice, by redoubled ingenuity of tenderness and of care. And so God does with us. When you and I, who deserve—oh! so different treatment—get, as we do get, daily care and providential blessings from Him, is not that His saying to us, 'I beseech you to cherish no alienation, enmity, indifference, but to come back and live in the love'? When He draws near to us in these outward gifts of His mercy, is He not doing Himself what He has bid us to do; and what He never could have bid us to do, nor our hearts have recognised to be the highest strain of human virtue to do, unless He Himself were doing it first? 'If thine enemy hunger, feed him. If he thirst, give him drink; for in so doing thou shalt heap coals of fire upon his head.'

Not only by the great demonstration of His stooping and infinite desire for our love which lies in the life and death of Jesus Christ, nor only by His outward work, nor by His providence, but by many an inward touch on our spirits, by many a prick of conscience, by many a strange longing that has swept across our souls, sudden as some perfumed air in the scentless atmosphere; by many an inward voice, coming we know not whence, that has spoken to us of Him, of His love, of our duty; by many a drawing which has brought us nearer to the Cross of Jesus Christ, only, alas! in some cases that we might recoil further from it,—has He been beseeching, beseeching us all.

2 B

Brethren! God pleads with you. He pleads with you because there is nothing in His heart to any of you but love, and a desire to bless you; He pleads with you because, unless you will let Him, He cannot lavish upon you His richest gifts and His highest blessings. He pleads with you, bowing to the level, and beneath the level, of your alienation and reluctance. And the sum and substance of all His dealings with every soul is, 'My son! give Me thy heart.' 'Be ye reconciled to God.'

II. And now turn, very briefly, to the next suggestion arising from this text, the terrible obverse, so to speak, of the coin: Man refusing a beseeching God.

That is the great paradox and mystery. Nobody has ever fathomed that yet, and nobody will. How it comes, how it is possible, there is no need for us to inquire. It is an awful and a solemn power that every poor little speck of humanity has, to lift itself up in God's face, and say, in answer to all His pleadings, 'I will not!' as if the dwellers in some little island, a mere pin-point of black, barren rock, jutting up at sea, were to declare war against a kingdom that stretched through twenty degrees of longitude on the mainland. So we, on our little bit of island, our pin-point of rock in the great waste ocean, we can separate ourselves from the great Continent; or, rather, God has, in a fashion, made us separate in order that we may either unite ourselves with Him, by our willing yielding, or wrench ourselves away from Him by our antagonism and rebellion. God beseeches because God has so settled the relations between Him and us, that that is what He has to do in order to get men to love Him. He cannot force them. He cannot prise open a man's heart with a crowbar, as it were, and force Himself inside.

The door opens from within. 'Behold! I stand at the door and knock.' There is an 'if.' 'If any man open I will come in.' Hence the beseeching, hence the wail of wisdom that cries aloud and no man regards it; of love that stands at the entering in of the city, and pleads in vain, and says, 'I have called, and ye have refused. . . . How often would I have gathered . . . and ye would not.' Oh, brethren! it is an awful responsibility, a mysterious prerogative, which each one of us, whether consciously or no, has to exercise, to accept or to refuse the pleadings of an entreating Christ.

And let me remind you that the act of refusal is a very simple one. Not to accept is to reject; not to yield is to rebel. You have only to do nothing, to do it all. There are dozens of people in our churches and chapels listening with self-satisfied unconcern, who have all their lives been refusing a beseeching God. And they do not know that they ever did it! They say, 'Oh! I will be a Christian some time or other.' They cherish vague ideas that, somehow or other, they are so already. They have done nothing at all, they have simply been absolutely indifferent and passive. Some of you have heard sermons like this so often that they produce no effect. 'It is the right kind of thing to say. It is the thing we have heard a hundred times.' Perhaps you wonder why I should be so much in earnest about the matter, and then you go outside, and discuss me or the weather, and forget all about the sermon.

And thus, once more, you reject Christ. It is done without knowing it; done simply by doing nothing. My brother! do not stop your ears any more against that tender, imploring love.

Then let me remind you that this refusing the

beseechings of God is the climax of all folly. For consider what it is,—a man refusing his highest good and choosing his certain ruin. I am afraid that people have been arguing and fighting so much of late years over disputable points in reference to the doctrine of future retribution that the indisputable fact of such retribution has lost much of its solemn power.

I pray you, brethren, to ask yourselves one·question: Is there anything, in the present or in the future condition of a man that is not reconciled to God, which explains God's beseeching urgency? Why this energy and intensity of divine desire? Why this which, if it were human only, would be called *passionate* entreaty? Why was it needful for Jesus Christ to die? Why was it worth His while to bear the punishment of man's sin? Why should God and Christ, through all the ages, plead with unintermittent voice? There must be some explanation of it all, and here is the explanation, 'They that hate Me love *death*.' 'Be ye reconciled to God,' for enmity is ruin and destruction.

And finally, dear friends, this turning away from Him that speaketh from Heaven, of which some of you have all your lives been guilty, is not only supreme folly, but it is the climax of all guilt. For there can be nothing worse, darker, arguing a nature more averse or indifferent to the highest good, than that God should plead, and I should steel my heart and deafen mine ear against His voice. The crown· of a man's sin, because it is the disclosure of the secrets of his deepest heart as loving darkness rather than light, is turning away from the divine voice that woos us to love and to God.

Oh! there are some of you that have heard that Voice too often to be much touched by it. There are some of you too busy to attend to it, who hear it not because of the clatter of the streets and the whir of the spindles. There are some of you that are seeking to drown it in the shouts of mirth and revelry. There are some of you to whom it comes muffled in the mists of doubt; but I beseech you all, look at the Cross, *look at the Cross!* and hear Him that hangs there pleading with you.

Before the battle there comes out the captain of the twenty thousand to the King with the ten thousand, who in His loftiness is not afraid to stoop to sue for peace from the weaker power. My brother! the moment is precious; the white flag may never be waved before your eyes again. Do not; do not refuse! or the next instant the clarion of the assault may sound, and where will you be then?

It is vain for thee to rush against the thick bosses of the Almighty buckler. 'We beseech, in Christ's behalf, be ye reconciled with God.'

CPSIA information can be obtained
at www.ICGtesting.com
Printed in the USA
LVHW081102160820
663326LV00005B/52